October 1969

Inscribed to Bob Hubbard, valued friend and colleague — with esteem and best regards —

Dave Holly

EXODUS 1947

President Warfield, *flagship of the Old Bay Line, in 1930*

EXODUS 1947

by David C. Holly

Little, Brown and Company Boston Toronto

LIBRARY OF CONGRESS CATALOG CARD NO. 75-79370

FIRST EDITION

Published simultaneously in Canada
by Little, Brown & Company (Canada) Limited

PRINTED IN THE UNITED STATES OF AMERICA

To the men and women who gave life
and meaning to a gallant ship

Author's Note

To SUGGEST THAT A MEANINGFUL BIOGRAPHY can be created from the life of an old steamboat is perhaps presumptuous on the part of the author. He certainly confesses to his prejudices and acknowledges that he may be overwhelmed by them. As a boy, he rode on the old boat down the Chesapeake Bay on glorious days in summer. Nostalgia can be piquant; it can also be stifling. As a young man, he saw the old ship in the grimness of her later years. Compassion can be sentimental; it can also be maudlin.

The subject of this biography could be made to appear heroic. Those who knew her best would not agree. She carried with her too much sentiment and too much pathos for any stance of grandeur. Too often, she was the object of humor, ridicule, and pity.

The story of this ship has never been told before in its entirety. Novels have been written about it. Journalism has exaggerated it. In many ways, the factual narrative is more dramatic than the fiction or the journalism.

The purpose is to present a simple story of a ship in the setting of history. To this end, much of the history must be told. Also, the people who made the history must enter. In so large an epic, at times the ship itself must take a subordinate place as one of the pieces in a very large game.

While the research for this undertaking has been extensive, inadvertent errors of both omission and commission may appear. The author offers deep apologies.

The intent is to tell an accurate story, to the extent possible, not an unkind one. The story, unfortunately, is not always a pleasant one, and people involved in its making were themselves caught in the bitterness which characterized so much of the environment. The author's thought was to present the story, however unpleasant, with sympathy and contemplation of the universality of human fallibility. His hope is that readers will perceive this purpose.

The book carries with it the profound gratitude of the author to all who assisted in its production. It carries also his dedication to the men and women who gave life to the ship and made it famous.

The author is heavily indebted to many generous people who gave hours of their time and experience to the substantive details of the narrative.

Most of the people to whom the author is most deeply obligated will remain forever anonymous at their own request.

Others, to whom the burden of obligation is equally great, include the following: Mr. Richard Randall of the Maryland Historical Society, Baltimore; Mr. John Le Veck of the Hercules Company, Baltimore; Captain Patrick L. Parker, last Old Bay Line skipper of *President Warfield;* Mr. Jean Hofmeister, Harbor Master of Baltimore; Lieutenant-Commander P. K. Kemp, O.B.E., Royal Navy (Ret.), Naval Historical Branch, British Ministry of Defence; Mr. Alexander C. Brown, literary editor of the Newport News *Daily News;* Messrs. Robert H. Burgess and John L. Lochhead, curator and librarian, respectively, of the Mariners' Museum, Newport News; Mr. William M. Bernard, public relations director of the Baltimore *Sun;* Mr. A. Spencer Marsellis, president of the Steamship Historical Society of America; Lieutenant George W. Boyer, U.S. Navy (Ret.), first commanding officer of the U.S.S. *President Warfield* (IX–169); Lieutenant Commander Alfred S. Harer, U.S. Navy (Ret.), her last commanding officer; Commander Donald C. Du Brul, U.S. Naval Reserve, her executive officer; Mr. Raymond

L. Jones, passenger traffic manager of the Old Bay Line for over forty years; Mr. Samuel Meisel, ship chandler of Baltimore; Captain William S. Schlegel, the ship's master during the storm; Captain Edward H. Eaton, former skipper of *District of Columbia* and partner in the Potomac Shipwrecking Company; two very helpful graduate students, Mr. Harold Lippman and Mr. Richard Fraenkel; and Mr. Peter Youngblood, photographer. Among the many, without whose assistance the story of the ship could not have been accurately portrayed, the author would gratefully single out Captain William C. Ash, who recounted the days of preparation in the United States with candor and color. In addition, the author wishes to extend his particular gratitude to Mr. Bernard Marks, chief mate and last master of *Exodus 1947*, for the use of his photographs and for invaluable technical advice, although this acknowledgment by no means implies that the book gains any official sanction thereby. The use of photographs furnished by other sources and included within private collections is also gratefully acknowledged. Most especially, the author wishes to extend his gratitude to the Reverend John Stanley Grauel, passenger and observer on *Exodus 1947* from start to finish, for a detailed story and a perceptive and sensitive presentation of the entire epic.

To the innumerable people who helped immeasurably along the way — the officials of the National Archives, the Zionist Library and Archives, the Israeli Information Office, the United States Navy Archives, the British Ministry of Defence, the British Embassy, the Enoch Pratt Free Library, and the United States Maritime Commission — the author extends his deepest gratitude. He wishes he could include all those by name whose substantive contributions were so significant.

Perhaps it seems exceptional for an author to single out his editor for special thanks; however, in this instance, the inspiration and constructive efforts of Mr. Harry Sions of Little, Brown and Company were so important to the final outcome of this book that the author wishes to express most particularly his very great appreciation.

To all those who tolerated the annoyance of dealing with a researcher, the author extends his thanks and good wishes.

DAVID C. HOLLY

January 1969

Contents

Illustrations

EXODUS
1947

Prologue

THIS BOOK IS THE BIOGRAPHY OF A SHIP.

Like a person, a ship is alive, drawing personality and definition from the people around her. Her life can be described in facts alone, but her very essence requires more than their simple narration. Great ships, like great people, have drawn their importance from the times. They have stood at the crossroads of history and symbolized the events which made them great.

Why should an obscure steamboat be singled out for greatness?

Surely there was nothing in the nightly sailings of *President Warfield* from Baltimore or Norfolk in the 1930's to excite the historian. He might reflect a little and suggest that she was probably the last of her class, the end of a dying era in inland transportation in the United States. But, surely, this fact alone was not enough to put her in a class with the great merchant ships of the past, like *Flying Cloud,* or *Great Eastern,* or *Robert E. Lee.* Certainly, there was nothing to suggest that this white steam packet, plying the peaceful waters of the Chesapeake every night, could have an illustrious career, worthy of the records of history.

Even the historian of 1942 would have been hard put to perceive a naval hero in the boarded-up, freakish-looking craft — a conversion of *President Warfield* — moored in her gray paint of war at a pier in Baltimore. Certainly there was no *Constitution* here, no *Monitor*, no *Victory*. What shots would be fired at this monstrous caricature of a ship? What enemy would ever engage her?

In 1946, the historian would have turned away in dismay and disgust at the sight of the dilapidated, bedraggled hulk of *President Warfield* moored again at a pier in Baltimore. Not even the most sentimental of steamboat buffs could look at this ancient, decrepit craft and see more than the scrap-yard ahead. Where was her history?

But this ship ran with destiny. Her life was a succession of dramas enacted in the graveyard of steamboats in America, in the roar of battle off the coast of Normandy, and in a silent, savage war that created a new nation. In the quarter-century of her span, she lived three lives, each a separate fulfillment.

Her life began quietly on the placid, majestic waters of the Chesapeake, with a honeymoon of music and gentle laughter. It ended in the harsh glare of battle, fought passionately and despairingly for a cause.

Within sight of the Promised Land, she was given a new name — *Exodus 1947*.

Exodus 1947 divided the world and became a symbol of hope for a scattered people.

She was no ordinary ship.

Part One

The Beginnings and the Years of Youth

ONE

The genesis was quiet, scarcely ruffling the local press.

The life of the ship began with the death of a man. Solomon Davies Warfield, known only to the world of finance and certain hunt club circles around Baltimore and the Chesapeake Bay country, died quietly of a heart attack in Union Memorial Hospital on October 24, 1927. A month beforehand, the keel of a new Chesapeake steamer had been laid at Wilmington, Delaware. Each event gained only back-page notice in the local newspapers.

Both the ship and the man would have remained in oblivion without the other. He gave the ship life. Without him, the keel would never have been laid. The ship, in turn, made his name known in history. The link was ironic. At the climax of a tumultuous career — at a magnificent moment of victory rising from defeat — the ship was to expunge his name from her side in a gesture of supreme defiance. The gesture was destined to change the world.

When Solomon Davies Warfield decided in 1920 to devote his full attention and the weight of his wealth to the sagging fortunes of the Seaboard Air Line Railroad and the nearly century-old Baltimore Steam Packet Company it controlled, his associates in the world of finance could only interpret his astonishing interest in a decrepit steamship line

S. Davies Warfield, president of the Seaboard Air Line Railroad and Baltimore Steam Packet Company (Old Bay Line). President Warfield *was named for him after his death.*

and an ailing railroad as a shrewd move for eventual financial advantage.

The truth stunned those who read his will in 1928. Here was an act of pure sentimentality — irrational and emotional, born of overweening pride and abstract attachment to a lost generation. Here was an anachronism, a step backward into another era.

His will disclaimed any expectation of profit from the Seaboard and Baltimore Steam Packet investments. Instead, the will declared that his investments were made solely to help the cause of the South. This attachment to the South, the will explained, came from his own Southern birth and his slave-owning ancestry.* Furthermore, he said, the imprisonment of his father, a member of the Maryland legislature, by Federal forces in 1861 had only deepened the intensity of his feeling for the cause of the South. Therefore, he would leave his fortune, some four million dollars — what was left of a much larger estate already shrunk by other financial enterprises in support of the South — in trust to the Seaboard Air Line Railroad and its subsidiary, known affectionately as the Old Bay Line. These were the transportation links to his beloved South, the land of plantations and graceful living where Warfield fancied he belonged. Here was an act of sentimentality, of attachment to a romantic myth out of step with the times.†

* One would have to accept the Baltimore suburb of Mount Washington, therefore, as part of the South.

† In his will, Warfield left a paltry $15,000 trust fund to his niece, Bessie Wallis Warfield. Sentimental attachment was certainly not displayed here. Apparently she had been something of an embarrassment to him. When his brother Teakle died a failure in 1899, leaving a widow and three-year-old daughter to fend for themselves in a rooming house on Biddle Street, Warfield had claimed the young girl as his ward, educated her in the fashionable schools where Warfields, in his view, were supposed to be educated, and launched her properly in Baltimore society. Even then, any attachment to her did not let him go so far as to permit lavishness. He even advertised in the newspapers of 1914 that he was not going to give a "big ball" for his niece prior to the Bachelors' Cotillion "while thousands [were] being slaughtered in Europe." The skimpiness of his bequest probably reflected his disap-

Between 1920 and 1928, Warfield worked mightily to restore the Seaboard and the Old Bay Line, both worn out by hard wartime use. The plight of the latter was particularly precarious. Its two passenger steamers, *Alabama* and *Florida*, were old and small. A dramatic leap was necessary, and Warfield spurred the Old Bay Line to build three new ships, the largest and finest ever seen on the Bay. *State of Maryland* and *State of Virginia*, launched in 1922 at the Pusey and Jones yards in Wilmington, Delaware, were handsome boats, 330 feet of yachtlike grace, the latest word in steamer packet luxury. The third sister ship, intended to be named *Florida* for the ship she replaced, gained special significance. Subtle changes were made in her specifications — a slightly heavier tonnage, a more pretentious interior, and staterooms earmarked for distinguished guests and the president of the line. This ship was to carry the pennant on the Chesapeake, to be the undisputed aristocrat of the Bay.

The aristocrat who planned the flagship died one month after the laying of the keel. He deserved better. For many years, S. Davies Warfield had labored mightily for the Old Bay Line and the South it served. Without him, the pageant of the Line might have ended before its hundredth anniversary, which it was destined to celebrate on board his flagship — the sentimental verse he had started but never found time to finish. Legh Powell, his successor and companion even in the hospital room when he died, suggested to the board of the company that the new ship be named *President Warfield*.*

---

proval of her first divorce and her gallivanting about the globe pursued by admirers. One could only speculate what his temper might have been in 1936, when the same woman shook an empire to its foundations and stood in the spotlight on the stage of the world.

* Even the name became a subject of ironic argument. Mrs. E. R. Clotworthy, a Warfield appointee to the vice presidency of the company, raised objections to the form of the name — first, in her view, it connoted a ferryboat (an earlier governor of Maryland was named Warfield and two ferryboats on the Bay were named *Governor Ritchie* and *Governor Harrington*); second, in her view, it connoted a steam engine (the Baltimore and Ohio Railroad was currently naming its locomotives

President Warfield's *hull on the launching ways prior to launching ceremonies, February 6, 1928, in the yard of Pusey and Jones. Wilmington, Delaware*

Christening of President Warfield *by Mrs. Zachary D. Lewis, niece of S. Davies Warfield, on February 6, 1928*

The ship was launched at high noon on Monday, February 6, 1928. The sun broke through a slight overcast just before noon, and the temperature mounted to forty-five. Four hundred people who had shivered through the morning in the shipyard of Pusey and Jones, on the banks of the Christiana River at Wilmington, Delaware, perceptibly stirred at the improvement in the weather.

The long, low, knifelike hull rested on the 400-foot ways. Its sponsons were tapered outward to the guard rail. The main deck was open, showing the framing. It hardly looked like even the beginning of a Bay steamer, since the elaborate superstructure was absent. Only the steel hull was here, the part of the boat little seen and mostly under water when a Bay steamer with its gingerbread of housing was underway.

The sponsor, Mrs. Zachary D. Lewis, arrived, buried under an enormous bouquet of roses, a huge fur collar, and a cloche hat in the highest fashion of the late Twenties.

She performed valiantly. The white hull slid down the ways into the narrow confines of the Christiana River and remained surprisingly upright. The crowd cheered lustily. The year 1928 being the eighth anniversary of the Volstead Act, the bottle used for christening was advertised as containing spring water. There were those several decades later, however, who were willing to swear that a bottle of bootleg champagne was aboard the special train from Baltimore.

As evening wore on — the guests long since having departed — the hull of *President Warfield* was warped alongside her building and outfitting berth in the shipyard. Night descended on the lonely ways, and a chill settled over the

---

after its presidents); and, third, in her view, the name should be S. Davies Warfield. Mrs. Clotworthy furthermore hoped that the board would consider as sponsor Miss Rosa Ponselle, the opera star and friend of Mr. Warfield. However, the board stood firm on the name of *President Warfield* and selected as sponsor Mrs. Zachary D. Lewis, the daughter of the president's living brother, General Henry M. Warfield. President Warfield's ward and other niece, Bessie Wallis Warfield, was in London acquiring her second husband, Ernest Aldrich Simpson, and therefore unavailable.

river. The sky darkened, and there was a strong hint of cold rain in the air. The dockside watchman shivered and turned to the warmth of his shack. In the half-light of the shipyard, the framing of *Warfield*'s painted hull glowed starkly on the surface of the water, like the bones of a scrapper's hulk from another, more distant day.

The winter of 1928 was hard, and only in the spring did *Warfield* emerge as the queen she was intended to be. Although she was designed along the lines of *State of Maryland* and *State of Virginia*, certain features were unique.* Her hull, for example, was flared out rather than straight-sided and was heavily reinforced with transverse steel beams and stringers; furthermore, instead of the wood normally used in Bay boats, the exterior steel was carried one deck above the main deck for added strength. Her interior was elegant: the ivory-paneled saloon, aft on the main deck, offered an unobstructed view of the Bay through windows all around the stern; the smoking room was heavily pilastered in mahogany; a palm room aft on the gallery deck was glass-enclosed and bright with blue-green and pink chintz; and a grand double stairway in the main saloon extended through two decks of self-conscious post-Edwardian sumptuousness, replete with chandeliers, gilt trim, and oil paintings of Mr. Warfield's hunting preserve at Carroll Island and his home at Glen Manor. Many of the staterooms had bathrooms (with tubs!). One in particular, number 203, on the hurricane deck, boasted a handsome mahogany bed, tile bath, and special wicker furniture; it had been reserved a year beforehand for the president of the line.

Underway, with her flags flying at full dress, smoke streaming from her tall stack and water curling along her white, glistening sides, *President Warfield* was an impressive sight — indeed, a thing of beauty. So thought her new owners on the early morning of Friday, July 13, 1928, when she rounded Cape Charles and entered the waters of the Chesapeake Bay

* See the Appendix for details of *Warfield*'s specifications.

for the first time. Off to port were the lights of Norfolk and the fleet at anchor in Hampton Roads. To the north stretched the wide expanse of the Bay, over two hundred miles long, in most places too wide to see across. In the semidarkness of dawn, it looked like open ocean. If any of her officers or company officials had been moved by superstition, they might have stirred uneasily at the fact that it was Friday the thirteenth.

As it was, the occasion was too auspicious for dark thoughts. *Warfield* was home. She was plowing the channel she was to navigate for many years. She was passing through the waters made famous by the pungies and the skipjacks, the schooners and the clippers of the Chesapeake. Ocean freighters slipped by on their way to sea. The sun rising over Pocomoke Sound illuminated the tranquil majesty of the Bay, welcoming *Warfield* to the waters over which she would rule for fourteen years.*

By late afternoon, she was standing in the Patapsco channel. White steamers of other lines heading for river landings all over tidewater Maryland and Virginia passed her one by one, a picturesque procession of another day. Neat white packets, gracefully sheered, their thin stacks belching smoke, they passed *Warfield* close aboard and saluted the splendid newcomer with a sonorous blast of the whistle. Passengers crowded the decks to see her. The parade was straight from the past, a nostalgic reminder of a century of steamboating on the Chesapeake Bay.†

* She came down from the Delaware River under command of Captain William C. Almy, senior captain of the line. The "outside" pilot for the brief Atlantic transit was Homer Almy, the captain's brother. First officer was John L. Marshall, a young man of thirteen years' service, destined to command the *State of Maryland* in the great Bay hurricane of 1933.

† The old sidewheelers *Eastern Shore, Virginia,* and *Talbot* would be making landings in the rivers of the Eastern Shore by morning; *Middlesex* and *Dorchester* would be in the lower reaches of the Potomac and Rappahannock rivers by dawn. The screw steamers *Potomac, Anne Arundel,* and *Piankatank* would be making their way in and out of the river landings of the lower Bay to serve the rich farm land of tidewater

Captain Almy, *Warfield*'s square-jawed, heavy-set skipper, was not given to showing his feelings. He was quiet, terse in rasping out his orders to bring the ship alongside her temporary berth on Pratt Street. As six bells chimed on the wheelhouse clock, he reached for the whistle control and sent a throaty, strident sound echoing over the harbor and around the buildings of Baltimore. It broke sharply upon the quiet of evening, sending gulls and pigeons circling above the piers. Unlike the deep melodious sounds of other steamers on the Bay, this was a high-pitched contralto. Baltimoreans who set their watches by familiar whistles were startled by its raucous wail. On the wing of the bridge, Captain Almy looked down the three hundred feet of *Warfield,* at her superstructure catching the evening's glow, and felt a momentary twinge of exultation. She was the finest of them all, the reigning queen of the Chesapeake, the latest in a century's procession of packets on the Bay.* Momentarily the thought struck him that she might be the last, a splendid finale in a long parade.†

Virginia. The *John Cadwalader* would arrive in Philadelphia the next day. And one boat, the *Calvert,* would turn a two-hour train ride from Baltimore to Washington into a forty-hour sojourn by water on the Chesapeake Bay and the Potomac River. All of these boats left Baltimore about 4:30 each evening and steamed in file down the channel.

* There was nothing very queenly about *Warfield*'s arrival the next morning at her permanent berth, Pier 10, Light Street, the Old Bay Line's Terminal. When it came time to depart from her temporary berth on Pratt Street, and crowds gathered about the pier, her steering gear refused to budge. If the superstitious had wanted to make a case of it, *Warfield*'s ignominious arrival was scarcely a heartening omen. She arrived at the end of a tow line!

† Captain Almy would hardly have considered *Yorktown* of the rival Chesapeake Steamship Company as in the same class with *President Warfield. Yorktown* was indeed launched on February 25, 1928, almost three weeks after *Warfield;* but *Yorktown,* fast as she was, in actual fact was a much smaller vessel, some fifty feet shorter and 300 tons lighter than *Warfield,* and much less sumptuous.

TWO

Many observers, including a number of steamboatmen, realized that *Warfield* was an anachronism from the start. When she appeared on the scene, the colorful drama of steamboating on the Bay was playing out its denouement. While steamers still plied the rivers of tidewater Maryland and Virginia and turned in a modest profit in the process, there was more than a hint that steamboating on the Chesapeake was resting precariously on little more than nostalgia.

The feeling was one of a very "late Victorian afterglow." Anyone who rode at the time as a passenger on the boats of the Chesapeake had the euphoric sensation of having stepped into another era, certainly into a more leisurely way of life. It smacked of the old South, of plantations and good living, and of the traditions of the Chesapeake Bay country.

Those who rode the ships and attempted to write about the experience found their prose turning saccharine. Cynics found themselves moved, whether they liked it or not; and even the most hardheaded of transportation experts felt a tug of nostalgia for a passing scene.

Negro roustabouts on the docks were a smelly and dirty lot. But one remained haunted by their chanting as they worked. The little steamers were sometimes cramped, and the plumbing was often sparse and leaky. But one remembered their deep-throated whistles blowing for river landings — or a lookout calling a long "all's well" to the mate in the wheelhouse at night. The shores of the Bay often carried the stench of dead fish and decaying seaweed. But one never forgot the stimulating smell of oysters and crabs and salt air. Baltimore harbor was filthy, and the streets that adjoined the wharves abounded in crushed garbage, occasional dead rats, and slimy water. But one remembered the smell of spices in the air, and the excitement of boarding a boat and watching it back clear of its slip and turn about in the harbor. One remembered sun-drenched days on white steamers with very tall stacks and gingerbread paddleboxes, churning a slow wake on the Bay — or groping up a river channel by night. There was a carefree quality to the scene, as though efficiency mattered none at all and speed could only be equated to original sin.

The romance of the Mississippi found its counterpart on the Chesapeake in a century of colorful history. The raconteur of the Mississippi would have reaped a literary harvest of steamboats that blew up without warning, of rescues in hurricanes and from burning boats, and of gamblers who lost plantations on a flick of the cards. Through rate wars, monopolies, and depressions, the steamboats of the Chesapeake somehow survived, and no one in 1928 wanted to make explicit his disquiet at the sight of macadam roads and trucking lines reaching into tidewater country — and at the statistics of a burgeoning automobile industry that made steamboating already a thing of the past.

Certainly, 1928 was not a time of somber thoughts. *Warfield* was entering her youth — carefree days of warmth and innocence. They began with her maiden voyage on Wednesday, July 18, 1928, and continued for over a decade.* In that time, she plowed up more than a half-million miles of water

* On her maiden voyage, a new quartermaster by the name of Patrick Parker took the wheel. He was destined to play a key role in the subsequent history of the ship.

between Baltimore and Norfolk — at the beginning, at least, a happy wake of song and laughter.

The wharves of Light Street at sailing time presented a scene of chaos. To get to the two-story wooden piers lining the far side of the street, a passenger gathered his courage, raced between horse-drawn drays and trucks thundering over the cobblestones, dodged the chanting stevedores trundling produce and crates of foul-smelling poultry about the wharves, and mounted some stairs to the safety of a reception room. There, in a moment of getting his breath, he might speculate on his good fortune at escaping alive from the tumult below. He might take time, in the bustle created by the arrival of other passengers, to note the particular sounds of the melodious din, of chirping tugs, shouting roustabouts, and sonorous ship whistles — or to savor the smell of oily harbor water, wooden piers, tar, and the aroma of roasting coffee from a local spice plant. Baltimoreans have grown sentimental over this nauseous, yet stimulating, concoction of sound and smell for generations.

A passenger arriving in late afternoon for a *Warfield* sailing from Pier 10, Light Street, got his bearings on the second floor of the dark green, clock-dominated building that served as the Old Bay Line terminal. From this room, he stepped across the gangway to the *Warfield*'s foredeck, often to meet the captain, who with outstretched hand played the role of host as well as master. The routine called for the passenger to pay his respects to the purser's office, where he obtained a huge brass stateroom key attached to a wooden tag large enough to keep the key afloat. Like other passengers, he pushed through the crowd on the upper deck to gape at the bustling scene prior to sailing.

Departure of *President Warfield* from Baltimore was promptly at 6:30. The time of departure was carefully chosen to accommodate the speed of the ship and the habits of its clientele. Seventeen statute miles per hour had been deemed to be quite sufficient as a cruising speed by her designers; any additional speed would have been superfluous, since passengers expected to enjoy a good dinner and an evening of festivities on board, without arriving in Norfolk, 185 miles away, at too inconvenient an hour the next morning. After all, riding a steamboat was different from faster means of travel. One boarded a steamboat for more than mere transportation.

At 6:30, with passengers blackening her rails and spectators waving from the pier, she would sound one stentorian blast and back clear, using a tug because her length made it difficult to pivot in the narrow confines of the basin. A series of whistle salutes between ship and tug would be exchanged as she finally steamed off down the channel, the etiquette due a queen.

In summertime, she would be loaded with vacationers and honeymooners, bound for Virginia Beach. They crowded the decks on the way down the channel past Fort McHenry.

There was an exhilaration in staying on the open decks while the ship steamed down the open Bay. It was almost like going to sea. The shore disappeared as night descended, and the distant lighthouses could be picked up, looming briefly on the horizon. The air freshened, and there was the clean smell of salt and the sea. The swish of waves at the cutwater and along the side could be heard as the boat knifed along at fifteen knots. In the bow stood the lookout, calling back his sightings to the wheelhouse two decks above. The bells would sound the hours and half-hours. Occasionally, out of the darkness would come a stab of light as the mate turned on the searchlight above the wheelhouse to locate a buoy. To the uninitiated, the ship plowing on into the night, through a whispering sea, was little short of romance at its best.

Below, the dining room presented a glowing spectacle of shining tablecloths and silverware and crowds of festive diners. The menu was a staggering offering of Bay delicacies — diamondback terrapin, canvasback duck, quail, turkey,

Mobjack Bay oysters, roe, Norfolk spot, and the side dishes that have made the South famous.

In the leather-chaired smoking room, card games would engage many of the male passengers. Strollers would roam around the balustraded, mirrored gallery deck and down the stairway. The ship's social directress would lead off the music, singing and dancing in the social hall or in the glass-enclosed palm room on the upper deck. Sometimes, she would inveigle passengers to start off games of "horse racing," accomplished by using small wooden horses racing over numbered squares on the deck. An air of comfortable elegance and leisure enveloped the spectacle — a reflection of a way of life and a mental attitude fast disappearing from the American scene.

Sometime during the evening, before one could see Wolf Trap Light flickering to starboard, the decks would clear of passengers. *Warfield*, after all, was a honeymoon ship. The night breeze on the Bay in summertime was downright sensual. Here and there, a couple blending in the shadow of the upper deck, would disappear to a waiting stateroom. The lights glimmering through louvred windows went out, one by one, all over the ship. To some imaginative sentimentalists who sailed her time and time again, the moments from midnight to dawn seemed intimate, the ship cradling young honeymooners and giving a gentle rhythm to their essays in love. Some cynics wondered how everything worked out in the cheaper staterooms equipped with double-deck bunks. There were surprises from peeping toms and pranksters.* But, for the most part, the sighs and little sounds from the staterooms were those of contentment.

Below, in the smoking room, where the barbershop had

* There were indeed surprises. A few crew members remembered the case of the buxom "mother" and her voluptuous "daughter," who were frequent passengers. When it came to light that they were engaging separate staterooms — one on the lower deck for the run of the mill, and a bridal suite for the carriage trade, the nature of their sojourn on *Warfield* was all too clear.

become a bar as soon as the Eighteenth Amendment was repealed, the parties might go on till daybreak, and the lower decks would ring with lusty choruses, less and less coherent as the night wore on, of the old familiar saws from "Harvest Moon" to "I've Been Working on the Railroad." A trip on *Warfield* was intended for pleasure, and those who rode her found their fun in different ways.

In the darkened pilothouse on the hurricane deck, far above the cabin lights and festivities, there was quiet and the work of navigation. On either side of the four-foot mahogany wheel were the brass binnacle to the right and the engine-room telegraph to the left, and around the front of the pilothouse, with its eleven windows, was a wooden grating where the officer of the watch paced. In the darkness, the mate would take his stand usually to one side of the middle window — the captain to the right if he was still on deck — and give quiet orders to the quartermaster at the wheel, "left rudder a spoke," "steady." He was alert for the lighthouses marking the major river entrances of the Bay, for the channel buoys flashing and sounding their deep bells with the rolling waves, and for the running lights of ocean freighters moving up the Bay. To qualify for his job, he had to know the thousand miles of the Chesapeake and its tributaries like a book.

Around daybreak, *Warfield* would round Thimble Shoal Light and feel underfoot the long swell of the Atlantic. Passengers awakened by the sound of the whistle could lower their stateroom windows and see in the half-light the pier at Old Point Comfort and the Hotel Chamberlain in the background; they could hear the jangle of engine-room bells far below, feel the pulse of the engines cease and then the vibration as they backed down, then the scrape of the fender along the piling, and the thump of mooring lines and gangplank on the dock. After a brief layover, the ship was underway again, across Hampton Roads and alongside the

Old Bay Line terminal in Norfolk, to arrive at 6:30 A.M., precisely.

The schedule was the same, winter and summer. This was not an excursion which could be canceled when the weather turned bad; it was a service, operated with the precision of a railroad, in spite of the weather.

Wintertime was a trying period. Ice in the upper Bay, sometimes a foot thick, could stop a boat in mid-channel until the icebreaker arrived to free her; hurricanes sweeping out of the Caribbean could build up heavy seas over the wide expanses of the Bay and drive a boat into the shoals. Fog was a continuing hazard, and a captain in the absence of modern radar had to depend on his memory of the Bay, its currents and its whims, and on a sixth sense of approaching danger.

In wintertime, one of the warmest spots on board was the engine room. To the casual spectator, the sight of the reciprocating engines, with their great flailing piston rods driving the propeller shaft at over one hundred revolutions per minute, was a startling sight — or the firerooms with white-hot flames from the firedoor licking out at firemen and stokers.

Steamboating in the 1930's was a leisurely, pleasant, graceful way of life — the last page of a book that was already written. The tranquillity was to last for almost a decade.*

President Warfield was the symbol of the end of a century of pageantry. The centennial of the Old Bay Line came to

* Very little disturbed the tranquillity. In March 1929, *Warfield* was stopped by a Coast Guard cutter, whose skipper found contraband gin in a roadster on board. The owner, abandoning his car, walked ashore at Old Point Comfort and escaped apprehension. To earn her keep in 1929 and again in 1931, *Warfield* was loaned away for runs on Long Island Sound under charter to the Eastern Steamship Company and the Colonial Line. People changed in the decade: Captain Almy retired, succeeded by Captain R. Sidney Foster, dean of Old Bay Line masters; Patrick Parker went off to *Maryland* and *Virginia*; and C. M. ("Skeeter") Walker became second engineer. To *Warfield* came Willie Harris, a waiter whose father had served on *Alabama* for thirty-eight years. Willie was famous for his dinner call, a magnificent "din-n-n-e-r-r-r now being served," with a trilling of the "r" which could last two full minutes by the clock.

President Warfield *alongside the wharf at Old Point Comfort, Virginia, in 1939*

The main saloon of President Warfield. *Shown is a skit marking the one hundreth anniversary of the Old Bay Line, May 23, 1940.*

Willie Harris, beloved steward on Warfield, *famous for his dinner call*

fulfillment on Thursday, May 23, 1940, in a touch of fanfare that turned back the pages of history.

On that day, the Old Bay Line pier, festooned with streamers and flags, displayed huge cutouts of old paddle-wheel steamers of the past. A costumed crowd of revelers swarmed through the reception rooms and lined the windows and sidewalks in a flutter of hoopskirts, crinolines, parasols, beaver hats and whiskers. In midafternoon, a parade through the streets brought an official party, including Governor O'Connor, Mayor Jackson of Baltimore, and the city managers of Norfolk, Portsmouth and Newport News, to the Old Bay Line pier in a procession of ancient victorias, broughams, and horsecars, escorted by horsemen in Confederate and Union uniforms and bands playing "Yankee Doodle" and "Dixie." In the reception room stood white-haired Captain Foster, commodore of the line, greeting each reveler with a stately bow. The crowd sang "Carry Me Back to Old Virginny" and trooped aboard *Warfield* to a thunderous salute from her whistle.

In the smoking room on the lower deck, a fountain bubbled with centennial cocktails and an orchestra serenaded with Stephen Foster melodies. The Governor led the way into the dining room to a banquet of terrapin and pheasant, topped by toasts in madeira of 1870 and Jesuitgarden 1934. By 6:30 it was quite clear that Mr. Raymond L. Jones, passenger manager, had been quite correct in his earlier prediction that *Warfield* would miss its sailing. Baltimoreans who for twelve years now had set their watches by the ship's blast were led astray. But no one really cared. After all, birthday celebrations like this did not come very often — only once in a hundred years — and maybe never again.

At length, *Warfield* sailed, with the costumed crowd still aboard and the ship a Mardi Gras of singing, dancing revelers. All along the waterfront, oceangoing and Bay ships, decked in flags, serenaded *Warfield* as she passed. Down the Bay she steamed in the ghostly wake of a half-hundred boats of the line, little sidewheelers and pretentious packets that had carried the red flag with the white "B" through a hundred years of history.

That evening on the trip down the Bay, a group of musicians and actors presented a series of skits in the social hall. One of the skits depicted the predicament and consternation of a young honeymoon couple in the early days of steamboating when they discovered that men's sleeping quarters were separated by the length of the boat from the women's. The skits and the festivities lasted into the night, and Miss Louise Lazenby, *Warfield*'s social directress, had indeed produced a centennial triumph. *Warfield*'s guests straggled wearily off at Old Point Comfort the next morning, some for the Cavalier Hotel. When some of them returned immediately by plane to Baltimore, the contrast between past and present, modern and rococo, was never more explicit.

While the operators of the Old Bay Line refused to accept the inevitable,* the destiny of *President Warfield* and the era she symbolized was being shaped by forces beyond their control. On the one hand, there were the inexorable economic trends of the times, forcing the steamboat to a position of irrelevance in an age of advancing technology. On the other hand, there was the somber spectacle of war, once more spreading a bloody pattern across the face of Europe.

Even as May 23, 1940, was celebrated on *Warfield*, the day was filled with heavy tidings in Europe. The German advance through Belgium had broken the French center, threatened to cut off the Allied armies from the south, and brought the contingency of emergency evacuation of the British Expeditionary Force to the very edge of Dunkirk. Just a week before, Churchill almost in his first act as Prime

* They reported that in January 1940, the company had marked up its most profitable month since 1923 and that it had never defaulted on interest payment on a debt of $700,000. However, there seemed little point in continuing the competition between the Old Bay Line and the Chesapeake Line, the latter owned jointly by the Atlantic Coast Line Railroad and the Southern Railway. Arrangements at the time of the centennial were virtually complete for merger.

Minister had pled with Roosevelt for fifty older destroyers to fill the gap in defense against the German U-boats; the resulting agreement was the beginning of lend-lease.

Warfield's fate was being cast in Europe, even as the anniversary cocktails bubbled in the fountain and "Auld Lang Syne" rose from the forward deck. Just as the curtain of war descended, her future was being sealed — in the vast and incomprehensible tragedy of Eastern and Central Europe where the racial theme of *Mein Kampf* was being played out in full measure.

For *Warfield*, May 23, 1940, was the end of youth and adolescence. Her sublime world of tranquil waters and song-filled evenings on the Bay came to an end.

Military cargoes began to fill her freight deck. Her passengers became servicemen bound for the ships and bases at Norfolk who crowded her decks and slept, sprawled about her saloon and public spaces, for want of staterooms. Elegance gave way to utility, and utility to shabbiness. *Warfield* lost her gaiety. About her were the echoes of marching feet, sad farewells, and the grim tidings of battle.

For *President Warfield* — as for many Americans — the age of innocence had come to an end.

Part Two

The War and Oblivion

THREE

THE WAR struck *President Warfield* swiftly and harshly.

She had stood by stoically, as her two sister ships one by one marched off to war, leaving her and the three former Chesapeake Line steamers (two of them worn and ancient) to maintain a pressing service.

Even as the officials of the Old Bay Line were recovering from the shock of seeing two of their best steamers drafted by the Army, more drastic events were developing behind the scenes. In early April of 1942, President Roosevelt set forth to a certain "Former Naval Person" in Whitehall a proposition concerning the launching of an offensive in Western Europe. One contingency, as perceived by the Combined Chiefs of Staff, was the procurement as quickly as possible of shallow-draft ships suitable for cross-Channel transport operations. Under lend-lease, therefore, the U.S. War Shipping Administration in mid-June was asked to furnish the British Ministry of War Transport up to fifteen small, fast, shallow-draft vessels. A conference, held quietly on June 26, 1942, in the Commerce Building office of Mr. D. S. Brierley, Director of Maintenance of WSA, attended by the Hon. J. F. Maclay of the British Merchant Shipping Mission and David Boyd of the British Ministry of War Transport, set about to select suitable vessels from a list of some twenty-five candidates.

Spread out on the conference table were photographs and drawings of these inland steamers available on the East Coast of the United States. The decrepit were quickly rejected. The best were picked.* Two of these were Old Bay Line boats. *Yorktown*, the newest of the former Chesapeake Line steamers, was selected. So was *President Warfield*.

Like a soldier, *Warfield* gained a number (requisition number 227,753) and orders — to be transferred as soon as possible by WSA to a repair yard designated by Messrs. Lemon and Bovring of the British Mission for alteration to make her seaworthy for a transatlantic voyage. Mr. David Boyd of the British Ministry in New York, because of his experience in fitting out small vessels for ocean crossing, was to approve the plans for conversion. The ship was to be manned by crews assigned by the British Ministry. Upon sailing, she was to carry British registry and flag.

To Captain Patrick Parker, her first quartermaster on the maiden voyage — a tall, heavyset, spectacled man, with a kindly bearing — and "Skeeter" Walker, chief engineer, fell the unhappy lot of bringing her up from Norfolk for the last time on July 11, 1942. The next day, at noon precisely, at her pier in Baltimore, *President Warfield* passed from the Old Bay Line to WSA under lend-lease to the British Ministry of War Transport. There was no ceremony. It was a quiet Sunday. *Warfield*, shorn of her flag, stood alone. Her days on the Bay were at an end.

By midafternoon, she had been moved to the west side of Pier 3, Pratt Street, where the machine shop and temporary wartime repair facilities of the Maryland Drydock Company were located. Workmen swarmed aboard. Already the race against time had begun — the race against military deadlines in Europe — and the race against the weather in the North

* In addition to *Yorktown* and *President Warfield*, the following were selected: *Northland* and *Southland* (Washington-to-Norfolk steamers), *Virginia Lee* (Cape Charles to Norfolk steamer), *Boston*, *Naushon*, and *New York* (New York-to-Boston steamers); *John Cadwalader* (Baltimore-to-Philadelphia steamer) was picked as an alternate.

From Chesapeake Bay to France

★ ★ ★

OLD BAY LINE
STEAMERS SERVING IN WORLD WAR II

The Steamer "PRESIDENT WARFIELD" shown here in pre-war days, now sails in French Waters. The "PRESIDENT WARFIELD" was requisitioned for the British Ministry on July 12th, 1942. She crossed the Atlantic during the most critical period of enemy submarine activity. She was later turned back to the U. S. Navy and participated in the Normandy invasion.

The Steamer "YORKTOWN" was also requisitioned for the British Ministry on July 13th, 1942 and sailed in same convoy with the "PRESIDENT WARFIELD".

The Steamers "STATE OF MARYLAND" and "STATE OF VIRGINIA" sister ships of the "PRESIDENT WARFIELD", were requisitioned by the U. S. Army on April 1st and April 2nd, 1942 and are now serving in the Army Transport Service.

DECEMBER 1944

Plaque on model of President Warfield *in the reception room of the Old Bay Line terminal, Pier 10, Light Street, Baltimore*

Atlantic when midsummer calm gave way to the gales of fall and winter. Sir Ashley Sparks of the British Mission was already flogging the War Shipping Administration in his demands for priority, for speed.

To their chagrin, Parker and Walker were assigned as liaison men to assist the British in *Warfield*'s conversion and to watch her torn to pieces.

Indeed, it seemed that the conversion would destroy her. In the interior, all of the staterooms on the saloon deck (except four for gun crews) were ripped out, leaving one enormous room, like a dormitory. Raw, unpainted wood replaced the paneling. On the gallery deck, the staterooms were left intact, some converted into crew messrooms; but on the hurricane deck, the "well" was decked over and converted into a wardroom, the old resplendent skylight remaining as a last touch of grandeur.

To provide clear arcs of fire for guns, the afterdeck was cut back and reinforced. A twelve-pounder was mounted on a platform especially constructed for it at the saloon deck level; four 20-mm mounts were installed around the smokestack; and around the pilothouse was placed six inches of asphalt shielding. All told, her armor and armament were certainly not formidable, and *Warfield* wore what there was of it with bad grace.

The real problem was to ready the ship, built only to ride the quiet waters of the Chesapeake, for the rough seas of the North Atlantic. An immediate problem was the sponson, the overhang at main-deck level above the hull, characteristic of all Bay steamers; heavy seas pounding underneath it could introduce dangerous strains on both hull and superstructure. The solution, as set forth by Mr. David Boyd, was to box in the overhang with timbers secured to metal channeling welded to the hull. The whole appearance of *Warfield* changed; her slender hull disappeared in a tublike casing.

Over her foredeck, a wooden, planked-up turtleback was built to fend off the boarding seas. Heavy vertical planking completely covered the superstructure at the saloon-deck level, blocking out the windows and shielding the house from high waves; and around the former dining room, aft on the main deck, a similar wooden structure went around the entire stern. Trigger-release life rafts were installed on the upper decks; additional oil tanks were added below; hawsepipes and mooring chocks were cemented up; side cargo ports were reinforced. Boxed in, turtlebacked, the ship had little resemblance to the *Warfield* of an earlier day.

The final stroke was a coat of paint, a dreary, somber gray camouflage from stack to waterline. The gray smut of war, covering forever the white grace of youth, was to shroud *Warfield* to the bitter end.

The red British merchant flag rose to the masthead on the morning of Friday, August 20, 1942. She sounded one long, plaintive blast of farewell to Baltimore and headed for New York. By evening, off the Delaware capes, she was in convoy — her only comfort the old *Virginia Lee* of the Cape Charles line at her side — and a Coast Guard cutter on the flank for protection. A volunteer British crew manned her, commanded by Captain J. R. Williams, a ruddy six-footer, steel-jawed from the grim experience of the U-boat war in the Atlantic.

Three weeks later, *Warfield*, small and forlorn, nestled in the landlocked harbor of St. Johns, Newfoundland — one of eight gray, nondescript, boarded-up river steamers huddled together for shelter against the moment when they would set forth together for a far shore.

September 20, 1942, was a quiet Sunday in St. Johns. The long shadows of the hills crept up the misty slopes, and the bells of the cathedral above the city rang for evensong.

Below clustered the little ships, fragile in their boxlike superstructures and low, cased-in hulls, seemingly defenseless against the gales of the North Atlantic and the dangers of the U-boat war. One wit had called the ships "skimming dishes" and bet that they wouldn't make it. Still another called them the "maniac convoy" and was not intentionally humorous.

There was, indeed, much to fear. In September 1942, the U-boat war was intense.* In August, two convoys had been severely mauled; a total of 108 ships had been sunk, amounting to over a half-million tons of shipping. The Germans were working in "wolf packs" roaming the shipping lanes and striking at convoys in submerged attack, even in broad daylight.

In St. Johns, as the bells of evensong sounded on the slopes, the masters of the eight ships met the convoy commodore and the escort commander for orders and emergency instructions aboard the convoy flagship. These skippers were seamen, hardened by memories of recent convoys: Captain R. S. Young, commodore and master of *Boston* of the Eastern Steamship Line; Captain C. Mayers, vice commodore, skipper of *New York,* also of Eastern; Captain James Beckett and Captain John Williams, masters of *Northland* and *Southland,* respectively, both former Norfolk-Washington packets; Captain J. J. Murray and Captain R. Hardy of

* By the first of September, Allied shipping losses had already exceeded three million tons. U-boats were operating in the shipping lanes of the North Atlantic and along the eastern seaboard of the United States and Canada. With Allied development of the convoy system and increased number of escorts, the tide of battle was slowly beginning to turn. However, the Germans were tenaciously, even hysterically, fighting on.

In September, D-day for "Torch," the invasion of North Africa, was little over a month away. Convoys from the United States were already steaming for the Clyde and the west of England, where shipping and stockpiles were being concentrated. The concern of the Combined Chiefs of Staff was to hoodwink the Germans into believing that Dakar was the objective. The Germans bit on the bait and their own intelligence led them to concentrate more than forty submarines to the south and east of the Azores. Hopefully, the way was clear for the movement of troopships from Britain across the Bay of Biscay and for the advance of the main American task force from the United States direct to Casablanca.

But not all of the German submarines were out of the North Atlantic shipping lanes, by any means. The wolf packs were active, sinkings were frequent, and the toll in desperately needed war materiel and in lives was fearful.

Naushon and *New Bedford*, steamers of the New Bedford, Martha's Vineyard and Nantucket line; and Captains W. P. Boylan and J. R. Williams of the Old Bay Line steamers *Yorktown* and *President Warfield*. The Royal Navy was represented by the commanding officers of H.M.S. *Veteran* and H.M.S. *Vanoc*, destroyer escorts.

Early the next morning, the strange assortment of craft filed through the slot of St. Johns harbor and joined up in formation off the entrance. The day was clear and crisp. Flanking the eight ships in two columns were *Veteran* and *Vanoc* to herd their awkward charges across the Atlantic and protect them at all costs from the lurking enemy. Flags fluttered from the improvised yardarm of *Boston* and were repeated throughout the convoy. RB–1 was underway.* †

Uneasy tension made its unseen presence felt throughout the convoy on that first day at sea. The intelligence briefing on board *Boston* the evening before had been bad enough, but continuing Admiralty message reports on German submarine activity were particularly disquieting.

Each ship settled into a routine of quiet but wakeful vigilance. Lookouts searched their sectors endlessly with binoculars; the armed guard no longer simply stood by their weapons in the mount but occupied the gun positions in the 12-pounder and stood in the harnesses of the 20-mm batteries, watch on and watch off. Engineers went about their

* Several years later, a young U.S. Navy journalist in a news release wrote that convoy RB–1 had been earmarked as a decoy to attract the U-boats away from a "more formidable convoy [to the south] of warships, transports, and amphibious craft . . . headed toward North Africa [and] the invasion that was to turn the tide of war in that epochal year of 1942." The idea was certainly heroic enough, if the facts of history could be made to jibe. The sailing of RB–1 and the amphibious force movement from the United States to North Africa were unfortunately separated by approximately one month in time. Whether the routing of RB–1 was arranged to coincide with another, perhaps equally critical, movement of ships to Britain is another matter. The evidence of later events suggests, however, that these strange ships were, in their own way, important and not so readily expendable as decoys.

† The letters RB meant "riverboat."

duties below decks with life jackets in easy reach. Seamen on deck were tight-lipped, noncommittal; some searched the horizon in quick, almost furtive glances. A gusty wind whipped up the sea, and *Warfield* dipped her nose in a glistening spray which made rainbows in the slanting sun. As evening came, the ship blacked out: porthole and hatch covers were shut, blackout curtains were drawn, and the watch was warned about matches and cigarettes in the open. Night came heavily. Many men slept in their clothes.

The second day passed like the first.

On the third day, a message indicated that a surface raider was operating in the vicinity of the convoy.

On the fourth day, a series of radio messages reported submarine action in the general area of RB–1.

The fifth afternoon, Saturday, September 21, was clear and breezy. The convoy still steamed in two columns, destroyer escorts slightly ahead on either flank, the wake of each ship a white feather on a choppy, greenish ocean.

Suddenly, heavy explosions shook the sea. *Boston,* the commodore's ship, struck by two torpedoes, shuddered in a great cloud of spray and smoke. The shattered hulk staggered to starboard, sagged in collapse, then slowly upended and sank. Her bow hung for a moment, then slipped beneath the waves.

In the convoy, there was momentary stunned silence. The effect was almost eerie. Ships seemed to continue along as before; the afternoon was the same — except that *Boston* was no longer there.

Then frantic activity broke out. Bridge watches leaped to alarm signals and ships' whistles. Men raced to their emergency stations. Full gun crews clambered over the tubs and readied their weapons.

Northland, turning away from the sinking *Boston,* had her rudder jam at full speed, just as her lookouts spotted a submarine breaking the surface five hundred yards away. Hastily transferring steering to after control, she swung about to flee. *New Bedford*, designated as rescue ship in the sailing orders, steamed toward the sinking wreckage. The escort commander broke radio silence, and the convoy warning frequency crackled. Both escorts rang up flank speed and knifed through the seas toward the beleaguered ships. Their sonar was a jumble of echoes, confused by the turbulence of rapidly turning wakes. Captain Mayers, vice commodore on *New York*, ran up emergency flags ordering the convoy to take evasive action.

Southland was on the outboard side of the emergency turn. Suddenly her lookouts and gun crews sighted a periscope to starboard. The 12-pounder aft opened fire. Fourteen rounds landed in spurts of spray. The periscope disappeared. Hardly had the cease-fire sounded, when a cry arose: "Periscope to port." Around the gunners spun, opening up on the opposite side. Eighteen rounds emptied from the 12-pounder. Again, the periscope disappeared. Whether the *Southland* sank the submarine remained undetermined.

Captain Williams, aboard *President Warfield*, was on the bridge almost from the start. He shouted rudder orders to the helmsman and rang up full speed himself on the engine-room telegraph. He stepped to the port bridge wing, just as the lookout, almost incoherent, shouted "Torpedo!" There it was — the speeding, telltale streak, approaching from abaft the port beam. Williams's shouts were instantaneous: "Right wheel — amidships — steady." The ship swung on a parallel course, and the torpedo passed harmlessly down the side, not much more than thirty feet away.

Almost immediately, there were shouts from the deck. Off the port quarter there appeared the unmistakable shadow of a submarine lurking just beneath the surface. Poor weapon that it was, the 12-pounder aft opened fire. *Warfield*'s whistle screeched in alarm. H.M.S. *Veteran* wheeled and raced to the attack. All around, the sea heaved with depth charges.

Warfield and *Veteran* together credited themselves with a probable kill.*

The convoy scattered. At best speed, the little ships steamed off — putting as much distance as possible between them to evade the attacking submarines. The wolf pack was not through. Spread over a wide area, the submarines waited for the ships to appear and coordinated their attacks by open communications.

At dusk, the *New York* was torpedoed and sank in a fiery explosion. Captain Mayers went down with his ship.

Picking her way through the floating debris in search of survivors, H.M.S. *Veteran* herself was hit and sank with heavy loss of life. She was loaded with survivors from *Boston.*

Yorktown steamed into the evening at full speed, her crew fervently praying that they had escaped. About sunset, still in sight of some of the convoy, she found that her steering engine was developing difficulties which required her to stop. For several anxious hours, she hove to in the choppy sea, her crew expecting attack at any instant, her engineers working frantically to repair the trouble. Underway at last, she raced on a tangent course into the night. Alone the next morning, her crew looked out across an empty, heaving ocean, and their prayers seemed answered. But shortly after nine o'clock, without any warning, she was hit on the port side. The explosion of the torpedo broke her back and collapsed her superstructure. She sank in a few brief minutes. Captain Boylan and a few other crew members survived by clinging to a raft made of wreckage. They were located by a patrol plane and picked up by a British destroyer forty-six hours after the sinking. When they crawled from the timbers to the deck of the destroyer, they were barely recognizable — oil-soaked, filthy, grief-stricken from the loss of their ship and shipmates.

* German records in the British Admiralty of the attack by U-404 on RB-1 show that no German losses were sustained during the attack on September 21, 1942.

Warfield, too, sped on into the night. Swinging far to the north, she hoped to clear the area where the submarine pack was operating. Day after day, her lookouts fearfully searched the sullen, crested waters of the North Atlantic.

But the periscope never appeared; the torpedo never struck.

The sea was rough, and *Warfield* wallowed badly. Her sharp prow burrowed too deeply into the oncoming seas, and she shook herself free in a cloud of spray like a wet dog shaking itself. The decks streamed with water and spray filled the scuppers. At each heavy roll, loose gear clattered about the ship, and men off watch wedged themselves in their bunks with lifejackets about them and watched helplessly as masses of sodden clothes, books, and foul-weather gear slid around the stateroom decks.

For the men on watch, it was a brutal period of intense tedium — of anticipating the roll and the pitch and hanging on as they moved about, of endlessly bracing and wedging themselves even in fatigue, and of keeping warm in a cold salt spray that seemed to permeate the whole ship. There was warmth and refuge in the engine room, where the great piston rods sped up and slowed down with the rise and fall of the propeller in the rolling seas. But this refuge was sudden death if the torpedo struck. On the bridge, the hours passed in a strain of waiting and searching the gray waters, sometimes dappled with silver in a fleeting sun, for some sign of the lurking danger.

Then, on the last day of September 1942, she rounded Malin Head and headed down the North Channel past the Mull of Kintyre. In the afternoon, dark clouds let through shafts of sunlight which flickered on the quiet water and lit up in green patches the distant hills of Ballycastle to starboard. The calm of the Firth of Clyde stretched off to port.

Shelter at last. A steady deck. Haven from the storm. Shutters were lowered along the hurricane and gallery decks to let in the sweetening breeze, wet clothes were set out to dry, and furniture and disheveled gear about the ship were set to rights. There was the sound of radio music from the messrooms and the smell of cooking from the galley. Seagulls soared and wheeled about the stern. Peace at last — rest and sleep.

Warfield steamed up Belfast Lough and into her berth along the long Belfast quay crowded with deep-laden ships, veterans of the war at sea. Strange newcomer that she was, *Warfield* was a veteran, too — scarred in the heat and pain of battle.

Other veterans of convoy RB–1 made port, also — *Naushon* and *Northland* to Londonderry in Northern Ireland, *Southland* and *New Bedford* to Greenock near Glasgow. Radio Berlin gave unwitting praise to the gallantry of the little riverboats, declaring that Nazi submarines had sunk several ships "of the Queen Mary class," claiming two of them to be the converted liners *Reina del Pacifico* and *Duchess of Bedford,* and acknowledging that the tally was uncertain because the defense was "so fierce." Any humor was lost on the crews of RB–1. Their thoughts were of the 131 shipmates left behind in the cruel Atlantic.

All of the masters, chief engineers, and fourteen other officers were included in the next honors list of the King. Some were posthumous awards. Captain J. R. Williams and Chief Engineer J. S. Penwill of *Warfield* deserved their honor. Under their command, *President Warfield* had become more than an inland steamer abused by war. She had become, even then, somewhat of a legend.

FOUR

Along the Devon coast, near the village of Westward Ho, the great combers of the Atlantic break upon the beach in a surging surf. Close by, inside the Neck, the rivers Torridge and Taw flow past Appledore in a quiet ebb lapping the muddy shores and, when the tide floods, running in eddying currents from the sea.

In the last days of 1942, whispers of impending operations to leap the Channel and land the Allies on the coast of France were already being heard in Britain and felt more particularly in military planning. At Appledore, the British established a base to teach the new art of amphibious warfare, where quiet water inside the Neck favored the practice of fledgling coxswains, and surf on the outside, like that on the coast of Normandy, challenged those to graduate upon the beachheads.

There was a need for the equivalent of barracks. Casting about for a quick solution, Admiralty planners found an answer in *President Warfield.* Under orders, her crew of Coast Lines, Ltd., in October 1942 moved her from Belfast and Holyhead to Southampton. In the shipyard, they crammed her saloon deck with rows of bunks and installed enormous soup kettles in the galley. Then, under charter by the Ministry of Transport, they took her down to Appledore.

There, inside the Neck, they drove her firmly into the mud. Mooring lines held her to shore, and outstretched cables held her upright when the tide went out. As a grounded accommodation or barracks ship, her status was totally ignominious.

It was like KP duty with less prestige. Amphibious units of the Royal Navy arrived to be quartered for training; LCT's and other landing craft moored alongside, sometimes catching themselves in the makeshift grating under *Warfield*'s overhang; and boat crews moved aboard for food and shelter. In August 1943* American personnel began to join the British for training — one hundred officers and two hundred enlisted men at a time — to learn the techniques of the landing force and the coordination of large-scale amphibious assault. To all of these, *Warfield* was a kind of temporary home under the British flag.

Training abruptly came to an end in mid-April 1944. Everyone knew that the great event in the Channel was about to happen.

Warfield's KP duty came to an end, also. Once more, she was assigned to combat.

On April 24, 1944, Coast Lines, Ltd., received orders to move her to Barry Roads, Wales, for discharge from His Majesty's Service, reversion to the War Shipping Administration and simultaneous transfer to the United States Navy. Getting her off the mud, after being stranded for a year, was another matter; a tug pulled from astern and LCM's inched her counter from side to side; *Warfield*'s great engines strained in reverse. For an hour or two it seemed that she was wedged on the beach for good. Then suddenly she broke

* In August 1943, the British transferred the Appledore-Instow base to the U.S. Navy, and there was some exchange of correspondence between Commander Naval Forces Europe and CNO, Washington, on the subject of bringing *Warfield* under U.S. Navy control. However, the decision was made to allow the vessel to remain as a barracks ship under the British, even though American personnel would be using it.

free. With the red British flag streaming from her staff, she headed out to the open sea and up the Bristol Channel.

The British flag was lowered at 9:59 on Saturday evening, May 20, 1944, alongside a dock at Barry. The next morning — Sunday — a U.S. Navy crew, gathered up hastily from local sources, assembled at 7:30 quarters on the hurricane deck. A new skipper, Lieutenant (j.g.) George W. Boyer, USN, read his orders to the crew lined up in formation. A bright new commission pennant at the masthead and an American flag at the staff broke free in the early morning breeze. At that moment, the old ship became U.S.S. *President Warfield* (IX–169), a commissioned auxiliary in the United States Navy.*

Her new crewmen were universally outraged at their assignment to this old "tub." Sixty-five of the enlisted men and four of the officers were in a personnel draft of the cruiser *Milwaukee;* all of the men had been peremptorily scooped up from the personnel pool of ComLanCrabEleventhPhib.† None of them liked the looks of the weathered little steamer that bore not the slightest resemblance to a man-of-war; in fact, they questioned her very seaworthiness.

Even Boyer, the skipper, had many misgivings. A deep-draft sailor with prewar enlisted duty aboard the cruisers *Salt Lake City* and *Minneapolis,* he had been shipped out from training recruits at San Diego and Farragut, Idaho, at the start of the war to join the amphibious force at a new base being carved out of the red clay at Solomons, Maryland, and then — even more surprising — to join a draft in April 1944 with the mission of establishing an amphibious base at the picturesque Cornish seaport of Fowey, there on the south coast of England to train the landing force destined for the

* The letters IX stood for "Miscellaneous." No one knew what else in naval classification to call such a nondescript craft.

† Translated as Commander Landing Craft Battalion, Eleventh Amphibious Force, the operational command controlling *Warfield* from headquarters in Plymouth, England.

Officers of the U.S.S. President Warfield (IX 169) *in Plymouth, England, February 1945. First row: left to right: Lt. G. W. Boyer, USN, commanding officer; Lt. (j.g.) R. J. Mumford, USNR, first lieutenant. Second row: Lt. (j.g.) J. David Dyer, USNR, communications officer; Lt. (j.g.) D. C. DuBrul, USN, executive officer; Ch. Mach. F. Owings, USN, engineering officer; Lt. (j.g.) W. Armstrong USNR, supply officer.*

invasion of Europe. For a deep-water sailor, the amphibious force at first seemed like the lowest form of duty; its boats were misshapen craft that performed the unthinkable act of deliberately grounding themselves on the beach; and its new sailors were a maverick breed of "feather merchants" who had never known the respectability of the old Navy. Hardly had Boyer taken stock of the quaint town of Fowey, whose narrow streets had known the swagger of Elizabethan gallants of the sea and whose estuary now echoed to the staccato rattle of modern landing craft, when he was shaken once again by a phone call from his boss, Commodore Korns (the very person of ComLanCrabEleventhPhib). Would Boyer come over to Plymouth and discuss taking charge of an old ship the Navy was inheriting from the British? In Plymouth, Boyer discovered the ship in question was in Barry and he was to become her commanding officer.

"It's like something I want nothing to do with! It's not my idea of a *ship*, let alone a *warship!*" he exclaimed when he saw his frowzy prospective command, drooping against the dock in Barry. But he overcame his shock and loyally set about to make her fit for duty in the United States Navy and for the assignment that awaited her on the far shore. The time was short.

On June 5, the invasion of France began. Over the beaches of Normandy poured the assault waves of the Allied Expeditionary Force. In the first echelons were the coxswains, the crews, and the troops that had known *Warfield* as home on the training beaches of Devon.

Warfield went to drydock in Plymouth to remove the scars of her year in the mud and to take off the planking under the sponsons, thereby exposing once again the sleek hull not seen since Baltimore. Emerging from drydock on American Independence Day, she gathered the last of her crew and prepared to sail for Normandy.

Boyer took a hard look at his assembled crew — a cross section of America's wartime Navy — the farmer, the scion of Madison Avenue, the bum. He decided that his experience with recruits would pay dividends. A neat, soft-spoken man, Boyer managed by his ministrations to remove some of the bedraggled appearance of crew and ship alike. Some of the men began to appreciate the comforts of the old ship — in fact, even to develop a kind of humorous pride in her. A semblance of unity augured well for the months ahead.

The officers had the same reaction as the crew. The new Executive Officer, Ensign Donald C. Du Brul, even after feeling the sting of the Japanese attack at Pearl Harbor and losing his own ship on D-Day at Normandy, said that his first sight of *Warfield* was the biggest jolt he ever had. A tall, thin chap in his twenties, Du Brul as navigator and second-in-command was to ride her through to the end of her naval career and to adapt himself over time to the mellow comforts of the old boat. Floyd Owings, chief machinist from San Diego with experience in major combatant ships behind him, was both amused by his assignment as chief engineer to an ancient river boat and worried about keeping her running. But the rugged reciprocating engines, in the end, won his grudging respect. The junior officers were generally a happy-go-lucky lot, young enough to shrug off assignment to this grotesque caricature of a man-of-war as just another lark. However, one who never got over the shock of his assignment to *Warfield* was the supply officer, Lieutenant (j.g.) William J. Armstrong. A rather solemn man, he looked at his job of supplying a floating hotel with downright astonishment. He seemed to be in a perpetual state of rush and confusion. Usually at mealtime, he could be depended upon to come sailing into the wardroom — water from hasty ablutions dripping from his nose — just a hairsbreadth ahead of the captain, who by protocol was the last to arrive and first to be seated. Each meal began with a bet on Armstrong's race. Unwittingly, in his own way, he unified the wardroom.

Warfield was ready. At eight in the evening of July 6, she slipped her wire from buoy number 8 in Plymouth harbor; an hour later she had joined a convoy offshore and turned her bow toward the beaches of Normandy.

As darkness fell on July 7, she crept into the vast roadstead of Omaha Beach. In the waning light, the anchorage seemed filled with ships; landing craft shuttled back and forth through the "mulberry" breakwater of sunken ships to the shore; and on the distant beach motor convoys rumbled up the steep cliffs and disappeared into France. Off Sector 23, *Warfield* let go her anchor.

Early the next morning, the harbor authorities moved her to her permanent berth, secured fore and aft to large mooring can buoys, and on the starboard side to the upper works of the old British battleship *Centurion* sunk to form part of the artificial harbor.

Warfield took up her duties. On board came the harbor master, the port director, movement control officer, and War Shipping Administration representative with all their staffs. *Warfield* became the focal point for the unloading of ships bringing supplies to the Normandy beachhead, the routing office for North Atlantic shipping reaching these shores, and the control point for logistic echelons bringing munitions over Omaha Beach to the front lines. Every ship entering or leaving port exchanged calls by blinker with *Warfield*; they seemed like salutes to an old veteran.

German air raids struck the very first night. *Warfield*'s decks were cluttered with shrapnel from antiaircraft fire which crisscrossed above the anchorage. Air raids became a nocturnal nuisance after a while. *Warfield*'s crew went routinely to general quarters for an hour or two when the alarm sounded, hardly interrupting the movie, the poker game in progress, or even their sleep in the process.

Not all air raids were without their sting. Early Sunday morning, July 30, a German plane dropped an aerial mine 700 yards astern of *Warfield*. At first light, a British hydrographic team quartered on *Warfield* approached it in a small boat and marked it with a buoy. About 10 A.M., British

U.S.S. President Warfield (*IX 169*) *off the Normandy beachhead, 1944. Behind her is the superstructure of the sunken battleship* Centurion. *Moored alongside are various landing craft and MTB's.*

LCT–7036 came boiling through the anchorage. Petrified, men on the deck of *Warfield* watched it bear down on the buoy — sure to the end that it would take notice and veer off. Suddenly, the LCT and the sea around it erupted in a thundering mushroom. As the debris and spray settled, *Warfield*'s boat crews raced to their LCVP's and roared off to the scene. Nine badly wounded survivors were brought back to the ship; two immediately died.

But the climax of combat had already passed. In a week or so, the air raids petered out. And *Warfield* settled down to the weeks of routine duty, punctuated by the little emergencies and discipline problems which characterized any ship in the combat zone. As fall came, the weather and not combat duty created one crisis after another. Across the exposed roadstead, the wind straight off the Atlantic hit at gale force time and time again, carrying away mooring lines, bits, and even capstans in the fury of the storms. Du Brul, the executive officer, nearly got swept away or mangled when a wire and bit broke loose aft. *Warfield* bucked like a wild animal, leashed by her crew in a net of heavy cables and even chains to her moorings.

Then, abruptly, one day she found herself all alone in a deserted anchorage. As far as one could see, there were only the lonely beaches and the hulls of sunken ships around her. Gulls and land birds circled over the water and perched, calling, on the upturned hulks. The day was Sunday, November 12, and church bells rang faintly beyond the cliffs above the beach.

Warfield's mission was at an end. With the opening of Channel ports to Allied shipping, the beachhead at Normandy was no longer needed, and, indeed, was too dangerous in its exposure to the wintry blasts from the Atlantic. When all the other ships had left, *Warfield*, suddenly irrelevant, had been utterly ignored. On the quiet Sunday, she cast loose her chains and crept off across the Channel to Plymouth — alone.

U.S.S. President Warfield (*IX 169*) *in Plymouth, England, February 1945*

FIVE

WARFIELD'S DUTIES IN EUROPE WERE NOT YET OVER. Like a veteran soldier coming back fatigued from the front lines, she was given a physical examination, patched up a little, and returned to duty. In Plymouth, they took off her trappings of war: gun tubs came off, the heavy concrete around her wheelhouse disappeared, and *Warfield* regained a little of her youthful figure. But each jabbing hammer left its mark. And the old ship, already badly beaten by her days in Devon and Normandy, looked a shambles.

Nevertheless, on February 17, she found herself in thick fog, groping out of Plymouth harbor, bound once again for France.

Her last assignment was not heroic. On George Washington's Birthday of 1945, she loaded troops at the Promenade Jetty, Le Havre, and steamed seventy miles up the Seine to discharge them at the so-called "Cigarette Camp," the forward staging area established at Duclair. Moving replacement troops up the river for staging to the front lines, she had, in effect, become a ferry. In three months, she made fifteen trips, handling an average of 800 "passengers" each time and as many as 1,028 on one occasion. On one trip in March 1945, she embarked 840 Italian ex-POW's, a work battalion operating with the U.S. Army after the withdrawal of Italy from combat. On the last few trips, she brought personnel down the river on rotation from the forward area. In effect, *Warfield* ran a commuter service on the Seine.

The river was like the Potomac, winding through the countryside in deep bends and long reaches. In a way, *Warfield* came into her own, harking back to the stately history of steamboating in America. The officers on watch loved to blow the whistle "comin' round the bend." *Warfield*'s old steam whistle, a clear musical note in contrast to the air whistles of Seine river craft, echoed along the banks and across the fields. Peasants came down to the shore to wave, and little villages emptied to watch the steamer glide by. For a moment in time, the old ship gathered around her some of the dignity and glamour of the past.

And, for the times, *Warfield* was a happy ship. But the war was coming to an end.

Lights were coming on again all over Europe, and weary, hungry people were emerging to look at the strange, disfigured world left in the wake of thundering armies. The little villages along the Seine came to life, and Le Havre, in spite of its scars, became once again the lusty seaport it had always been.

Some young sailors turned up AWOL, as they found the beds and beverages of France overwhelmingly tempting. The stairs of one establishment in Le Havre were as busy as the beds above with sailors on the way up and down. Pent-up tensions of discipline and war were released in an emotional overflow. War had come to an end. This was spring, and here was France!

But the crew developed a solid affection for the old ship. At Omaha Beach, they had named her the Statler. It was only partly in jest. In the forward area, even worn as she was, the old boat offered comfortable staterooms, running water, and baths, which were rare indeed.

The sailors were an exuberant lot. Once they caught the Army napping. Forty-two Army nurses appeared in Le Havre for transit. Before the GI's could grab them, the *Warfield* crew had the nurses on board. Their horseplay was fun enough. But the girls suddenly found *Warfield* was unique in two fascinating ways. She had lots of bathrooms — with tubs! And she had in her crew a boy who had been a hairdresser for Lilly Daché in New York. The nurses squealed with pleasure. The Army sulked.

A few wits in the engineering force, the "black gang," threw a song together to the tune of "MacNamara's Band":

OOH — *We call our ship the* Warfield;
She's the finest in the fleet.
And when it comes to making time,
She simply can't be beat.

Her boiler's old and rusty,
But they're full of dynamite.
One puff of smoke — one splash of brine,
And then she's out of sight.

OOH — *Her pistons clang and her engines bang,*
And the whistle toots away.
The captain cries "full speed ahead,"
And then there's hell to pay.

Her top three decks are made of wood,
And her hull is made of tin.
A credit to our Navy is
This Grand Old Hulk we're in!

A hulk she was, and grand indeed!

On May 8, 1945, as the war came to an end in Europe, she lay at the Quai d'Escole, Le Havre, with a hawser wrapped around her propeller shaft and two blades of her propeller bent from striking a submerged object in the river. About to arrive on board was her new commanding officer, Lieutenant Alfred Sanford Harer, USN, a thin-faced, solid-looking man in his early fifties, who brought with him a firm conviction that the traditions of the old Navy could be made to work, even on an old tub like *Warfield*. He refused to be depressed by the dreariness of his assignment.

She was an unbelievable mess. Her canvas decks were cracked and worn. Her interior was a dingy shambles. Here and there were small touches of elegance from another day, a splendid gilt-framed mirror over the grand stairway, now shabby with the scuffing of thousands of feet, a hint of carved mahogany near an entrance port where duffle bags and cargo were stacked high. She looked a gray-streaked wreck, which fine lines and a graceful sheer could not disguise — a drab and ugly wreck.

Scuttlebutt began in early May that the ship was going home. Lieutenant Boyer confirmed the news before his departure. When she went to the bombed-out drydock in Le Havre in anticipation of a second transatlantic crossing, a certain amount of genuine concern developed among the crew — not so much for themselves as for the old *Warfield*.

"The ship is wonderful and we love her," said Chief Engineer Floyd Owings, "but she just wasn't built for the open sea." His words echoed the misgivings of the British in Baltimore and St. Johns in 1942. Their echo would be long in dying out; shadowy whispers would be heard again — and yet again.

She celebrated her imminent departure for the States on Independence Day. Her thirty-odd passengers were aboard for transportation to the United States. At noon on July Fourth, the crew sat down to a ham and turkey dinner, topped by an angel food cake prepared for the occasion by the Scotch baker who was a master of his trade.

In the wardroom, Captain Harer suddenly accosted Mr. Armstrong, the supply officer, with a request that he go ashore in Le Havre and find some watermelons for the crew. Everybody looked at the captain in stunned amazement. Watermelons — in wartorn Le Havre? Armstrong looked ashen.

At the forward staging area on the Seine sometime during March 1945 when U.S.S. President Warfield *(IX 169) acted as a river ferry carrying troops to the forward area*

U.S.S. President Warfield *(IX 169) in bombed-out drydock, Bassin de l'Eure, Le Havre, France, June 20–30, 1945, preparatory to returning to the United States*

"That's an order, Mr. Armstrong," intoned the captain.

The supply officer was gone for the rest of the day. Late in the evening, he came struggling aboard with eight watermelons. He refused to disclose where he got them.

They made a big hit with the crew. Captain Harer took their appearance as a matter of course.

Mr. Armstrong went to bed.

On the afternoon of July 7, *Warfield* stood out from Le Havre — the cliffs of Normandy receding on the starboard quarter. During all of Sunday, July 8, she lay quietly at anchor in Plymouth — in the shadow of the green hills of Devon — beside the city, broken and jagged from the edge of war, slowly coming to life in the promise of peace. In the communion of that Sunday, *Warfield* said farewell to England, where, before her transfer to the U.S. Navy a year earlier, she had grown old in the service of the King. The mist of the following morning shrouded her as she put Land's End astern, and in convoy, turned her bow for home.

Home for a ship, weary with war, was different from home for the returning soldier. On the LST's, which made up the convoy, were Seabees who had risked their lives preparing the beachheads of Normandy and Sicily for the landings; other passengers were fighter pilots and bomber crews of the Eighth Air Force recently released from German prison camps. For reasons individual to each man, tangible and intangible, going home at the end of the war was a moving experience, not easily shared even with one's closest buddy — and masked in a light banter of chitchat about Times Square and the corner drugstore. For the *Warfield*, going home with weariness and the scars of war indelibly upon her, the future was most uncertain.

And yet, cloudy as her future seemed and dowdy as she appeared, there was vigor left in the old ship. It was shown when she gathered speed and left the convoy on Wednesday, July 11, to seek replenishment in the Azores which her limited fuel capacity required. Her trim hull cleaving the seas as she went through the ranks of the convoy excited the admiration of several LST skippers; there was grace about the old ship, even tattered and disheveled. In an hour, she had shown the convoy her heels and disappeared over the horizon.

There was a toughness about her, too, which refused to surrender to the seas which challenged her. As she approached the Azores, the wind and sea picked up. By Friday, she found herself in heavy weather. Long swells born in the North Atlantic caught her on the starboard beam and rolled her, scuppers under. To compound her difficulties, engine trouble developed, and her crew at considerable risk had to rig out a sea anchor to keep her from broaching in the troughs, until a gasket could be tightened. Underway again, she was forced to slow down and alter course to put the seas on the quarter. Even then, the seas played havoc, sending loose gear cascading about the mess decks, fracturing the ribs of a machinist's mate when he fell. Green, capped seas, riding up under the counter, sent *Warfield* in a steep skid down their slopes to dangerous troughs that taxed the helmsman in a desperate fight to keep the ship from broaching.

In watching the working of the old ship in the seas, both the chief engineer and the captain had been disquieted. Her wallowing, and a rather obvious loosening of the framing of the superstructure as the waves lifted her by the overhang, were not reassuring. Du Brul said that she acted like an old wooden trolley car on a bumpy track, and there was grim humor in the analogy. Among the crew, there was apprehension that this voyage might turn out to be more than anyone bargained for.

But then Arnel Light glowed in the evening on the starboard bow. At one in the morning, *Warfield* slipped into Ponta Delgada and loaded fuel alongside the long oil jetty. The wind was still blowing, and the town was dark. A few lights showed bleakly here and there, and the harbor lights glimmered at the end of the jetty. At four o'clock a sleepy pilot boarded, and the ship was underway again at first light. *Warfield* had come and gone in darkness.

By Sunday midnight, *Warfield* was back in station in the convoy — no mean navigational feat for Du Brul, since the gyro had been taken off in Plymouth and the ship was reduced to one magnetic compass.

Warfield had been tried on the run to the Azores; but the anger of the Atlantic at the trespassing of this river craft had not yet spent itself. Three days out of Norfolk the barometer dropped sharply. Rain squalls, blotting out the convoy, preceded the buildup in wind and seas that soon assumed the proportions of a widely gathering storm. In the midst of it, five of the LST's left the convoy and headed northeast for New York. *Warfield* and the remaining ships found themselves fighting for their very lives in a full Atlantic gale.

Warfield began to pound heavily in the boarding seas. Leaks began to show themselves here and there, as plating buckled and loosened in the heavy working of the ship. Without planking under the guards and overhang, the seas under the sponson created forces tending to tear hull and superstructure apart. Water began to deepen in forward compartments and in the bilges. Even the ship's steam pumps could not keep up with the inflow. In the lurching confusion, the engineers managed to rig three portable gasoline pumps (Navy handy-billies) and to keep the level of water from rising. For two hours in the evening, all the lights went out in the engine room and in the lower decks as salt water shorted the circuits. Only by rigging a jumper over the existing wiring were the engineers able to restore essential power.

All through Sunday and Monday, July 22 and 23, the storm raged. Somehow *Warfield* was holding her own. The wind and seas veered around to the southwest, and the ship buried her nose in each oncoming comber and sent the breaking green water in cascades of spray down her wooden sides. Lieutenant Harer, stocky and sturdy, wedged himself in the wheelhouse. The helmsman braced himself painfully against each sickening and shuddering lurch.

The laboring of the ship could be seen by those who groped through the open stretches of the saloon deck. There was a definite working of the flooring, a vertical bending with the flexing of the ship. Furthermore, in the forward part of the ship, the superstructure would shift back and forth at each roll. Water streamed down the bulkheads from the canvas decks leaking above. Sturdy as she was, *Warfield* had suffered much from the weight of troops and cargo in the preceding years. Grounding for a year in the mud beaches of Devon and the storms off Normandy had taken their toll in structural soundness. And now the North Atlantic was driving her hard.

Then, suddenly, a white light flashed off to starboard — the entrance to Chesapeake Bay. At daybreak of July 25, she passed Cape Henry Light to port. The seas abruptly quieted, and the calm of the Chesapeake once again cradled *Warfield.*

A three-year odyssey had ended. *President Warfield* was home again.

Her crew was jubilant: "The old bucket made it . . . she got us home safe." They cut up the forty-foot "homeward bound" pennant made by the signalman out of old bunting and each man in the crew got a piece as a souvenir. At times they had hated her, perhaps as much as Navy men could ever hate a ship. About to leave her now, they were a little proud of her, too. A bit of vintage, a bit of a lady — but a doughty fighter in stress and storm.

The newspapers of Maryland and Virginia editorialized in tribute to the old ship. From his vacation in Maine, Mayor McKeldin of Baltimore sent some "purple passages," as he called them, to the Baltimore *Sun:* "Back from the wars! Ravaged by trials endured, worn and washed out, weatherbeaten, almost scarred, by the dangers borne and fears surmounted . . . now the sailor is home again, covered with

U.S.S. President Warfield (IX 169) *shortly after arrival at the Naval Operating Base, Norfolk, Virginia, in late July 1945*

the ribbons of service and the stars of combat . . . Our gallant veteran . . . in liberty's cause, the old steamer, General [sic] Warfield."

A few at a time, her crew deserted her, in drafts for reassignment or discharge. The process of decommissioning began — out came the radio and navigation equipment, the evaporators and signaling gear — all of the paraphernalia that gave the ship a military life and a naval semblance. Then at 1:20 P.M., September 13, 1945, Lieutenant Commander Boykin of the Fifth Naval District read the orders of decommissioning before the final remnant of the crew; the commission pennant was folded and handed to the commanding officer, Lieutenant Harer; and the ensign slowly descended for the last time from the staff. *President Warfield*'s naval duties were at an end. She was a veteran — a rejected and lonely outcast — but a veteran.

Her loneliness was bittersweet. Old friends came to visit her — and left in sadness. One was Captain Patrick L. Parker, her first quartermaster and her last Old Bay Line skipper, who came aboard at noon on the very day she arrived in Norfolk. Mr. Raymond L. Jones, the Old Bay Line's passenger traffic manager, and later Mr. Robert E. Dunn, the Old Bay Line's president since 1941, came to see her. All came with one question in mind, the feasibility of repairing *Warfield* and restoring her as an Old Bay Line steamer. Times were not good for steamers on the Bay. Each visitor left with an unexpressed but heart-rending conclusion that the cost of putting her to rights would be staggering — probably prohibitive.* The Board of Directors of the Old Bay

* Through the war years, there had been extensive correspondence between the Old Bay Line and the War Shipping Administration on the appraised value of *President Warfield*. In 1944, a firm of marine engineers had determined her original cost (plus "betterments") at $1,003,117.90 in 1928 and the cost of replacement to comply with contemporary laws and regulations at $2,522,536.00. In 1946, however, the Maritime Commission placed the replacement costs at $1,730,000.00 and the depreciated value at $360,000.00. In November 1945, the Old Bay Line received checks aggregating $1,347,996.39

Line, elected to leave *President Warfield* with the War Shipping Administration for disposition.

The days of *Warfield* seemed numbered. On November 14, 1945, they dragged her out from her berth in Norfolk and delivered her in the afternoon to the James River Reserve Fleet at Lee Hall, Virginia. That night, *President Warfield* found herself moored outboard in an enormous nest of spent, weary, derelict ships — the outcasts, the forgotten — the gray, unwanted hulks of war.

Here were the ghosts of convoys, their wakes streaked with oil-sodden corpses and burned wreckage. There were the shadows of invasion fleets, echoing with the rattle of anti-aircraft batteries and the humming din of landing craft marching to a hostile shore. In the stillness of the autumn night, there were haunting notes of hawsers creaking and fenders riding; but each muffled sound was the echo of an immediate past — grim and somber.

Then the rats came. Over the hawsers and around the guards. Old gray rats that had thrived somehow on the derelict ships. Their scuffling could be heard on *Warfield*'s decks and behind the paneling.

The winter snow fell and turned the lonely decks white.

---

representing 75 per cent of the award made by WSA for the *four* vessels (*State of Maryland, State of Virginia, Yorktown,* and *President Warfield*). The Old Bay Line filed suit, and the Court of Claims raised the compensation to $4,151,425.00. Excluding legal costs, taxes, and expenses, the compensation for *Warfield* was somewhat short of $990,000.00. The amount was far short of replacement. According to Maritime Commission estimates, mechanical and structural repairs alone would amount to $976,700.00, and these would not include the costs of at least a quarter of a million dollars to furnish the ship with adequate passenger quarters.

And with all this expense, the Old Bay Line would still have a badly worn ship nearly twenty years old on its hands.

SIX

THE LONG YEAR PASSED SLOWLY. *President Warfield,* rotting in the James River, was all but forgotten.

Only the Maritime Commission and a few steamboat buffs remembered her, and the interest of the Commission was solely in getting rid of her, along with all the other hulks cluttering up the channel of the James.

During the early months of 1946, the Commission advertised her for sale for purposes of scrap only. Three companies bid: Patapsco Scrap Corporation, $1,500; Boston Metals Corporation, $5,100; and the Potomac Shipwrecking Company, $6,255. These bids were rejected by the Maritime Commission as below the minimum price.

Then the Commission, in an effort to get rid of the hulk, decided to place no restriction on the sale and on June 18, 1946, offered *President Warfield* for sale "as is, where is" for "purposes of operation" without limitation.

Interestingly enough, a number of brokers had been pressing the Commission for this very decision. One broker in mid-July sarcastically addressed a memorandum thanking the Commission for its "momentous decision" to sell *President Warfield* for operational use and congratulating it on its "speed and efficiency" in reaching that decision — "it only took about four months." The broker proposed to find out if his principals were still interested in buying *Warfield*, but only if the Commission was prepared to do immediate business. "There are a lot of admirals in the Maritime Commission and possibly some of them might have heard of the Monsoon seasons which are a controlling factor in sending vessels such as . . . the *President Warfield* to China."

The mention of China as a possible home for *Warfield* had an odd ring about it. A few old-timers in the Maritime Commission began to prick up their ears.

Still without a sale, however, the Commission, in accordance with its customary practice, advertised *President Warfield* for sale on August 6, 1946, in the principal newspapers of Washington, New York, Boston, Philadelphia, Baltimore, Chicago, Cleveland, Norfolk, New Orleans, and San Francisco. A number of ship brokers made inquiries.

Then, suddenly during October, the news spread around the Baltimore shipping world that the old *President Warfield* had been purchased for scrap. On November 9, 1946, when she was towed out of the Reserve Fleet and up to Baltimore, the worst fears of the old buffs who loved *Warfield* seemed confirmed. The word was out that she had been sold for scrap to the Potomac Shipwrecking Company of Pope's Creek, Maryland, and Washington, D.C., for the ignominious sum of $8,056.

She was seen in Baltimore during December 1946 at the face of Pier 5, Pratt Street, and then alongside the old, rotting municipal wharf, Pier 8, Lancaster Street — in the midst of sagging warehouses and a lumberyard. Across the basin, a chemical plant belched noxious fumes; the city fireboat tied up at an adjacent pier. A complicated maze of cobblestone streets, lined by dilapidated buildings and ancient row houses, led to the pier. This was the oldest part of Baltimore, now a mixture of slum and half-abandoned warehouses.

On January 23, 1947, the Baltimore *Sun* electrified the steamboat buffs with an article entitled "Warfield, Old Bay

Line Queen, Exiled to China as Riverboat." The ship, according to Captain William C. Ash, a marine surveyor apparently in charge of her, was destined to perform the same type of service in China as when she plied between Baltimore and Norfolk in the old days. Her new owner was the Chinese-American Industrial Company of New York.

"Even if she is sold by them to other concerns," stated Captain Ash, "she still will go to China as a riverboat, as she is not equipped to do any other type of work."

Her skipper, according to Captain Ash, would probably be Captain William Schlegel of Baltimore. The ship would sail as soon as registry proceedings with the Honduran government were completed and a special certificate issued — like that granted *Warfield* under British registry in 1942 — to permit her to cross the Atlantic with minimum cargo and no passengers in good weather. He disclosed that about $25,000 had been spent on her to make her seaworthy. According to him, the ship would make the trip in easy stages via the Mediterranean, where she would drop a little cargo, until she reached her destination in Hong Kong.

The *Sun* followed the article with a two-page pictorial in the Sunday rotogravure section of February 2, entitled "From Canton to Canton." The caption noted that the ship, which once took on her fuel in the part of Baltimore harbor called Canton, was headed overseas to operate from Hong Kong up the Pearl River to Canton, China.

The Baltimore *News-Post* picked up the story the next day. It reported that Captain Schlegel planned to go via the Azores, Gibraltar, the Mediterranean, Suez, the Arabian Sea, Gulf of Bengal and the China Sea, and quoted him as dismissing a route across the Pacific with the following: "Once you start across the Pacific, it's too far between fueling stations for a ship as small as the *President Warfield*. If the weather was all right we might make it, but a little bit of heavy weather might easily leave us out of fuel in the middle of the ocean."

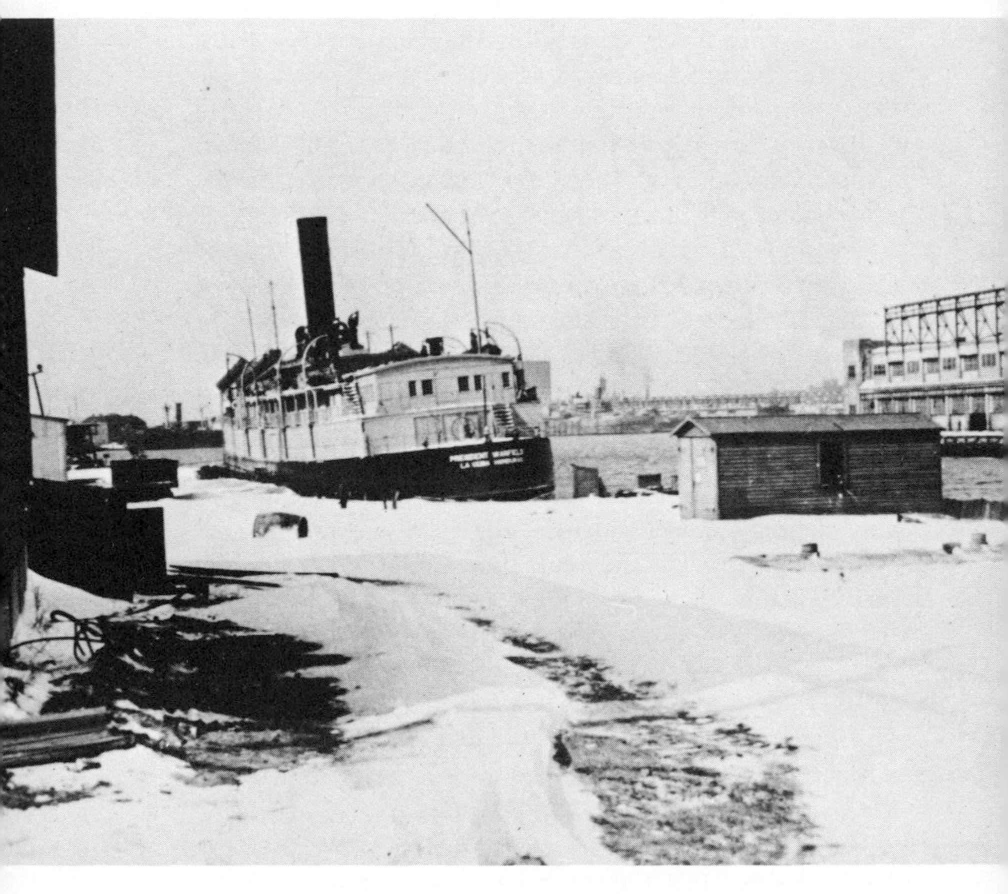

President Warfield *lying at a dock in Baltimore, February 1947. Her stern shows her home port as Le Ceiba, Honduras. Her destination had been announced as China.*

Several curious pieces of apparently irrelevant information accompanied the articles in both the *Sun* and the *News-Post*. In the January *Sun* article, for example, Captain Ash was quoted as announcing that the former Coast Guard cutter *Northland*, originally built for the Alaska icefields and the first American vessel to see active duty against Germany in the late war, had recently been bought for resale to the Danish Government by the Weston Trading Company, who paid fifty thousand dollars for her as surplus. *Northland* was undergoing repairs at Pier 4, Pratt Street. Another piece of oblique information was contained in the *News-Post* article, when it added that Captain Schlegel, assigned to take *Warfield* to China via the Mediterranean, had recently delivered the former Coast Guard cutter *Ulua* to her new owners in Marseilles. Had the newswriter been more inquisitive, he might have reported that the name *Ulua* had never been shown on any listing of U.S. Coast Guard vessels, and that no listing of the "Weston Trading Company" appeared in any phone book or directory in the United States.

The *News-Post* article reported that Captain Schlegel was a Bavarian who in 1910 persuaded his parents to allow him to visit his aunt and uncle in Pittsburgh. Schlegel instead came to Baltimore, sailed as a seaman with the Merchants and Miners Steamship Company, and later joined the old Baltimore–New York Steamship Company. According to the article, Schlegel and another seaman both fell in love with the daughter of the skipper of the steamer *Manahata* and smuggled her aboard on one voyage. The young lady reportedly suggested that they fight it out at the top of the mast; Schlegel toppled (and had the scar to prove it); whereupon the lady denounced the rival as a bully and spent the rest of the voyage nursing Schlegel.

Nothing further on *President Warfield* stirred the press until February 26, 1947. The news report of that date was almost melodramatic. *Warfield* was in distress in heavy seas, seventy-five miles east of Diamond Shoals off the North

Carolina coast. She had flashed an SOS and radioed the Coast Guard for assistance. Her message stated that her forward hold was flooded, that she was leaking badly and listing heavily to starboard, and that her engine room would be flooded within the hour. She had turned around and was headed for Norfolk at three knots.

News reports of the weather had not been exaggerated. Fierce, sporadic storms, with winds up to sixty miles an hour, had whipped up mountainous seas across the Atlantic, sinking a fishing schooner and endangering seven other ships. The storm had lasted for five days and showed no signs of abating. Heavy ice locked the upper Chesapeake, and cold midwinter gales swept the whole Eastern seaboard. Ships all along the coast were imperiled by raging seas.

According to the Associated Press, the tankers *H. C. Sinclair* and *Gulfhawk* had picked up *Warfield*'s message and had headed for her. At 9:30 P.M., *H. C. Sinclair* had reached the scene and was standing by. *Gulfhawk* and the Coast Guard cutter *Cherokee* were expected to arrive by two o'clock in the morning.

Warfield had sailed, according to a number of reports, on February 25 from Baltimore for Marseilles and carried a crew of about forty in command of Captain William S. Schlegel, who had stated he would leave the vessel at the French port. The reports showed that a large number of the crew appeared to be Jewish, an Egyptian and a Lithuanian were listed aboard, and the chief mate and another crew member were said to be natives of Palestine.

A Baltimore *Sun* reporter interviewed the ship's agent in Norfolk, after *Warfield* limped into Hampton Roads. Mr. R. W. Weiss, a retired Norwegian seaman and district manager of the Alcoa Steamship Company, whose offices adjoined those of the vice consul of Panama, stated that the heavy seas had ripped the wooden fenders or guard rails from the sides of the ship and that water had entered in the holes left by the rivets. Chief Engineer John Crabson of Baltimore, who was injured in the storm and sent to the Marine Hospital in Norfolk, said the ship with minor repairs could undertake her journey again. He explained that in the storm, the ship's seams opened forward and three compartments were flooded; but the watertight bulkheads had held and prevented flooding of the engine room. As to the ship's destination, he would state only that he would leave her in Marseilles where his contract expired.

By now, *President Warfield* had become a mystery ship. The storm which had brought her back to port exposed her to a scrutiny that was obviously unwelcome. Explanations of her destination and mission simply did not ring true.

In the first week of March, George Horne of the New York *Times* set about to lift the veil. He found himself running in circles. He noted in his news story of March 6, 1947, that the ship carried a cargo of only thirty-five tons, most of it made up of life jackets and mess kits. Advertising her destination as China, she admittedly carried no charts for Chinese waters. The ship's crew members, he declared, were eighty per cent Jewish, some of them natives of Palestine. From the crew members there were veiled admissions that they were going there. The implication was startling. If the information was true, *Warfield* was to become a blockade runner, to break through the barrier imposed by the British against illegal entrance of Jews into the mandate of Palestine. Captain Schlegel was now denying that he knew anything of the ship's ultimate destination.

Investigation by the New York *Times* reporter led back to *Warfield*'s reported sale on November 11, 1946, by the Maritime Commission to the Potomac Shipwrecking Company for about eight thousand dollars. Two days later, according to an unconfirmed report, the ship had been resold for forty thousand dollars to an unidentified New York concern. Horne found out from the ship's agent, Alcoa in Norfolk, that the new owner was the Weston Trading

Company of 24 Stone Street, New York. The firm was not listed in the phone book.

Alcoa Steamship Company headquarters in New York denied knowledge of *Warfield*. However, on the fifth floor of the old building at 24 Stone Street, the reporter found the office he sought — a small space cramped by a desk and a number of busy men. On the glass door were the words: "Marine Surveyor — Weston Trading Company." One man agreed that the firm had indeed bought *Warfield* but stated that all inquiries could be handled only by Captain Weiss of the Alcoa Steamship Company in Norfolk. There seemed no way off the merry-go-round.

The reporter found a source in New York who knew much more than he confessed about what was happening. He declared that *President Warfield* was now owned by Haganah, the Jewish military underground, and he gave Horne a telephone number to call.

On the other end of the phone a man's voice said: "*Warfield?* How do you spell it?"

Part Three

The Grasp of History

SEVEN

FORGOTTEN, A WORTHLESS HULK, *President Warfield* had been caught up by the merest chance in the current of a mighty stream, a current of history that had been gathering force through the centuries. An understanding of the place of the ship in this history requires a digression into some of its details.

The story reaches back 1,900 years to the expulsion of the Jews from Palestine and the conquest of the region by the Arabs in the wake of Roman rule. It spans the tragic history of the Diaspora — the dispersion of the Jews over the world — and their persecution in lands they adopted. It gains momentum in the birth of Zionism, profoundly rooted in the origins of the Jewish race in Palestine and in the spiritual and intellectual devotion of the people to the bond of Israel — Eretz Israel, a symbol at once of escape and of national identity. Turbulence came with the growth of Arab nationalism, awaiting only the disintegration of the Ottoman Empire for its fulfillment and for its collision with the forces of Zionism.

World War I was the watershed. The alliance of the Ottoman Empire with Germany posed political and strategic problems of the first magnitude for Britain. These problems stemmed from a number of sources — the position of the

Middle East as a critical bridgehead to the British Empire, the greed of her allies in dividing up the spoils of a defeated Turkey, the demands of the Arabs for guarantees of independence and statehood as the price for their attack against the Turks, and the need for quieting Zionist fears about Arab aspirations. Related to the latter was the necessity of gaining the support of international Jewry on a wide front.

For Britain the problem of solidifying Jewish backing for the war contained many perplexing elements. The aid of Jewish financial interests was required, particularly as gold and marketable securities available for American munitions purchases neared exhaustion; the initial apathy — even pro-German sentiment — of many prominent American Jews, among them influential publicists, had to be overcome as the war advanced; the Jews in Russia, left disorganized in the wake of political disintegration, needed to be rallied; with Russia out of the running as a contender for the spoils, France became the sole competitor of Britain for the Levant and the need was perceived by the British to reduce French influence in that region by holding out the prospects for an extended Jewish presence in Palestine, perhaps even the emergence of a Jewish buffer state; the rug had to be pulled somehow from under the German competition for Zionist sympathies, thus undermining the German regime or, at the least, isolating the Jews in Germany; and finally, on the home-front, some twenty thousand Russian Jews of draft age who had managed to escape conscription by their alien status needed a clarion call to arms which Zionism might provide. To gain the support of Jewry on many fronts became for Britain an urgent task.

The history shows that the exigencies of World War I presented the British with the necessity of making substantial concessions, particularly to the Arabs and the Jews. That these concessions resulted in conflicting commitments meant little at the time, since the objective was victory and any tactic that contributed to that end was worthy; any differences in wartime understandings could be sorted out diplomatically when hostilities ceased.

To Sherif Hussein of Mecca, the British in the McMahon Pledge of 1916 obligated themselves to support the independence of the Arabs in large areas of the Middle East, excluding the coastal belt of Syria but leaving the fate of Palestine uncertain, and therefore by implication subject to the eventual demands of the Arabs for national identity like the other Arab states emerging as Palestine's neighbors. To Walter, second Lord Rothschild, the British issued the Balfour Declaration of 1917. Its principal paragraph stated: "His Majesty's Government view with favour the establishment in Palestine of a national home for the Jewish people, and will use their best endeavours to facilitate the achievement of this object, it being clearly understood that nothing shall be done which may prejudice the civil and religious rights of existing non-Jewish communities in Palestine."

Both the Arabs and the Jews responded, the first with revolt against the Ottoman Empire, the second with support for the Allied cause. Both chose to interpret the ambiguous British commitments in their own way: the Arabs looking to the incorporation of Palestine in an independent Arab state, the Zionists viewing the "national home" as meaning the establishment of an autonomous state of Israel. The Arabs and Jews, two Semitic peoples with no natural enmity, were now divided by competitive nationalism, by emotional attachment to a common land and aspirations to exercise exclusive control over it when the temporary authority of the British ceased, and by external forces of dangerous international proportions. Palestine on its basic terms became a problem essentially refractory to settlement. Here was the explosive setting which Britain brought to her duties as Mandatory Power for Palestine under the Covenant of the League of Nations.

The history of Palestine turned on the issue of Jewish immigration. For the British, immigration of the Jews into

Palestine became a painful dilemma. The terms of the Mandate required her to facilitate Jewish immigration and land settlement; however, the influx of skillful and aggressive Jews, bent on the acquisition of land and the establishment of a prosperous agricultural and industrial economy in Palestine, disquieted the Arabs and, as the flow of Jews increased, stirred them to commit acts of violence. In the view of the Arabs, their whole economic and social structure stood on the brink of disruption with the loss of the land which they had occupied for centuries.

Almost immediately upon assumption of authority as the Mandatory Power, Britain instituted implicit restrictions on the Jews to placate the Arabs. The Churchill Memorandum of 1922 denied that the Balfour Declaration contemplated the conversion of all Palestine into a Jewish national state and proclaimed that Jewish immigration in any given year would be limited to the "economic absorptive capacity" of the country. The pressure of Jewish immigration continued, impelled by the growing weight of the World Zionist Organization, and Arab violence increased. After the Wailing Wall incident of 1928 with its overtones of religious hatred, unrest became acute. It developed into an accelerating pattern of insurrection during the 1930's, as the Jews driven by persecution in Europe clamored to enter Palestine. Peace was never restored to the Mandate. The Arab rebellion in 1937 against Jews and British alike brought the country to the edge of civil war.

The British, in attempts to placate the Arabs and to restore peace to the country, issued yearly immigration quotas, which progressively reduced the number of entry certificates given to Jews. The 1935 immigration quota was sixty thousand per year; in 1936, the number was cut in half. The White Paper for Palestine prepared by the British in 1939, proposed to limit Jewish immigration to a total of seventy-five thousand over the next five years, after which it was to cease altogether. In 1945, the quota was 1,500 per month, set by Ernest Bevin, the British Foreign Minister. Against the restrictions and quotas, which were pitifully small, stood the dammed-up hordes of Jews frantic to escape the pogroms of Europe and bent on one objective, to reach the Promised Land. At the same time, there stood the Arabs in Palestine in open revolt against the preemption of their ancestral land and in defiance of the British who turned a deaf ear to their demands for statehood. Room for the British to maneuver in was narrow indeed.

The rise of totalitarian power in Europe and the threat of war exacerbated the problem of Palestine. In Eastern and Central Europe, anti-Semitism in the racial policy of Nazism reached new heights of magnitude and violence, culminating in the pogroms in Germany in 1938. A grip of fear closed upon European Jewry; among Jews abroad, a new note of hysteria crept in, as they recognized that they had to get their people out of Europe and that the price of failure might run high. In Palestine, quotas ceased to have meaning, as frightened refugees circumvented the restrictions with the active help of the Zionist Organization.

The violent extremes of anti-Semitism brought forth a wave of protest worldwide from Jews and non-Jews alike, directed at the governments of the Western powers, urging them to extricate the Jews in Europe from their desperate predicament. As time went on, the Jews came to realize that remedies rested in self-help and in the primordial instinct of self-preservation. Upon France, Britain and the United States fell the mantle of responsibility in the period between the wars. Their failure to act in behalf of the Jews was, in a sense, part of a larger breakdown in the whole fabric of postwar settlement. Isolationism, revulsion from the horror of the last war, sympathy for Germany as the underdog at Versailles, economic weakness from deep depression, and the specter of severe political stress engendered in the extremes of Fascism and Communism all contributed to their lack of moral fiber and their ineptitude in the face of German excesses. In the aggregate, democracy as a whole failed not only to uphold the peace but also to develop soon enough the internal resolve to meet the dynamism of totalitarian power and of a catastrophic demogogy constructed from a senseless, romantic myth of racial purity.

In spite of the pleas of the Jews, immigration quotas into Palestine were not revised upward. Nor were immigration quotas into the United States or Western European countries changed materially either. The Western powers did not want thousands of refugee Jews inside their borders, and many of the Jews wanted to go nowhere but to Palestine. In 1936, there was talk in Britain of resettling some one hundred thousand to two hundred and fifty thousand Jews in various territories of the British Empire. Rumania suggested resettlement in Northern Rhodesia. Italy considered opening up Ethiopia, contingent upon the development of a "favorable" attitude of world Jewry toward Fascism. And after the 1938 pogroms, Cuba, Southern Rhodesia, Tanganyika, and a number of South American countries expressed their readiness to receive Jewish refugees. But they were barely heard and went unheeded. For the harried Jew, there existed no home but Eretz Israel.

In the Middle East as the war drew near, both Germany and Italy were inciting the Arabs to rebellion against the British and furnishing the arms and the money for insurrection. The Jews invariably found themselves the objects of Arab terrorism. The response of the British to outbreaks of violence was almost rhythmic. A commission was appointed; a report was written for consideration. Nothing proved effective. The Jews, no more than the Arabs, would accept compromise. After the 1939 Round Table Conference broke down because the Palestinian Arabs refused to sit with the Jews, and after the White Paper for Palestine in the same year met with the animosity of the Arabs because it did not go far enough in restricting the Jews, and with the shocked dismay of the Jews because it appeared to violate the Balfour

Declaration, the British threw up their hands. "His Majesty's Government cannot hope to satisfy the partisans of one party or the other in such controversy as the Mandate has aroused," stated the White Paper.

The nearness of war magnified the strategic dilemma for the British — the hold of the Arab world on the lifeline of Britain's empire, on the communication links of the Mediterranean and the Indian Ocean, setting apart Britain from her Commonwealth partners in Africa and Asia. The truculence of the Arabs, fanned into rebellion by the Germans and Italians and stirred to greater heights by Jewish illegal immigration, constituted a manifest danger. To complicate the problem, American public opinion, strengthened by the support of President Roosevelt, ranged itself more and more on the side of the Zionists.

The war itself diluted the tension. However, even then, when a tacit Arab-Jewish truce existed, violence continued in Palestine, stemming from the activity of Jewish extremists who sought to undermine British rule. The Stern Gang, one group of extremists, practiced unrestrained violence; in November 1944 its members murdered Lord Moyne, the British Minister of State, in Cairo. Irgun Zwai Leumi, a militant offshoot of Haganah, the unofficial Jewish army, joined in the insurrection, keeping world attention focused on Palestine.

Throughout the war years, the Nazi "solution" to the "Jewish question" was being implemented. Hints of the magnitude of the "solution" reached the Allies from intelligence sources and the lips of the few who escaped. Then, as the Nazis retreated before the Allied advance, the world saw exposed the full horror of the extermination of six million Jews. Also revealed was the desperate condition of the surviving millions, the broken remnants from the concentration camps and the hiding places. The response was a worldwide upsurge of emotion. Here was a verdict, final and irreducible — rendered not only upon a demagogic despotism which debased the very sanctity of life but also upon the democracies of the West for previous neglect.

There began the exodus of Jews from Eastern and Central Europe, not only the survivors of the Nazi terror but also Jews who saw little hope for themselves in the Communist-dominated countries. The mass movement of the Jews constituted a humanitarian problem of the first magnitude. On August 31, 1945, President Truman addressed an appeal to Prime Minister Attlee, asking for the immediate admission of one hundred thousand Jewish immigrants into Palestine. The British proposed a joint commission of inquiry; its recommendations to continue the existing government in Palestine pending a trusteeship agreement with the United Nations, to issue one hundred thousand entry certificates for Jewish victims of Nazi persecution, and to rescind land transfer restrictions on Jews remained in suspension while still another commission was appointed to consider their feasibility.

For the United States and its allies, the intransigence of the Soviet Union in the immediate aftermath of war threw a vexing variable into the Palestine equation. Not all officials were persuaded by any means that Zionist aspirations should be encouraged, and in rational terms their attitude had the force of logic. Many, like Secretary of Defense James V. Forrestal and Loy Henderson, head of the State Department's Office of Near Eastern and African Affairs, held that the strategic interest of the West in standing firm against Soviet expansionism came above all other objectives; that this interest rested in the protection of the oil reserves in the Middle East, vital to the economic and military posture of the West, but held by the Arabs; and that this interest demanded the friendship of the Arab world as a bulwark against possible Soviet probes into the important crossroads of the Near East. In addition, in their view, nothing should be allowed to come between the United States and Britain, the two bastions of democracy, in the face of Soviet animosity.

Valid as the argument seemed for the West to court Arab support, the prevailing mood on the question of Palestine was not rational; it was visceral and passionate. There was no damming up the flood. The Jews would not be held.

The flight of the Jews from Europe became an epic — a vast and melancholy drama played on the stage of Europe, the Mediterranean, and the Middle East — the panorama of an exodus springing full-blown from the annals of an ancient past to the harsh glare of the twentieth century.

Part Four

Aliyah Beth

EIGHT

President Warfield, lurking around the old piers of Baltimore harbor in late 1946 and early 1947, was being prepared to play a role in history which could be dimly foreseen.

She was joining a long procession of wretched little ships, aged and derelict, which since 1934 had been limping surreptitiously around the coastline of the Mediterranean and the Black Sea, eluding the patrol boats of the British and landing Jewish refugees on the shores of Palestine in defiance of immigration quotas and restrictions. Some ships were successful. Others were captured and the immigrants on board interned; some foundered with tragic loss of life.

Warfield was joining one of the great mass movements of history — the postwar exodus of the Jews from Europe. The movement began feebly in the mid-1930's and swelled in volume. For the Jews in any numbers to escape from Europe, the problems were critical enough, but for them to enter Palestine, the situation seemed immoderately complicated. Under pressure from events in Europe, the only recourse of the Zionists was to circumvent the immigration quotas set by the British.

Unwittingly, the British themselves originated the apparatus to do the job. During the Arab rebellion of 1936–1937, when the Arabs, in response to Jewish immigration, began a campaign of uncontrolled terror, the British set up an intelligence network under Orde Wingate, then a rising officer in the British army.* The network included a paramilitary force of Jews operating as guerrilla units without explicit authority of the British government. Haganah, the earlier underground organization which developed formal structure from these guerrilla units, was from the outset a defensive force without legal standing. With the assumption of its role as Mandatory Power, Britain could not acknowledge the existence of such a force, since the training of indigenous military units was expressly forbidden by the restrictions of the League of Nations. Nevertheless, the existence of Haganah had tacit British acceptance.

As it developed in strength and substance, Haganah under the control of the Jewish Agency became the underground military force not only of the Jews in Palestine but also of the Zionist movement as a whole. The activities of Haganah, as the situation in Europe developed, became international; its units were organized by capable, dedicated people to meet Jewish needs whatever they might be.

Palmach was the general name given to the ground forces of Haganah. Palyam was its naval unit. Aliyah Beth was the branch that operated with the utmost secrecy in the management of illegal immigration. Bri'ha referred to the units responsible for guiding refugees across frontiers, irrespective of their geography, for movement to Palestine. Rekhesh was responsible for the procurement of arms and their covert entry into Palestine. And Shai was Haganah's intelligence service — performing a counterintelligence mission against British efforts to penetrate the entire Jewish underground — and also serving Haganah, and with it the whole immigration effort, in positive intelligence collected and disseminated where needed throughout Europe and the Middle East.

* Wingate, who received the Distinguished Service Order for this operation, achieved fame in World War II for his organization and leadership of the "Chindits," a brigade of guerrillas that operated behind the Japanese lines in Burma.

Haganah, from a simplistic defense concept of the British, became in a relatively short time a highly sophisticated and complex organization, reaching out from Palestine into areas of Europe and the Middle East, and even into the Western Hemisphere, when its services were required.

Movement into Palestine from Europe, even from the beginning, was almost exclusively by sea. It began in the summer of 1934, even before Haganah, not yet organized for its future mission, and the Jewish Agency, preoccupied with diplomatic confrontation with the British, were quite prepared to approve its operations.* *Velos,* the first of the frail craft of a series to sail from the shores of Greece, landed over three hundred immigrants on the beaches north of Tel Aviv. The operation, mounted by overzealous members of the Jewish underground in Greece, startled the leadership. David Ben-Gurion, the executive of the Jewish Agency, and Eliahu Golomb, leader of the underground, both feared that illegal immigration might backfire in the face of negotiations with the British and ultimately prove adverse to the best interests of the Jews and the Zionist movement. Nevertheless, they were unwilling to order the enthusiastic efforts of these agents in Greece to cease; with only the barest of nods from the leadership in Palestine, the operations continued.

On its second trip, *Velos* was caught at the beaches by the British on September 12, 1934. Fifty immigrants made it ashore. But the escaping ship carried with it three hundred refugees. A filthy hulk crowded beyond belief with its human

* The Jewish Agency, representing the Jewish community, was recognized by the Mandatory Power as the authority with which it would deal in the establishment of the Jewish home, in many administrative functions of Palestine itself, and in the selection of immigrants for certificates to enter Palestine. This agency also was the instrument of the World Zionist Organization, and Dr. Chaim Weizmann was president of both during most of the period of the Mandate. In Palestine, the agency's executive was David Ben-Gurion. External affairs were under Moshe Shertok. The dualistic nature of the Jewish Agency — at once administratively responsible to Britain in Palestine and universally accredited as leading the Zionist movement — became of substantive consequence.

cargo, it wandered month after month about the Mediterranean, from port to port, until it came to be known as a phantom ship without a home.

Other shiploads from Greece followed. In January 1938, the little 60-ton *Poseidon*, followed by the 230-ton *Artemisia*, both creaking derelicts, made the trip to the beaches of Palestine and offloaded their refugee cargoes from small boats carried on board without interception by the British. However, knowledge of these landings had an immediate effect on the British government, which applied strong diplomatic pressure through its consulate in Athens to persuade the Greeks to halt the sailing of such craft bent on illegal immigration to Palestine.

The success of these landings was not lost on the Jewish Agency and the Haganah leadership. They catalogued it for immediate use.

The year of 1938 was a year of crisis. Hitler's subjection of the Jews to new heights of terror seemed to portend the immediate swing of the Nazis toward radical measures designed to force the Jews out of Germany and German areas of control. With the Western capitals rendering little more than verbal expressions of sympathy, the Jews found the question of immigration into Palestine even more pressing than ever before. The Jewish Agency promptly urged the British government to admit one hundred thousand refugees at once as within "the absorptive capacity" of Jewish Palestine. With war signals in the air and with an eye to the Moslem bridgehead across the Middle East, Britain was in no mood to exacerbate its problems with the Arabs by approving such a move.

Confronted with a door slammed shut by the British in the face of the frantic hordes of European Jewry, the Jewish Agency turned to illegal immigration and the remembered success of the little ships from Greece. Ben-Gurion, now pressed by Golomb to permit operations to start, gave his approval. In addition, American sources, notably the American Joint Distribution Committee, agreed to support the illegal undertakings in spite of fears of the physical dangers which the operations entailed for the refugees and the implications of the American involvement. At once, the apparatus of Haganah gained a vast new dimension in planning and mounting an operation of international scope, which by its very nature had to remain clandestine.

The operation gained a name: Mossad le Aliyah Beth (Illegal Immigration Bureau). Its agents set up secret headquarters in London, Paris, Vienna, and other strategic locations where they could establish an effective network to extricate the afflicted Jews.

For a time, the Nazis themselves, obsessed with getting the Jews out of their territory by any means possible, actually cooperated with agents of Mossad le Aliyah Beth for movement of the refugees through Austria and Yugoslavia to ports of transit to Palestine. Even Adolf Eichmann, from his suite in the Vienna palace of the Rothschilds, for a time and for his own reasons was helpful. German assistance, however, was short-lived.

From May 1939 until early 1942, a stream of ancient hulks sailed from Black Sea ports for Palestine. They had been bought at an initial financial burden by agents of Aliyah Beth. Risking their very lives upon these precarious vessels were refugee groups, shepherded from Germany, Austria, Czechoslovakia, and Poland by Haganah emissaries and shipped out from Rumanian and Bulgarian ports for Palestine. Conditions aboard these ships were unbelievably harsh — hundreds jammed into tiny, reeking craft never intended for passengers; sanitary facilities lacking or utterly primitive; food resembling emergency rations barely adequate; water supply low and often failing altogether; incompetent crews that frequently got drunk and fought; and operators who were nothing short of racketeers. The risk was enormous, and the chances of escaping shipwreck, fatal illness, or the blockade were relatively small. But it was the best that Haganah could do. Shipowners under the circumstances would risk nothing but ships ready for scrap; logistics in a covert situation were not only uncertain but necessarily limited enough to be concealed; and the pressing flow of refugees meant crowding into whatever hulks could be found. There was little complaint among the refugees, even in disaster; hope was infinitely better than a desolate end in Europe.

In spite of catastrophes, Mossad le Aliyah Beth by the start of the war in 1939 had successfully landed almost seven thousand refugees on the shores of Palestine. The effort required to move so large a group over many hundreds of miles inside Europe; to procure, provision and sail nearly unobtainable craft in an environment of total secrecy; and to land their exhausted cargoes on the shores of Palestine in the face of a hostile blockade was large. But the total number put ashore in Palestine stood in grim contrast to the yearning millions still in Europe.

While the plight of the Jews in Central and Eastern Europe seemed real enough — and the courage of those who risked the dangers of the sea and the British opposition appeared symbolic of an overwhelming need — there were sharp misgivings in the Zionist organization, indeed in its high command, about illegal immigration. Many of the more statesmanlike of the leadership feared that they were being led by the more impetuous members of the underground into a rather cruel crusade just to prove the point that the British blockade could be breached. There was just enough truth in the statement of Malcolm MacDonald, the British Colonial Secretary, in the Commons on July 20, 1939, that there was "an organized movement to break the immigration law of Palestine for the sake of breaking the immigration law of Palestine" to give the Zionist leadership momentary pause. When the twenty-first Zionist Congress convened in Geneva, there was a round of sharp dissension over illegal immigration; some saw it generating antagonism among non-Jewish opinion; others even called it potential murder. The war descending suddenly upon Europe made the dissension irrelevant.

In spite of the grip of German military might upon Europe and the contest for the Mediterranean being waged by the British, the operation of Mossad le Aliyah Beth continued for three years until 1942.

Hilda carried a group from Berlin who came down the Danube in midwinter. Their riverboat at one point froze to a dock, with the frightened refugees jammed tightly inside for warmth. At sea aboard *Hilda,* they were pounced upon by British warships near Istanbul and taken into Haifa. There, they were made to stay on board the stinking craft for over three months, the British threatening meanwhile to send them to Paraguay, the ship's declared destination. *Libertad,* a little ship flying the Uruguayan flag, after suffering a dangerous and difficult trip, was captured within sight of Palestine. *Pencho,* with five hundred Czechoslovakian refugees, burst its boiler in the Aegean, and its passengers and crew barely made it to a deserted island. Rescued by an Italian warship, they became POW's in Italy. *Salvador* sank in a storm off Istanbul with few survivors.

Two ships, the *Patria* and the *Struma,* brought worldwide attention when the facts were broadcast. *Patria,* a French ship taken over by the British and sitting idle in Haifa, was loaded with over eighteen hundred immigrants taken from three little ships, *Pacific, Atlantic* and *Milos,* arriving from the Black Sea. The British, determined to use the incident as a deterrent to further illegal immigration, announced *Patria* would sail with its human cargo for Mauritius. Haganah was equally determined that the ship would not sail. On November 25, 1940, there was an explosion deep in the hold of *Patria.* She rolled over in the harbor and sank in twelve minutes. Two hundred immigrants and fifty crew and Palestinian policemen died. Haganah agents, disguised as workmen, had secreted a bomb on board, expecting it to damage the ship but not to sink it so quickly. They had miscalculated on *Patria*'s age and the condition of her plating. Haganah was stricken with remorse.

Struma, a ramshackle cattleboat, had spent some of her years before salvage sunk in the Danube. Loaded with seven hundred and fifty refugees from Rumania, she was stopped and turned around by Turkish authorities at Istanbul. On this occasion, the Germans had applied the pressure, since the refugees held British-authorized entry certificates. The refugees and Mossad pled with the Turkish authorities for two months. Shortly after *Struma* turned about to reenter the Black Sea, there was an explosion, and the ship sank. Only one man survived. The news shocked the world. The bitter cup overflowed. Mossad le Aliyah Beth forbade the sailing of any more ships from Rumania, and for a year and a half the seaward movement of refugees from Europe ceased.

The shocking disclosure of the state of the Jews in Europe in 1944 at long last led the British Colonial Secretary, Lord Cranbourne, to declare that thirty thousand entry permits would be issued for Jews emigrating from Nazi-held countries. Haganah immediately set about the risky business of secretly extricating the refugees through German-held Europe to ports of departure and then making it through contested and dangerous waters to Palestine. For a time, the smuggling of Jewish emissaries behind enemy lines was actively assisted by British intelligence. By the end of 1944, nearly eight thousand people had been rescued. Eight wretched 400-ton wooden boats — *Milka, Mariza, Kazbak, Marina, Bulbul, Mafkura, Saleh-ad-Din,* and *Taurus* — performed the impossible.* Late as the British action came, the Jewish organization responded as best it could to a precarious and dangerous situation.

Goaded by Arab pressure and startled by the rapid acceleration of Jewish immigration, the British in December 1944

* Two were sunk: *Mariza* on a return trip, *Mafkura* with 359 refugees aboard, the victim of machine-gun fire from a Nazi submarine.

canceled the Cranbourne Declaration. Legal immigration into Palestine was closed once again.

By now, however, Haganah agents were deep into Europe. They had slipped behind the lines by ship, submarine, border crossing — even by parachute. They had moved eastward into Soviet-held areas. Their chain of secret headquarters, way stations, and border crossing units stretched across Eastern Europe to ports in Yugoslavia, and — with Italy out of the war — to Italian ports in the Adriatic and Mediterranean. In Bari, they linked up with units of the Jewish Brigade. As the war in Europe came to an end, these units, still in uniform, continued the effort in the utmost secrecy and became the means by which additional agents, using the identification papers of men returning on leave to Palestine, gained access to Europe. The organizational structure of Mossad le Aliyah Beth in the last months of the war quickly developed into a widespread, highly efficient system, bent on rendering rapid assistance to the remnants of Jewry in Europe and evacuating them to Palestine. Now that the incomprehensible facts were known, no other destination was acceptable — in the face of the tragedy that had befallen the Jews in Europe. At the end of the war, the fierce determination to reassert a racial and national identity in Eretz Israel was overriding.

The mass flight of the Jews from Europe was an epic of classic proportions. Seldom has history witnessed such an exodus, the compulsive, simultaneous, organized movement of a people, turning in revulsion from the ghettoes and the degradation of the past, and clamoring — even in the misery of camps all over Europe — to get to Palestine. There was no stemming the flood of hundreds of thousands of wretched people driven in a single purpose.

Into the DP camps in the American zone of Germany, already swamped with remnants of German Jewry, came the flood from Eastern Europe. In January 1946, the chief of UNRRA in Germany, Lieutenant General Sir Frederick E.

Morgan, made public the contents of a U.S. Third Army intelligence report which indicated that the migration of some two thousand Polish Jews per week into the U.S. occupation Zone of Germany was sponsored by an unidentified Jewish Zionist organization which operated an extensive underground route in Europe. The report was at least partially confirmed by General Joseph T. McNarney, Commanding General, U.S. Forces, European theater, in his report to President Truman on January 29, 1946.

The Jews never denied it. On the other hand, they never pulled aside the veil of secrecy which covered the organization and its workings. Not once, during the entire period of operations, was there a damaging disclosure. There were some defectors, to be sure; but the success of the operation as a whole was never impaired by breakdowns in the chain of security. The British intelligence services, directed to the task of penetrating the organization and alerting their government to its moves, confronted a problem of formidable and international magnitude.

Planning for the operation came from Jerusalem and Tel Aviv under the active scrutiny of David Ben-Gurion. In Europe, the implementation of the plans was directed from the Jewish Agency's headquarters in Paris, hidden in a travel agency's office which served as a front. The network spread all over Europe. In Germany, Haganah representatives served on the staff of Dr. Chaim Hoffman, the Jewish Agency's representatives. There were offices in Munich, Vienna, Rome, Milan, London, and outposts all over Europe. Agents of Bri'ha operated over the mountain passes and across the valleys — along the highways — and aboard the trains. They scraped together the little ships wherever they could procure them and coordinated the movement of refugee groups through the escape routes across Europe to the ports where the ships were ready.

While the escape routes were covert, the organization depended on the functioning of the DP camps in Germany for success. In Munich, the building at Number 3 Sieberstrasse was the focal point of assembly and movement through the major DP camps. Landsberg and Fedalfing were nearby; new camps near Stuttgart, Frankfort, Hassel, and in southern Bavaria were being organized in a frenzied effort on the part of UNRRA and the American authorities to meet the immediate arrival of a hundred thousand refugees from Eastern Europe. Groups of orphaned children appeared — located originally by Aliyah Beth agents in places of concealment, largely Catholic homes and institutions in Hungary and Poland — and placed in centers established for them at Rosenheim, Lindenfels, Indersdorf, and Dornstadt. The offices in Munich hummed in 1946 with the endless flow of refugees from the East and the visits of high officials and philanthropists from the West. In the inner offices, there was a huge map of operations, the movement of liberated Jews.

The organization depended also upon the vast humanitarian efforts of the American Joint Distribution Committee (JOINT). This private organization was engaged in a colossal international program over much of Eurasia to provide food, clothing and minimum essentials to the Jewish remnants. The conditions they found were appalling — the Jews in Poland reduced to a hundred thousand in dire want and without the means of livelihood; a half-million in Hungary and Rumania existing on less than a thousand calories a day; hordes of refugees on the move with little but the clothes they wore. By the end of 1946, JOINT had spent on the order of sixty million dollars. Its mainstay was the United Jewish Appeal in the United States. Dr. Joseph Schwartz, a tall, gaunt man, a product of social administration in New York and a rare combination of ambassador and executive, directed the operation from 19 Rue de Teheran, Paris. With its huge machinery functioning all over Europe and parts of Asia, JOINT was an open ally of the Jewish exodus.

But the organized movement of refugees from the interior

of Europe — from DP camps where they assembled, across national frontiers, by night over mountain passes, in trucks in hiding, on foot across borders — was the half-lit world of secrecy. In the face of entry restrictions and British representations to the countries of Europe to stop immigration flow to Palestine, there was no such thing as legal movement. Instead, there were the gendarmes, the border and customs guards, the ever-present military authorities, the police, the Sûreté, and the heavily augmented British intelligence operatives. The work of Aliyah Beth and Bri'ha was covert — performed by shrewd, talented and determined men and women.

The techniques were nearly as old as the "oldest profession" and had fewer scruples. There were many stories of the Jewish underground — stories of cleverness and high courage.

One such example — and it is a true story — concerns an American chief mate on one of the illegal ships, a man by the name of Morgan. He was a Roman Catholic. Originally signing up with the ship only for money, he became interested in its destination and its passengers, enough to stay on after arrival in Marseilles. The ship was intercepted and seized by the British on its way to Palestine. He, of course, ended up in one of the British internment camps on Cyprus. The British were unable to identify him as a crew member, because like the Palestinian crew, he was given forged identity papers. The British, at that point, had yet to capture an identifiable crew member and were avidly trying to catch one. Under the guise of a shell-shocked Polish soldier, he marched off in Cyprus with a child on his shoulder and a Jewish girl of Haganah, his ostensible wife, on his arm. He was told by the Jews to say nothing; his "wife" would explain his silence as the result of shell shock.

In Cyprus, he was eventually scheduled for entry into Palestine under the limited quota. One day, he was actually on the way to the boat. Suddenly, the line of refugees was stopped and reversed. Typhus had been discovered in the camp, and the departing group had to be examined by a physician before departure.

In the course of the examination, Morgan's lack of circumcision was discovered. As a non-Jew, there was circumstantial evidence that he was a crew member, long sought by the British. Badly frightened, he was thrown into solitary confinement in a barbed wire stockade. Three hours later, a British colonel, very military with his ribbons, swagger stick and moustache, entered and sat down at a little table. Without saying a word, he handed Morgan a card.

"I am a member of the Jewish underground" was written on the card. "Do not answer any of the questions that I will ask you."

Then the colonel said, "So, you're one of the crew! Who hired you?"

Morgan remained silent. The same question was repeated. Then more questions followed, delivered in an increasingly abusive torrent. Morgan remained silent, even under insult. In the midst of the tirade, the colonel produced another card.

"Tonight the Jews will storm the stockade, calling you a traitor and an informer," the card read. "Have no fear, you will not be hurt. But in order to protect you, the British will have to take you away from here in a motor torpedo boat to the prison at Acre to save your life. But do not worry. You will not be harmed."

After a final outburst, the colonel left. At nine o'clock that night, with a great shout a mob of a hundred men stormed the stockade, broke down the wire, and seized Morgan. They threw him in the air, tore his clothes, and bloodied his nose. British soldiers with Sten guns fired over the heads of the mob and dispersed them. The next day, as the colonel predicted, Morgan found himself on an MTB bound for the prison at Acre in Palestine.

In the prison yard at Acre, he was approached by some young Jewish men who gave him cigarettes and hasty assurances that he would be rescued. Two days later, they gave him an identity card for Palestine — with his picture, a new name, and an address in a kibbutz. For days on end, they drilled him on his new identity, the description of his kibbutz, every detail of the life he would have led to verify the validity of his papers. Then they arranged for his escape.

At a given moment, there was an explosion, and one wall of the prison yard collapsed. Prisoners poured outside. On the beach were more than three hundred people walking. Morgan, in the beach clothes quickly given him, joined the crowd and soon found himself carrying a beach tent and escorting some youngsters away from the scene of excitement created by the explosion.

At the checkpoint, he gave the right answers.

A few days later he was in Athens, then Paris, and Rome, and finally home in the United States — entertained well all the way by the underground. Morgan's story, like so many others of Haganah, revealed the subtlety and danger of its operations.

Bribery, sometimes on a large scale and dipping into the Zionist resources, was widespread and involved officials often of considerable rank who were in a position to assist. Passports, entry permits, identification papers, requisition forms — even official correspondence — were readily forged, on a mass scale, if necessary — sometimes with spurious results but usually with sufficient apparent validity to escape quick inspection. Military trucks, jeeps, and other equipment, huge quantities of which were standing idle in the motor pools and supply dumps all over postwar Europe, were simply "acquired," or "liberated." Haganah men, many still in uniform, operated from within the ranks of the military. Even whole logistic units, administratively dissolved and forgotten by their commands in the postwar wrap-up, managed to stand in place, fully operational with organic equipment intact, and escaped detection as bogus outfits. Haganah agents often carried letters of appeal from officials of the Jewish Agency which were useful in persuading Jewish commanding officers to render special assistance. Haganah even penetrated into high levels of government — in Britain, France and Italy.

In spite of its skill and resources, the task of Mossad le Aliyah Beth was enormously difficult. At every turn, the law and its apparatus stood in the way. At each juncture, the political pressures were brought to bear to inhibit the flow of refugees toward Palestine and cause them to return to their countries of residence from the DP camps. Furthermore, the chaos of Europe, filled with the rubble and disintegration of war and lacking in food and the basic elements of human needs, greatly compounded the logistic problems of such a vast, yet hidden, emigration. Where the Western powers might have helped, they were obsessed with a variety of problems — the restoration of unified control in a battered and divided France — the evacuation of the United States from Europe — the flow of the Soviet Union into a power vacuum. The complexity of immediate postwar adjustment in a torn and confused Europe and the perception of new strategic stresses in the international system left little to the assistance of the ragged and displaced Jews whose emigration might aggravate the stresses. For all its organization and its dedication, the Jewish leadership and Haganah confronted a difficult and treacherous job from which there was no retreat.

The picture of the migration of a people was at once epic, heroic, and ugly. Years of deprivation and degradation — then persecution — had driven many of the Jewish DP's into a mental makeup that was both menacing and demoralizing. Survival came to the clever, the wily, and the exploiters of human fallibility; the weak and righteous went to the gas chamber. The unity among them was compounded far less from the religious beckoning of Zionism than from raw hatred. They were enormously sensitive to suggestions of anti-Semitism, and they had few scruples about reprisals against the non-Jew. For Haganah, the conversion of this nihilistic, malignant hatred into a more constructive base of unity was an educational challenge of major proportions.

Haganah's agents were dedicated and courageous men and women, who put principle aside for a greater goal. Much of their success depended on their wits. Much depended, also, on the good will of others — the American soldier in the motor pool who looked the other way, the British officer who refused to notice, French and Italian authorities who were sympathetic, the farmer in the field who sheltered the sick and the weary, customs officials who never questioned the passports, the border guards who ignored the long line of marchers on the frontier trail, and the people along the way who looked upon the unfortunate refugees with compassion.

In the end, the element of compassion, felt in a numb but comprehensive way, was to prove decisive. Having, in effect, allowed the stage to be set — whether through ineptitude, lack of spine, corruption, or the pressure of circumstance — for the destruction of millions of Jews, the Western powers were left with little option but to allow the remnants, the survivors of Dachau and of all the other symbols of human degradation to seek new lives in the home of their choice. The sense of guilt was overriding. Sympathy indeed existed for the Arabs; and, certainly, strategic considerations demanded conciliation with the Arab world.

But the Jewish need was greater.

In the aftermath of war, the sense of guilt and of compassion for the Arabs could not ripen in the Western world as it did for the Jews. The memory of Arab cooperation with the Germans in the past lingered. But above all, there would be no putting aside the plight of the Jews — poignant and tangible in the horror of an immediate past. Furthermore, for the Jews but not for the Arabs, there existed a wealthy and well-organized structure in the United States, Britain, and France to keep the issue of the Jewish homeland a burning and critical one. Whether the Western powers liked it or not, the Jewish march to Palestine could not be stopped.

The network of Haganah spread over the map of Europe and the Middle East to facilitate the march. It poked into the shipping interests of the United States and around the fleet of abandoned derelicts in the James River to settle on an old steamer named *President Warfield* in which to infuse new life and a sense of mission.

They placed about her the same veil of secrecy that had always covered the work of Haganah. She was shielded from the inquiries of the press and the probes of British intelligence. The veil hid her to the very end of the saga.

NINE

THE FUTURE OF PRESIDENT WARFIELD, reborn with a new purpose but no inkling of her destiny, turned on events far from the Chesapeake Bay. What happened to her — and she had no way of knowing — depended on the shadowy panorama of an exodus in Europe and upon the dedicated people who, as supporting cast, were setting the stage for her dramatic entrance.

The men and women of Aliyah Beth, who operated the incredible network for the mass emigration of European Jews, were sturdy people who kept their counsels and lived rigorously by a stern discipline. They were known by their code names only: Ernst, Amos, Amnon, Ephraim, Reuben, Rudy, Zvi, and many others. The activities of some of them, prior to the appearance of *Warfield*, were as important to the role of *Warfield* as the ship itself was to the mission.

Overall direction of Haganah, from its beginnings as an organized force, was under Eliahu Golomb, who served as its chief-in-command until his death in 1945. Golomb was a moderate man, who urged restraint and rational decisions and who kept the leash on more extreme measures advocated by the militants in the organization. Moderation he preached, as he went about Palestine on his motorcycle and quietly met the members of his command. At various times he and his chief of staff, Ya'akov Dori, visited the United States and translated the needs of Haganah to perform its mission into funds raised from American Zionist sources.* Basic decisions governing the role and operation of Aliyah Beth were those of Golomb and Ya'akov Dori.

The active head of Aliyah Beth from 1939 on was Saul Avigur (originally Meiroll).† His life had been packed with melodrama. In 1920, he had been among the early defenders of Jewish settlers in Palestine. He had served on *Velos*, the phantom ship from Greece, in 1934. From then on, he had worked closely in coordinating immigration activities with the Haganah command. Just before the war began, he had set up headquarters in London. Then he moved to Paris, where he established himself in a cramped room in the Ceramic Hotel to run the underground immigration movement that had its tentacles all over Europe and Asia, and even into the Western Hemisphere. In 1940, he directed the *Patria* operation. When the war closed off the sea routes temporarily, he moved his headquarters in 1941 to Iraq. He arrived wearing a British army uniform to help him cross the frontiers and set about to move the Jews out of the pogroms there and, in addition, to facilitate overland movement to Palestine. In 1942, he showed up in Istanbul, there conniving to get Jews out of Europe via Bulgaria and Rumania. As the war came to an end, he slipped back into Europe to effect the release of an immigrant ship held by the Italians at La Spezia. Eventually, he set up headquarters near the Madeleine in Paris. From there he directed once again the far-flung network of Aliyah Beth in Europe. An intelligent, highly resourceful man, tough and shrewd, he moved surely and swiftly. The network of Aliyah Beth was never beyond his reach, and sooner or later most of its operations knew the touch of his hand.

* Ya'akov Dori (originally Dostrowski) became the first chief of staff of the armed forces of Israel.

† He was the brother-in-law of Moshe Shertok, then in charge of foreign relations of the Jewish Agency.

Operations in Italy were closely associated with the name of Ada Sereni. A gentle, black-haired, stout little woman, she was the wife of Enzo Sereni, a member of Haganah from the start. A Ph.D. himself, Enzo was the son of the physician to the King of Italy. In 1941, he led the way into Iraq to establish the headquarters for land movement there, where he was joined by Saul Avigur. He spoke several languages fluently. During the war, he worked with the British in Cairo to produce propaganda directed to Italian prisoners. For a while, he was Haganah's coordinator with the British Army Secret Service for operations with the German underground. As the war came to an end, he volunteered to parachute behind the enemy lines in Italy. He was captured and killed by the Germans. Ada, a widow and the mother of three children, entered Italy even while the war continued, to search for her husband. She became the mainstay of Aliyah Beth operations in Italy. Her connections in the Italian government proved invaluable. With Yehuda Arazi, she worked to acquire and outfit ships, establish transit depots, acquire villas near the ports of embarkation, and to obtain the gasoline, trucks, food and endless needs to be hidden in secret warehouses for last-minute use. To the men of Aliyah Beth, her quiet voice was a command.

Yehuda Arazi (his former name was Tannenbaum) was a formidable antagonist for the British to confront. His code name was Alon, or oak; the British thought of him as fox. His seven years in the Criminal Investigation Department of the Palestine Police served Haganah well. When he left the police force, he knew the techniques it used in searching out its quarry. He worked for Rekhesh in the acquirement of arms and ammunition. During the war, he joined a special Haganah sabotage team, which under the British operated in the Balkans for three years. His talents, his training, and his raw courage led him to the high command of Haganah. He became its operations officer — and simultaneously a hunted man, with a price on his head.

In Europe, he saw the vast traffic in military stores illegally diverted to the black market and decided that the support of Jews in the pipeline of Aliyah Beth could be procured by the same means. Shortly, the whiskey and cigarette rations of Palestinian troops were being used to acquire estates and farms for camps, transmitters and receivers for communications stations, canned food by the truckload for the DP camps and the refugees. With the telephone system virtually destroyed in postwar Europe and the postal services disorganized, Arazi set up a radiocommunications link between Paris, Tel Aviv, Milan, Naples, Antwerp, Marseilles and Athens that was more efficient than most of the diplomatic channels then in operation.

He arranged to smuggle Palmach members into Italy. These were the hard core of Haganah who accompanied each shipload of refugees as "commandants," who knew the operation of Aliyah Beth and coordinated the specific details of movement and logistics. With these people, Arazi developed to a fine art the procedures of secretly embarking refugees at clandestine spots along the coast. The effort involved a complex, smoothly working organization. Training and organizing the refugees, setting up local warning and defense, devising rapid embarkation techniques, establishing effective and secure communications, and forging passports, visas and requisitions, required the resources equivalent to an Army division. To coordinate all these far-flung functions required the thoroughness of a military commander. Arazi was equal to the task. He was a wily, dangerous fighter.

The incident of *Fede* proved to the British that they had a shrewd opponent who was capable of using any weapon. Arazi had decided to try an open port for embarkation, rather than the secret spots along the Italian coast where support and communications were difficult. His choice of a port was La Spezia; his choice of ships for the trial run was an old coaster of 512 tons, named *Fede,* into which Arazi decided to jam one thousand refugees. As a cover, he sent her under a fictitious agent to Sardinia with a load of salt, then bribed the port authorities in La Spezia into a bad case of blindness when she returned. Twenty trucks were "borrowed" from the last two Palestinian companies in Italy. On the night of April 4, 1946, they were to load refugees from the camps and converge from different directions on La Spezia. At the last critical instant, Arazi appeared out of nowhere in his black sports car and turned them back; the Italian police had decided to inspect *Fede*. They tried again the next night, but the police threw up a roadblock and stopped the convoy. To the amazement of the Italians — who were looking for Fascists escaping to Spain — British Palestinian soldiers in uniform with a thousand Jewish refugees emerged from the trucks. The Italians consented to let the refugees board *Fede* at La Spezia, but they simultaneously called the British authorities. However, by the time the British stirred, the trucks were back in their motor pools, polished up, with altered travel logs — and no one the wiser.

At British instigation, an Italian gunboat blocked *Fede*'s path to sea. Arazi, with a British price on his head, decided — right under the noses of the British — to use the sharp weapon of public opinion. When British military units on board demanded that the refugees leave the ship, Arazi brazenly announced that the ship would be blown up the instant a British soldier laid hands on a refugee. Abruptly the British soldiers left the ship and sealed off the port area. A great public outcry went up. Arazi added fuel to the fire by sending public telegrams to Attlee, Truman and Stalin, denouncing the British action and pleading for the miserable refugees jammed aboard *Fede*.

Next, Arazi announced a hunger strike. He put up a signboard on *Fede*'s deckhouse announcing the hours the strike had lasted and the number of refugees incapacitated by hunger. As both numbers mounted and shocked the observers of the press on the dock, world clamor mounted likewise. Harold Laski, chairman of the British Labor party, arriving in La Spezia with the British Ambassador, offered to negotiate with His Majesty's Government. With public opinion loud in their ears, the British capitulated, adding a stipulation to their agreement for the entry of *Fede* into Palestine that the refugees would be deducted from the immigration quota. Arazi held the quota in utter contempt. *Fede* (renamed *Dov Hos*) sailed for Palestine to the cheers of the dockside crowds and the raucous tunes of a local band.

For his exploits, Arazi was almost a legend in the annals of Mossad le Aliyah Beth. Another legend was Ze'ev Shind, known as Danny. His attachment to the Zionist cause came early. Born in Lithuania in 1909 of a Zionist family, he left home at seventeen to join the youth movement (Hehalutz) and to help establish an early training farm. In 1929, he managed to get himself included in a quota for Palestine and worked in the fields there until he could send for the rest of his family. He was one of the first to seize on the idea of ships to carry refugees out of Greece and one of the first to pressure the executive of the Jewish Agency in Palestine for authority to continue the operation. Danny's life was an active and dangerous one. He was in Iraq and Istanbul with Enzo Sereni and Saul Avigur. With other veterans in the game, notably Yehuda Ragin and Zvi Yehieli, he established in 1937 the headquarters in Paris which directed the immigration movement. In 1942, he was scheming with British naval intelligence officers and officials in the office of the American consul general in Istanbul to gain the assistance of the Turkish government in effecting movements of immigrants from Bulgaria to Palestine via Turkey. Teddy Kollek, to figure later in Aliyah Beth operations abroad, helped him develop contacts in Europe. After hostilities ceased, Danny seemed to be everywhere in Europe. His tall, muscular frame and red hair were familiar to the Haganah apparatus everywhere — at the borders, in headquarters meetings, at the dockside as refugees sailed, and in Baltimore aboard *President Warfield.*

Unsung in Haganah history were the emissaries, who established local headquarters and lived in the shadow of the police while they furthered the purposes of Aliyah Beth. One was Shmarya Zamaret, an early American settler in Palestine in the left-wing settlement of Bet Hashita. He was sent to Europe in 1937 as an emissary of the Union of Communal Settlements, and stayed on as an emissary of the Mossad in the Netherlands. In that year, he dispatched *Dora* from Holland with five hundred refugees for Palestine. At the end of the war, he was with Arazi in Italy as a Mossad operator in southern Europe. Like many Mossad operators, he managed to journey to Palestine and back into Europe under cover of a British uniform not his own. At one point, he had a narrow escape from British military intelligence, which suspected him of having a role in illegal immigration but couldn't prove it. He was picked up for interrogation, and he thought the end was in sight. But he managed to hoodwink his interrogators and escaped. Somehow he eluded pursuit. With the British looking for him all over Italy, he slipped over the border and began operations in southern France. From his headquarters in the vicinity of Marseilles, he directed large-scale refugee movements and immigrant ship departures under the very noses of French and British surveillance.

Shmarya Zamaret, like so many of the other unsung heroes of Mossad le Aliyah Beth, was destined to cross the path of *President Warfield.* They all came to know her sooner or later in the half shadows of a risky existence. Her resurrection and her fulfillment depended on the life they breathed into her. She had joined them in the backwashes of Baltimore, even as they started on its way down the long and hidden trails of Central Europe the human cargo which she was to carry. And she was only one — one in a long series of ships which had cradled the weary, the defiant, and the prayerful of Europe's outcast Jewry.

In staging areas — abandoned army camps, rented villas, even abandoned chateaux — along the French and Italian coasts, the refugees recovered from the arduous trek across Europe and prepared for the dangers of the sea route to Palestine. In time, they moved to the ships as they became available. A small but counterpart operation to that in France and Italy continued in Greece and Belgium. Slowly, the stream of seaborne immigration swelled into a flood. About a thousand refugees reached Palestine in 1945; by the end of 1946, the number of immigrants reached nearly twenty-two thousand. In 1947, over forty thousand had followed the sea route of Aliyah Beth. Most of them ended up in Cyprus, at Caraolos or Xyletymbou, the detention camps provided by the British. There, crowded behind barbed wire, they could wait out the quota which allowed only a trickle to enter Palestine per month. To Haganah, Cyprus was an outpost in a war — the last step to Palestine, when the British grip should weaken.

Nearly fifty ships had sailed under Aliyah Beth for Palestine by mid-1947. Their names chronicled the contemporary history of the Zionist movement and commemorated the men who gave it life and meaning: *Josiah Wedgwood* (1,039 tons) out of Savona with 1,260 passengers; *Hochelaga* (628 tons) out of Antwerp with 500; *The 23* (200 tons) out of northern Italy with 815; *Palmach* (360 tons) out of La Spezia with 626. There were many others — *Henrietta Szold, Eliahu Golomb, Orde Wingate* and *Enzo Sereni.* Ships from the United States in 1946 added a new dimension. In addition to *Josiah Wedgwood* (formerly *Beauharnois*), they included *Hagana* (formerly *Norsya*), *Hatikva* (formerly *Tradewinds*), *Ben Hecht* (formerly *Avril*), and *Chaim Arlossoroff* (the former Coast Guard cutter *Unalga* renamed *Ulua* by Captain Ash).

The exploit of *Chaim Arlossoroff* in running the blockade brought violence on a new scale to the sea routes of Aliyah Beth. In August 1946, when *Katriel Yaffe* docked in Haifa and the British announced for the first time the decision to deport the refugees to Cyprus, a fight started on board which quickly assumed the proportions of a battle. Mossad decided to strike back — not with firearms — but with fists and with any articles at hand that could be thrown. Therefore, when *Chaim Arlossoroff*, the next in line, approached the coast of Palestine, she was ready for battle. She was one of the first of the ships from the United States, a sturdy vessel by comparison to the wreckage available in Europe. She had been delivered in Marseilles, then moved to northern Europe. Picking up six hundred and fifty refugees in Sweden, she voyaged to Taranto, Italy, for another seven hundred. By then, the British had picked up her track; escort ships closed in on her and steamed with her toward Palestine.

Off Bat Galin, one of the two destroyers escorting her came alongside and ordered the ship to stop. *Chaim Arlossoroff*, abruptly jumping to full speed, made a dash for the beach. The British ship closed in at flank speed, rammed, dropped drawbridges, and boarded. The boarding party met with a barrage of tin cans and bottles. Some of its members were injured. The British sprayed tear gas and put a second boarding party over. Both boarding parties were captured and forced to jump overboard. The destroyers now used machine guns. But *Chaim Arlossoroff* drove herself upon the beach, and most of her passengers leaped into the surf. Most of them ran straight into the arms of a British shore patrol.

With the episode of *Chaim Arlossoroff*, the route of Aliyah Beth gained a new dimension of danger. The British and the Jews now knew that each arrival off the coast of Palestine could bring a virtual battle at sea — a battle in the classic mode, complete with boarding parties and hand-to-hand fighting.

For the Royal Navy, the problem presented was a stubborn and difficult one, for which its officers and men had no real stomach. Many had personal sympathies for the Jews, and very few felt any compulsion to use force against shiploads of helpless refugees. The operating Navy had little voice in the matter, however. All the decisions were made in London, and even the Admiralty was letting the Foreign Office call the tune.

The situation was a paradox. In it, the Labor government in Britain found itself totally beleaguered.

On the one hand, there seemed to be no solution to the ever-growing threat of Arab uprising. Now that the Arab League was organized, there existed for the first time a strong, articulate voice proclaiming unity in the Arab world and undying enmity for the encroaching Jew in Palestine. The voice was menacing and peremptory. For the British, the message was clear. If the recommendations of the Anglo-American Commission were accepted for the immediate admission of Jews in large numbers to Palestine, or even if Jewish immigration continued, legal or illegal, violence on a massive and widespread scale would erupt in the Middle East.

On the other hand, there seemed to be no way of stemming the avalanche of refugees pouring over Europe to the Promised Land. International pressure continued to mount. Britain's closest ally, the United States, virtually demanded that she admit a hundred thousand refugees into Palestine immediately. Public opinion worldwide, swayed by sympathy for the Jews, impelled by guilt for earlier omissions to prevent a genocide, and driven by the sheer weight of Zionist influence, smashed against the bulwark of government. Furthermore, within the British government itself, sympathy for the Jewish cause was strong.

Britain, near exhaustion at the end of a war that had already shattered her economically and left her a second-rate power with little potential in the postwar world, lacked the means of resolving a problem that even then was virtually refractory to settlement. A major decision was required, and shortly. Britain lacked a way of making it — or having made it, of backing it up. Under pressure from all sides, the situation of the British government rapidly became untenable.

The Jews thought the decision had been made with the ascendency of the Labor party to power. The Labor government had risen to majority with declarations of support for Zionist aspirations. Its platform included the statement: "There is surely neither hope nor meaning in a 'Jewish National Home' unless we are prepared to let the Jews, if they wish, enter this tiny land in such numbers as to become a majority. There was a strong case for this before the war. There is an irresistible case now . . . The Arabs have many wide territories of their own; they must not claim to exclude the Jews from this small area of Palestine . . . We should seek to win the full sympathy and support of both the American and Russian Governments for the execution of this policy."

After this statement, reaffirmed many times, the Jews were unprepared for the stern enforcement of the tight restrictive immigration policy of the past, which in effect choked off Jewish entry into Palestine to the barest trickle — piling up the refugees in Cyprus and damming up the exodus across Europe to dangerous levels. They were unprepared, also, for extreme and repressive measures by the British to restore the peace in Palestine — measures which seemed occasionally to approach the vindictive and irrational. They were unprepared, also, for the hostility which seemed to characterize the attitude of Ernest Bevin, the British Foreign Secretary, in his public utterances and in his policy positions concerning Palestine.

Bevin's attitude was an enigma. There were many who said that he was anti-Semitic from the start and made no pretense of concealing his strong dislike for the Jewish race. There were others who denied anti-Semitism in his makeup but conceded that he suffered from an acute case of "hoof-in-mouth disease" that made his public utterances a vulgar display of abuse for the sources of immediate irritation. But there were still others who said that he came to his job as Foreign Secretary in 1945 with a plan to make Palestine a showcase of the Middle East to be achieved with Jewish ingenuity and talent; that he was eventually persuaded by the Foreign Office and the Imperial General Staff to accept the immediate necessity of stabilizing Palestine by keeping the Arabs quiet; and that he gave in to the view that stability could only be brought about by restricting Jewish immigration to no more than fifteen hundred per month. Certainly, the evidence suggests that the storm that broke in response to this restriction was never fully comprehended by Bevin or the Attlee government. Some say that the anti-Semitism of Bevin, and indeed others in the British government, began then and there.

To them, the Jews were totally unreasonable. After all, others had suffered tragically in the war — the Poles, the Russians, even the British themselves. Why should the Jews single themselves out, as if they alone deserved restitution? Why was the unreasoning hostility of the Jews spent on the British soldier in Palestine or the British tar on the high seas — men who were doing their duty under orders, with the least force and often with the most compassion? Why were the Jews so uncompromising, offering nothing to offset their demands for all of Palestine? Why were the Jews jeopardizing their own people, driving them in an inhuman avalanche across Europe and upon the Mediterranean in dangerous and unseaworthy ships fit only for the scrapyard? Emotion, even passion, entered irrevocably into such thinking. Little by little, the attitude of the British hierarchy was heightened by emotionalism, less and less tempered as time went on by the capacity for rationality, objectivity, and fair play which the British themselves associated with their diplomacy.

The Jewish leadership had decisions to make, also. In the face of what they perceived to be an established British policy of exclusion and a deliberate postponement of the establishment of the Jewish national home in Palestine, the leadership decided that the only tactic was to force "illegal" immigration in ever-increasing numbers — to compel the British to reckon with a human flood and thereby to focus world attention so sharply on the Jewish plight in Palestine that a solution would prove inevitable.

The gallant men and women of Aliyah Beth readied themselves for a monumental task. Some gallant ships did, also.

Part Five

The Mission

TEN

In 1946 and 1947, the sea lanes of Aliyah Beth in the Mediterranean were active with ships of American origin. Each adventurous voyage was an odyssey in a relentless and impetuous epic.

The groundwork in the United States had been laid without very much warning or preparation. In fact, the idea of urgent and special support to Haganah from American Jewish sources was no older than July 1945, and the jump-off to aid this particular branch of the Zionist movement began no sooner than November.

Ben-Gurion's visit to New York in the summer of 1945 was the beginning. His conversation with Rudolph G. Sonnenborn, wealthy businessman and Zionist leader, led to the immediate conclusion that Haganah required early American financial and material assistance. The need was predicated on the necessity of the Jews of Palestine to defend themselves and, at the same time, to coordinate the accelerated movement of refugees out of Europe. The assistance could be provided only from the resources of the Zionist movement in the United States, and in particular by certain wealthy leaders who could be trusted in circumstances of the utmost secrecy.

On Sunday, July 1, 1945, there assembled in the drawing

room of Sonnenborn's home on Fifty-seventh Street in New York some eighteen prominent bankers, industrialists and professional men from all over the United States, brought hastily together at Sonnenborn's invitation to meet his guest from Palestine, David Ben-Gurion. For several hours, Ben-Gurion discussed the defenses of the Jewish community in Palestine and the status of immigration; then he grimly informed his listeners that, if the Labor government in Britain failed to fulfill its platform pledges and stood in the way of the exodus of the Jews from Europe to Palestine, there was little choice left but to force the issue by a flood of illegal immigration. The support would have to come from the United States — not only the source of money but also the source of adequate ships. In Europe, the only ships available after the war were no more than floating death traps.

His listeners, sworn to absolute secrecy, agreed to help to the limit. They formed what became known as the Sonnenborn Institute, a loosely organized, totally secret, but highly effective organization to put American substance behind Haganah and its branch, Mossad le Aliyah Beth. The signal for direct action, when the time was ripe, would come from Ben-Gurion.

After Bevin's speech of November 13, 1945, when he turned his back on unrestricted immigration, even on Truman's urgent appeal for the immediate admission of one hundred thousand refugees, and instead established a restricted quota of fifteen hundred entries per month, the members of the Sonnenborn Institute expected the signal. It came from Ben-Gurion by a telephone call to Sonnenborn via an English courier who simply said, "The time has come."

Funds were needed on a large scale. But their procurement could not compromise the necessity for secrecy. A quiet but highly effective campaign among American Zionists began. In most instances, the contributors never knew what the

Rudolph G. Sonnenborn (right) talks to Henry Morgenthau, Jr., former Secretary of the Treasury (left), and Eliezer Kaplan, treasurer of the Jewish Agency for Palestine (center), at the national conference, United Jewish Appeal, Atlantic City, New Jersey

money was for. Initiated by members of the Sonnenborn Institute or their trusted friends, there were gatherings in the living rooms of private homes in many cities — in New York, Philadelphia, Boston, Baltimore, Washington, among others — to raise the funds necessary for the purchase of perhaps a dozen ships in the United States and their outfitting. In addition, the money was used for arms — munitions of all kinds — to be placed in storage overseas, ready for use if and when required. The small American Friends of Haganah, already in existence, had its mission materially expanded by the Sonnenborn Institute.

Rudolph Sonnenborn was more than a fund-raiser. He was an active administrator in the whole operation, seen in unlikely warehouses and on the obscure docks where the ships were being readied. His influence was persuasive and reassuring.

There were prominent Americans involved — Dewey Stone, a Boston philanthropist; Abe Feinberg of the Kaiser-Roth Company; Morris Ginsberg, the shipping magnate; and many others who were active, but whose association with Haganah was certainly not public knowledge. Everywhere there were groups of prominent people — Zionists and sometimes Gentiles — who many years later were to say that they bought a Haganah ship and sent it to Palestine. The truth of the statement rests in the fact that the money came from a huge pot, the results of contributions from all over the United States.

Unknown to the immigration authorities and to the public was the presence of the leaders of Haganah itself in the United States. They had entered the country on some pretext or other under British passport. There was Theodore Kollek, an energetic Palestinian who had been engaged for some time in the risky running of the British blockade — who was destined to be Ben-Gurion's executive secretary and eventually mayor of Jerusalem in the new state of Israel.

In the United States, too, was Ya'akov Dori — chief of

staff of Haganah — future chief of staff of the Israeli armed forces. His voice was decisive in the whole procurement operation.

And Ze'ev Shind, the ever present "Danny," appeared. His tall, red-haired figure was beside Ben-Gurion in New York in July. It was seen in various ports of the Eastern seaboard; in the harbor slums where the little ships were being repaired; in the offices where discreet negotiations for purchase were being undertaken; among the crew members as they made ready for the one-way voyages. There was a quality of steel in Danny Shind. He symbolized Aliyah Beth. He had served it from the sailing of *Velos* in 1934; he had known all the years of never-ending danger; he had lived in constant risk of his life for months on end and had survived by his wits alone. His presence was a catalyst in getting the American operation into full swing.

These leaders of Haganah, supported by other members who functioned in various capacities, had entered the United States legally on British passports for various declared reasons, none of which related to the real purpose. One of their principal missions was to obtain ships from the surplus reserves and among the vintage craft in the United States that had outworn their usefulness. Quietly, they sought out American intermediaries who could help. They looked for men who knew the shipping world — who could negotiate in terms of price and availability of the ships selected, who could outfit and provide the crews — and who could be trusted with the confidential nature of the undertaking. The Haganah men, bringing with them the dark aura of their operations in Europe and Palestine, could perceive the process of procuring and readying the ships only as a clandestine operation, to be conducted in the utmost secrecy, hidden from the surveillance of government and the eyes of the British.

Morris Ginsberg, of the American Foreign Steamship Corporation in New York and a member of a family of successful ship operators, was one of the men initially approached. Through his good offices, there were shortly two Canadian corvettes, to be registered under the Panamanian flag, under conversion to cargo vessels in Brewer's Drydock, New York. Their destination was quietly announced as South America. They ended up some months later on the Mediterranean routes of Aliyah Beth. Morris Ginsberg was not just an agent for the procurement of ships; he was much more a financial guarantor of the whole operation in the United States, one of the channels for the disbursement of funds. The prestige of his name in the shipping world was often enough to spell success when the going got rough.

Captain William C. Ash was another American initially approached. A deep-water skipper, a leader in the labor organization of merchant seamen, a wartime officer in the U.S. Maritime Service, and an entrepreneur in the shipping world, Captain Ash was also a humanist — although his salty, bluff manner tended to disguise it. A Polish Jew who had emigrated to America from a Czarist regime, he had a deep compassion for the Jews in Eastern Europe. But Captain Ash was above all else a professional seaman. The Haganah men and the newly formed crews of the ships were soon to reckon with this stocky, swarthy, beret-capped figure, whose gravelly voice could be heard in a full gale and whose briny adjectives were devastating.

At the end of the war, shortly after being released from active duty in the Maritime Service, Ash served as port captain for the American Foreign Steamship Corporation. He started his own business as a marine surveyor, with an office in an old building at 24 Stone Street, New York, and was doing quite well; furthermore, he had become business manager of Local 88 of the Masters, Mates and Pilots Union, then vice president of the national organization.

One day his office phone rang. "This is the Jewish Agency for Palestine calling," a woman's voice announced.

"I make my contribution every year," Ash answered. "I can't afford any more."

"But it's not about a donation at all," the woman responded. "This is a matter of very great importance, which we would like to discuss with you confidentially. We're located at 342 Madison Avenue, near Forty-third Street. Can you come?"

Ash agreed to go on the following morning. Once there, he was taken into an inner office. There were three Palestinians present, two of whom left immediately. The third was Danny Shind.

From Danny Shind, Ash learned of the purposes of the Haganah deputation in the United States and their efforts to get ships. He learned, too, that Haganah had found him through Rabbi Joshua Goldberg, then on active duty as a chaplain in the Third Naval District; Ash had met him only once before at Sheepshead Bay, but the rabbi had a long memory.

Shind's plans smacked of the underground, of furtive methods of procurement, and of illegal procedures of registering, outfitting, and sailing. Ash balked.

"I want to impress upon you the fact that if there is anything illegal done here, you've got the wrong man," he asserted. "I know we can legally procure ships. We can legally send them wherever we want to. We can buy cargo and put it aboard. What you do with it on the other side, I don't care. But I will do my end legally. Now, how do American companies and shipowners legally get ships — and operate them — and get them out of the country? For five hundred dollars, they organize a Panamanian corporation. So we'll organize a Panamanian corporation for the purpose of operating and brokerage in ships. Then we'll go out and buy ships on the market in the name of that corporation. Why don't we take a leaf right out of the American shipowners' book and do the same thing they do? There's nothing illegal about it."

Ash's advice was followed.

Arias and Arias became the name of the new Panamanian company; like so many which operated ships under "flags of convenience," it was no more than a letter drop.

The company in the United States became the Weston Trading Company, improvised hastily to accomplish its specific procurement mission for Haganah. Ash became president, and the small fifth-floor office he had rented as a marine surveyor at 24 Stone Street became the headquarters of the company. The one stockholder, included in the instrument of incorporation for legal purposes, was Dewey Stone, the Brockton, Massachusetts, philanthropist. The other officers — Milton Pensack, Kieve Skidell, and Hyman Sobel — were window-dressing. Letterheads and envelopes were printed, and the name "Weston Trading Company" appeared next to the words "Marine Surveyor" on the frosted glass of Captain Ash's office door. In the initial stages of the operation, Danny Shind was always behind the scenes.

The first purchase was an obsolete Coast Guard cutter by the name of *Unalga,* still structurally and mechanically sound. She was acquired in Baltimore. Captain Ash moved to Baltimore and established himself there in the Mount Royal Hotel. The organization initiated accounts in the name of the Weston Trading Company with appropriate tradesmen in Baltimore and opened a bank account with the Chemical Bank and Trust Company. A bookkeeper employed by the organization kept disbursements in order from an office in Ash's hotel headquarters. *Unalga* went to the Maryland Drydock Company in Fairfield and then to a fitting-out dock, where she met the class standards of the French classification firm of Bureau Veritas and the inspection of Lloyds of London. Bureau Veritas standards, although not enough for U.S. registry, were sufficient to acquire Panamanian or Honduran flags. With Honduran registry, Weston renamed the cutter *Ulua* after a river in Honduras.

Ulua was ready for a crew. Here arose a conflict. The first thought of Haganah and the American organization which supported it was to put aboard a voluntary crew — young American Jews who wanted above all else to go to Palestine. These were the idealists, the dedicated — and also the adventurers and the opportunists. Young people from all over the United States volunteered through the mechanism of the American Zionist organization for a variety of reasons, both selfish and altruistic. Some came from recent service in the armed forces. A few had naval or merchant marine experience. But for the most part, they represented a cross-section of America, with zeal overweighing maritime competence. Haganah was especially anxious to have its own members — trusted agents who would be ultimately responsible for the ship and its conduct — on board, either active among the officers or unidentified as "sleepers" in the crew. Their status, in any circumstance, had to be kept secret.

The first concern of Captain Ash was to hire competent officers and crew members. He railed at the assortment of nonprofessional seamen recruited without his sanction. In his view they had only one characteristic that was suitable: they wanted to be of help to the Jewish people. In all other respects they were in the way, and Ash would gladly have gotten rid of them. "Some of them —— ——! Let alone tie a sailor's knot, I wonder how they tie their shoelaces!" he stormed. Under the circumstances he was more concerned to find seamen sufficiently competent to handle the ship even under the jurisdiction of professional officers.

The necessity of hiring a skipper with American master's paper was clear enough; it would ease the problem of clearance from a U.S. port. Captain Ash went to the Masters, Mates and Pilots Union in Baltimore and requested a master for a "one run job" to deliver a ship to the western Mediterranean at class "C" wages (Liberty ship, or equivalent), with return first-class transportation and wages paid until arrival back in the United States. His request found the union in the midst of the great maritime strike of 1946. However, since the person selected would be sailing under a foreign flag, he could accept the job offered by Ash without breaking the strike. Many officers with master's papers had been beached for a long time. The practice was to hire the man who had been the longest unemployed. William Scholastica Schlegel, out of over two hundred eligible candidates, had been the longest on the beach.

A Roman Catholic from Bavaria, William Schlegel was a good mariner. A little man in his forties with a paunch, a florid face and a German accent, Schlegel had a propensity or two, however, which tended to cross the grain of his employer and his crew — a peremptory tone of command which he assumed over his subordinates and an exceptional fondness for the bottle. Eventually both were to strain a relationship which from the outset was no more than utilitarian.

Ulua, with her repairs completed and a crew of sorts on board, was nearing her sailing date. There remained the matter of loading stores. For Captain Ash, the loading of stores became a problem often compounded in its complexity by the overzealous efforts of local Zionists.

For some time in Baltimore, a few native Zionists located by Danny Shind and friends of Haganah had been busy collecting stores which they considered invaluable to the success of the forthcoming immigration runs into Palestine. One of these men was Dr. Herman Seidel, a sixty-year-old general practitioner and leader of the pro-Histadrut movement in the United States, engaged in the procurement and support of labor for Palestine.* Another was Moses I. Speert, clothing manufacturer and a prominent figure among Baltimore Zionists.

Dr. Seidel was a little, drawn-up man with an inscrutable expression and a heavy accent. He had his offices in a row

* Histadrut in Palestine was the Jewish Federation of Labor, controlling agricultural cooperatives, industries, educational institutions, banks, and other activities. It was influential in the Jewish organization of Palestine.

Dr. Herman Seidel, Baltimore physician, who was an important benefactor in outfitting ships for Palestine

house at 2404 Eutaw Place, Baltimore, a few blocks from Druid Hill Park, in an area where apartment buildings and townhouses largely occupied by the Jewish community bordered a large Negro district. His outer office was lined with plaques and framed certificates commemorating his contributions to Histadrut. His inner office, lined with shelves of books in Hebrew, attested to his scholarship in Zionism and the history of the Jewish people. To his doors at all hours of day and night came his patients from both the Jewish and the Negro communities. He was a practitioner of the old school, deliberate, thorough, almost a hospital in himself.

His association with the Zionist cause was long. It started when as a boy in Lithuania he had watched the oppression under which the Jews lived. Shortly after his arrival in the United States and Baltimore in 1903, he became active in the Histadrut labor movement and spent the rest of his life in fund-raising for the Jewish homeland. In World War I, he played a key role in recruiting for the Jewish Brigade in its augmentation from Canadian sources, and he often suggested to young American Jews that they join up in Canada with that branch of the British Army. In view of his long and active role, Haganah sought his help in outfitting its ships in Baltimore.

Dr. Seidel raised money, although his efforts in parlor sessions and telephone calls around Baltimore took second place to several more important functions. Primarily, he collected medical supplies — drugs, dressings and instruments — from his contacts in the large pharmaceutical houses around the city. These supplies he assembled in his home and conveyed to the docks at night. In addition, to his door came the volunteers, the prospective crews of the ships, for physical examinations, inoculations and counsel. The fifteen or so Baltimoreans who enlisted in Haganah came to his office; a good portion of the four or five hundred Americans who joined the Haganah organization as crew members, liaison men and technicians passed through his door. One was a physician, another a former Navy pharmacist's mate. The latter was checked out by Dr. Seidel on his knowledge of obstetrics, in view of the number of pregnant women that journeyed the route of Aliyah Beth.

The organization in Baltimore associated with the work of Haganah and known to Dr. Seidel was quiet but effective. One leader was Joseph Allen, head of the Baltimore district of the Zionist Organization of America. Another was Samuel J. Keiser, chairman of the Baltimore Zionist Emergency Council. However, the Jewish community contributed heavily, often not knowing or even asking about the objectives for which contributions were asked. Only much later did the purposes of the drive become explicit.

Moses I. Speert, drawing upon his extensive contacts among the industrialists and commercial suppliers of Baltimore, served effectively as a kind of local quartermaster general. In a special warehouse, hidden away from public view, he collected the bedding, rations, ship equipment, stores, and even canned water that would be needed. Some of the materials even came from Haganah warehouses set up in New York. The collection of most of the supplies was scheduled well in advance of completion dates, so that ships could load quickly.

For a man experienced in the procedures of the export trade, any attempt to put aboard materials which could not be explained by customs declarations or crew's allowances could not be countenanced. Captain Ash looked in dismay at the pile of twenty-five hundred life preservers, a stack of messkits, a hundred firepumps of the canister type (to be used for dispensing soup), even a few obstetrical kits which would be difficult to explain in a crew's medicine chest. Under the code, he could load stores equivalent to a 180-day consumption period for a 30- to 40-man crew. How was he to explain this other mountain of stuff? How was he to explain three or four carloads of Canadian lumber (later to be used as bunks and partitions) which suddenly arrived at the dock?

He demanded that all the extra materials be crated and shipped as cargo, with proper declarations. There was a storm of dissent, but with U.S. customs officials always in the offing there was no ready alternative without jeopardy to the whole operation. *Ulua* sailed with legal credentials, her cargo consigned to a legal agent, Ginesta and Company in Marseilles.

Some weeks later *Ulua,* under yet another new name, *Chaim Arlossoroff*, sailed boldly through the British blockade and rammed herself on the beaches of Palestine in broad daylight. Her immigrant passengers plunged through the surf into the waiting arms of a British patrol. The exploit became a dramatic episode in the annals of Aliyah Beth and opened the route to Palestine to new heights of violence.

Captain Schlegel, by the time he left *Ulua* in Marseilles, must have comprehended something of her mission. He had been brought aboard by Ash almost at the last minute in Baltimore to keep down his suspicions. He had carried out his assignment to deliver the ship to Marseilles to the very letter of his contract.

By the time he flew back across the Atlantic via Shannon and reached Baltimore shortly after New Year's of 1947, Captain Ash had decided to hire him for the next run. *President Warfield* was nearly ready to receive him.

ELEVEN

A CHAIN OF ALTRUISM AND AVARICE linked *President Warfield* to Haganah.

On July 29, 1946, the U.S. Maritime Commission listed her for unrestricted sale and advertised the following week in newspapers all over the United States. A few brokers inquired. Interest lagged.

On August 28, the Potomac Shipwrecking Company, which had lost its earlier bid of $6,255 for *Warfield* as scrap when the Commission had rejected all bids as too low, submitted a second bid, this time for $8,028. This company maintained a small office and nondescript scrapyard at 1343 L Street, S.E., Washington, D.C., in a rundown area near the Navy Yard and the bridge to Anacostia. It also had a small facility at Pope's Creek on the Potomac River. Its partners included George Levin, Louis Levin, and Paul Backer. Captain Edward H. Eaton, soon to become master of *District of Columbia*, an Old Bay Line steamer operating between Norfolk and Washington, was a principal officer. The bid of $8,028 was intended to acquire *Warfield* for scrap only. On September 25 the Commission accepted the bid and notified the Potomac Shipwrecking Company by telegram on October 1, 1946, of its acceptance. Under the conditions of the award, the company had to take delivery within thirty days.

In the meantime, interest in *Warfield* had stirred in New York. The word had gotten around that certain Jewish interests in the United States were buying old ships. The speculators, seeing the Commission's advertising in the newspapers, responded with a sixth sense to this intelligence. For the most part, the speculators themselves were Jewish.

A few days after the Commission had published the name of the successful bidder on *Warfield,* the Potomac Shipwrecking Company received a telephone call from New York. George Levin answered. On the other end was Samuel Derecktor of the Chinese-American Industrial Company of 500 Fifth Avenue, who wanted to know their price for resale of *President Warfield.*

Levin cupped his hand over the mouthpiece and turned to Edward Eaton with Derecktor's proposal. "What price shall we ask?" he inquired.

"Forty thousand dollars," answered Eaton, almost without thinking. Levin shrugged and relayed the price. Derecktor in the very next breath invited them to come to New York at once to complete the sale.

A few days later, George Levin and Edward Eaton found themselves standing in the lower Broadway office of Herman Goldman, attorney for Samuel Derecktor. At the last minute, Derecktor began to hem and haw about the price.

"Let's get out of here," said Levin. Followed by Eaton, he abruptly left Goldman's office. Outside he said to Eaton, "He'll call us back. Just wait!"

Before they reached the elevator, Derecktor pursued them. He agreed to pay the $40,000. The sale was consummated on October 23, 1946. *President Warfield* was not now headed for the scrapyard, if indeed she ever had been.

The Chinese-American Industrial Company was legitimate enough, as one of Derecktor's promotions, to import bristles and skins from the Far East. But *President Warfield* was not bought for that purpose. Samuel Derecktor had smelled out the existence of the Palestinian underground in the United States and its purchasing of ships. He saw the possibilities that *President Warfield* would engage in a Mediterranean undertaking for which no great imagination was required. She was providentially suited for such a task. He negotiated immediately for her resale to Weston Trading Company—and in particular to Danny Shind.

The Maritime Commission was requested by Herman Goldman on November 4, 1946, to approve the transfer of *President Warfield* to Panamanian registry and her sale by Chinese-American Industrial Company to the Weston Trading Company. The application, dated November 2, contained some interesting statements: the ship had been placed on the "market" by Chinese-American less than a week before, one offer of $50,000 had been received from the Weston Trading Company, and the new owners intended to operate her, like *Ulua*, in "western European waters." The application was signed by Samuel Derecktor for Chinese-American and William C. Ash for Weston.

The Maritime Commission officially interposed no objections, and the transfer was approved on December 3, 1946. Unofficially, a number of responsible people in the United States government expressed deep concern on two counts. One stemmed from the increasing practice of profit-taking in surplus shipping. Too many ships, disposed of by the Commission in competitive bidding at ridiculous prices, had been resold in a short period of time at a handsome profit. The second worry stemmed from suspicions concerning the ultimate destination and employment of these vessels. Already the British were pressuring the Panamanians about the increasing number of hulks, formerly of American registry but now bearing the Panamanian flag, engaged in questionable preparations for the Mediterranean. The State Department spent time listening to complaints from the British Embassy. The Maritime Commission, with no legal grounds to withhold permission for transfer, could do no more than routinely alert Coast Guard intelligence to the transactions.

The Potomac Shipwrecking Company, in the meantime, had found itself in some difficulty. The terms of the original sale on October 1 required the removal of *President Warfield* from the James River Reserve Fleet within thirty days. When the period was about to expire and Potomac Shipwrecking had yet to make a move, the Commission pointedly issued a reminder. On November 6, George Levin responded by a letter explaining the delay by a tugboat strike, then a tugboat breakdown. He promised to effect the removal on the next day. The ship was pulled out of the Reserve Fleet on November 9. The significant fact is that George Levin's letter and his acceptance of responsibility to move *Warfield* was dated November 6 — two weeks *after* the sale to Chinese-American and two days following the application for transfer from Chinese-American to Weston Trading Company. Furthermore, actual removal was effected, not by Potomac, but with tugs hired by Weston. The evidence suggests that Potomac itself was not beyond knowledge of the web which tied *Warfield* to Haganah.

Captain Ash heard of *Warfield* from Danny Shind, who telephoned him with the information that Haganah had bought a new ship. Danny Shind stated that the contract would be signed the same day. The meeting was in Herman Goldman's office. It turned out to be a blustery session.

Ash's objections were based on the absence of a so-called "drydock clause" in the contract. In maritime sales contracts, such a clause provides protection to the purchaser by requiring drydocking for bottom inspection. Otherwise the buyer might find himself the possessor of a ship requiring major and costly repair to the hull. Danny Shind and the other Mossad agents, so sure that *Warfield*, with its shallow draft, speed, passenger capacity and cheap price, was the ideal ship for the mission, were willing to buy her without requiring the clause, indeed without any restrictions or stipulations of any sort. Ash was indignant that they would not accept his advice.

"Why'd you bring me here?" he fumed. "You made up your minds you're going to buy this ship anyway. What do you want me for? I tell you that you're making a mistake in buying that ship without the drydock clause. No one in his right mind would do it!"

"Now another thing," he thundered. "What about the expenses of breaking the ship out of the Reserve Fleet? Do you realize that you are going to have to go down there and tow away a dead ship? Where do you want to fit it out — Baltimore? — Norfolk? Remember the money you're going to have to spend once you get title. Have you got permission to transfer the flag, or are they going to sell you a ship with a flag on it? Let's get these things straight!"

No one seemed to take him seriously. Rebuffed, he threw up his hands. "What the hell! It's your money. You're paying for it."

Weston bought *Warfield* in spite of Ash's protestations. But Herman Goldman listened to him, and the actual terms of sale in the end met most of Ash's objections.

President Warfield was hauled out of the end of the long line of derelicts in the James River on a gloomy ninth of November and towed as a dead ship over her old route up the Bay to Baltimore. She was put immediately into drydock at the Fairfield yard of the Maryland Drydock Company. Less than three weeks later she was alongside the end of Pier 5, Pratt Street, for the initial stages of outfitting.

Later, she was moved by Captain Ash around the end of Jones Falls to Pier 8, Lancaster Street, an old, ramshackle municipal pier whose timbers had been untreated in the haste of construction during the WPA era and had been allowed to rot without replacement. The pier projected into a basin, always smelly from the discharge of sewage from Jones Falls and from the stench of a nearby chemical plant belching noxious fumes. To reach the pier one had to pick one's way through a warren of narrow streets of broken paving, lined by dilapidated warehouses and old slums with broken, empty windows. Here and there were vacant lots and lumberyards. At night it was a dark, eerie place, quiet except for the noise of distant city traffic, the whistles of ships in the harbor, and raucous sounds from an Italian bar a few blocks away. It was a place deserted except for the rats scuttling in the gutters and under the piers.

The old steamboat buffs of Baltimore, when they found her, looked in disbelief and dismay at *President Warfield* alongside the rotting pier. She was a pathetic sight, somehow shriveled and tiny now — an ugly, streaked craft, her canvas decks tattered, her railings sagging. An air of total neglect and utter fatigue encompassed her. Except for the jaunty angle of her tall stack and her neat, trim lines, there was nothing whatsoever left of the elegant and graceful past.

With her newest mission ahead of her, much work had to be done. Auxiliary equipment, refrigeration, pumps, steering engine, winches, all had to be repaired; the boilers had to be overhauled and cleaned. But her hull was in excellent condition — wrought iron, stout, built for a century of service. And her big reciprocating engines were operable, ready for thousands of miles of steaming. Electrical wiring, altered in 1942 by the British to fit their own appliances, was haphazard, and there were fourteen electrical fires on board before the ship was ready to sail.

Captain Ash found that his hands were full. With both *Warfield* in Baltimore and his business as a marine surveyor in New York requiring attention, he began to commute between the two cities. Husbanding the ship in Baltimore, playing customs broker, arranging berthing and pilotage, paying the bills was the Lone Star subsidiary of Lykes Brothers. The bills that poured in — $27,000 from the Maryland Drydock Company, large bills from ship chandlers — were guaranteed by Morris Ginsberg and met by disbursement from Weston's bank account. This fund was continu-

Raymond L. Jones (right), Old Bay Line Passenger traffic manager, shows the lower deck of the Warfield, *where the centennial celebration was held in 1940, to Nat Cohen, a merchant marine officer and shore engineer working with Captain Ash in the preparation of the ship for her adventures in the Mediterranean*

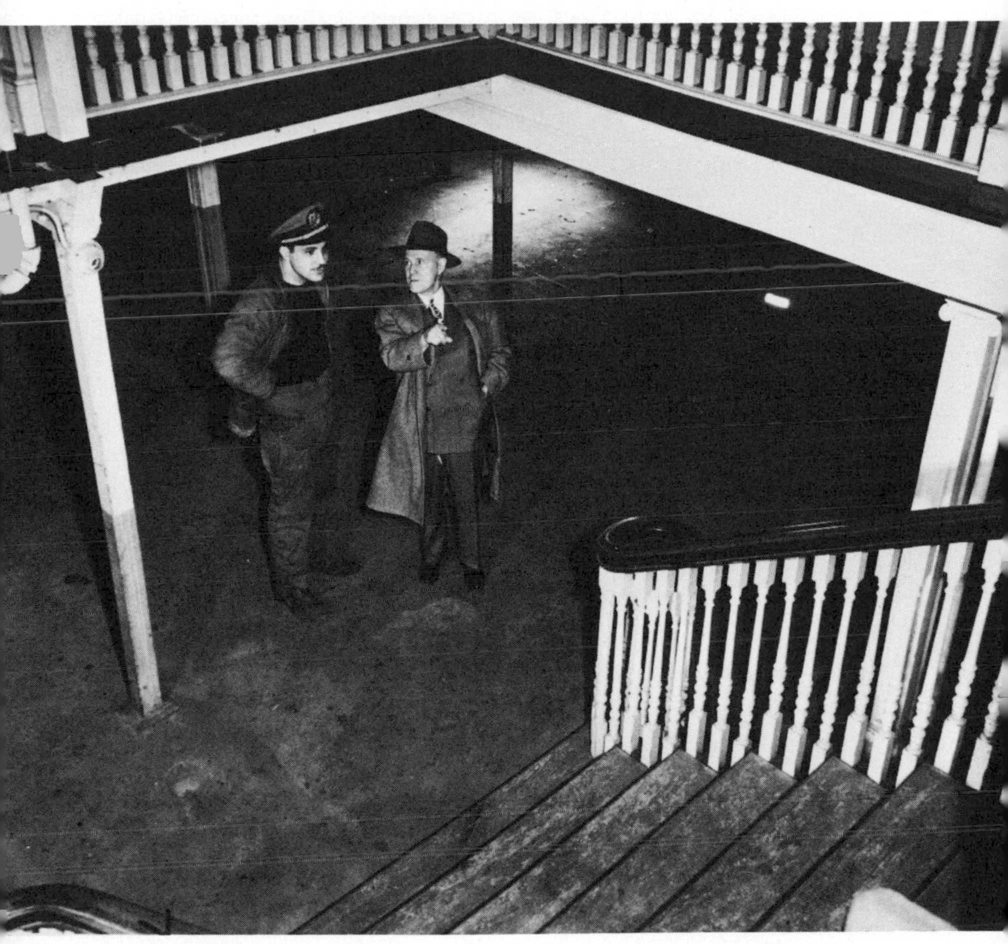

ously supplied from the flow of contributions. Estimates of total expenditures, including the initial cost, ran as high as $130,000; however, there was never any question about the availability of money.

Just as with *Ulua,* Captain Ash regarded the new crew skeptically. They began to assemble in Baltimore — young Jewish volunteers from all over the United States — the ex-GI's, the ex-Marines, the ex-sailors, former seamen in a wartime merchant marine, and the clerks and students — all stirred to go to Palestine for reasons of their own, altruistic and adventursome.

Many were real seamen. There was Bernard Marks from Cincinnati, an officer in the merchant marine who had come up from the bottom, now a member of the Masters, Mates and Pilots Union who had his master's papers. He had sailed on *Josiah Wedgwood* to Palestine with I. F. Stone, who on page 150 of his book *Underground to Palestine,* described Marks (called "Tom" in the book) as one of the Lamedvovnik — thirty-six saints supposedly scattered about the world "of such genuine, unaffected, and natural goodness of heart that God finds it worthwhile to let an otherwise wicked world go on for their sake." Marks was a sailor's man, competent and respected. At twenty-four, thin and boyish-looking, he scarcely looked his age. He became *Warfield*'s first mate.

The other mate was twenty-three-year-old William Bernstein of San Francisco, a graduate of the U.S. Merchant Marine Academy at Kings Point. Unaffected, curly-haired, quiet — an idealist in a nonreligious way — he exuded confidence and good cheer, often pulling things together when the going got rough. His training in the merchant service never left him, and his competence was apparent.

Cyril Weinstein filled the gangway when he came aboard. A polio victim who still walked with a slight limp, he had the massive shoulders and the general appearance of Franklin

Roosevelt. A New Yorker, he too had the experience in the merchant service so sorely needed.

Ben Foreman, a handsome youngster with no knowledge of the sea but a willingness to learn, became the right-hand man of Bernie Marks. During the war he served in the 82nd Airborne Division and intended, when he returned to civilian life, to study marine biology. The call to the side of Haganah was too strong, however, and he appeared in Baltimore on the gangway of *Warfield* one day in army uniform complete with Airborne insignia. The ship being cold and unready for habitation at the time, Marks shared his hotel room ashore with Foreman and placed him on the list of his watch at sea. Quiet, talented, he was worth far more than the rank of seaman which his inexperience prescribed.

Several of those who arrived carried their courage on their sleeves and in their fists. One was Murray Aronoff, a true New Yorker almost in the stereotype of the term, from accent to attitude. Somewhat aggressive, willing to tackle anyone or any situation that stood in the way, he managed to develop a following in the crew, largely because he was tough and others did not want to cross him, or because he was shrewd and led others into liking him. Another man, able with his fists, was Nat Nadler, clever as a mechanic, who quickly applied his genius to the onerous chore of keeping *Warfield*'s aging parts functioning.

A semiprofessional fighter arrived in the person of "Big Bill" Millman, who claimed the boxing championship of U.S.S. *Pittsburgh* during his wartime tour of duty as a sailor aboard the cruiser. Tall and muscular, he stood head and shoulders above the second Millman to show up in the crew, Dave, a bright but somewhat cynical chap who wound up in the galley. He was not related to Bill. The two Millmans, with their faces rimmed in full beards and with a conspicuous difference in height, came to be known as the "Smith Brothers."

And so they came: Harold Leidner, a college graduate with

MEMBERS OF THE CREW

Cyril Weinstein

Reverend John Stanley Grauel, Methodist minister who rode Exodus 1947 *from the beginning as a crew member, standing in the wheelhouse*

Eli Kalm with William Bernstein clowning behind him

William Bernstein, mate, later mortally wounded during the battle

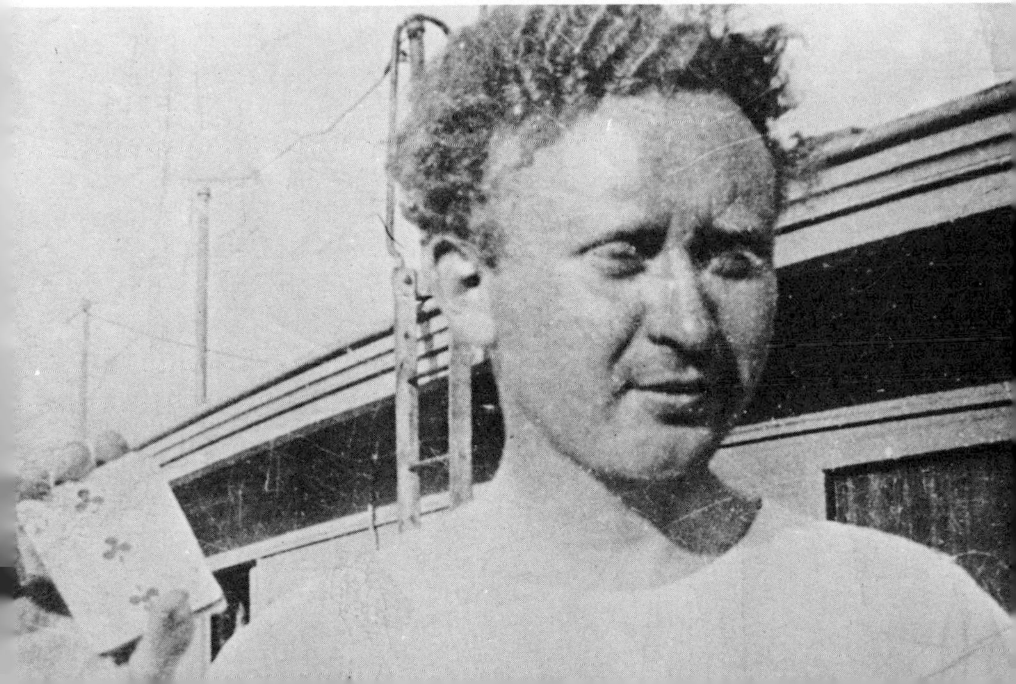

a career in patent law ahead of him, who elected instead to follow the trade of radioman in the merchant marine and found no end of difficulty with the radio equipment newly installed aboard *Warfield;* Danny Malovsky, an eighteen-year-old electrician who struggled with the wiring nightmare left by the British and fought the recurrent electrical fires in the switchboxes; Joe Miller, a swarthy, muscular young man about whom gathered a small colony of intellectuals among the crew; Abe Lippschitz, the pharmacist's mate of wartime experience; Leonard Sklar; Frank Levine; and all the rest of them from all walks of life. They numbered over forty, an improbable collection of young Americans brought to a miserable little ship in the harbor stench of Baltimore by a variety of impulses, with no common denominator other than the cause of Jewry.

And then in December came John Stanley Grauel, a twenty-nine-year-old Methodist minister from Worcester, Massachusetts.

John Grauel's link to Zionism and Haganah had come about by a chain of circumstances which could not have been foreseen in his early life. He had a father of German descent and an English mother. As a boy, he had grown up near the Kennedy boys at Hyannisport and, like them, was fascinated with sailing and the water. Narragansett Bay knew him by his twenty-six-foot boat, *Horizon.* He attended Randolph-Macon, the Methodist men's college at Ashland, Virginia, and the Bangor Theological Seminary in Maine. Subsequently, he was ordained as a Methodist minister. During the war years as a clergyman, he set to work for the *Churchman* at its Philadelphia offices. There, in pursuit of good causes, he became active in the American Christian Palestine Committee. Through this connection his association with the Jewish community became intimate; its members came to trust him, and in time, he learned about Haganah and its efforts in the United States. Fascinated, he became a recruit of Haganah and volunteered to ride *President Warfield* to Palestine.

He came aboard in Baltimore as a galley boy. A tall, cherubic-faced man with light wavy hair, he carried with him two important attributes: an abiding sense of balance and good humor, and a totally ecumenical spirit of compassion and mission. Like William Bernstein, he was a quiet and sustaining voice when the going got rough. At the same time, there was nothing obviously pious about him either. He could even resort to the necessary vernacular if the occasion required. And he was willing to work at the most menial tasks, even scrub the deck. His dedication to the mission was absolute.

But of the forty or so Americans who came aboard in late 1946 and early 1947 there were many whose credentials for deck, engineering and galley duties — and even some whose motivation for the trip — were not so well defined. In the face of the substantial task confronting the crew in getting the old ship in some semblance of readiness, they were often confused and stood about — or simply went ashore in search of entertainment which lower Baltimore Street with its burlesques, tattoo artists, and other skin shows was well prepared to provide.

The Palestinian members of Haganah circulated among the crew. Like the Americans, they had limited experience of ships. If they had sailed on any of the Haganah hulks from Greece or the Black Sea before or during the war, they were generally disposed to accept the deplorable condition of *Warfield* for what it was — remembering, as they did, the fate that befell the earlier ships — and were not too much excited about repairs and preparations for an Atlantic voyage. Dedicated, they were, and idealistic — but often not too practical.

Each time Captain Ash appeared, he railed at the crew. "You don't know your left foot from your right . . . I think you should keep out of here and away from the ship until it's ready to sail. I don't want you around her. You're down here to work, and you haven't put in a day's work yet!"

But the work went on somehow. An utterly uninhibited, democratic spirit prevailed among a volunteer crew which Ash's denunciation could not quell. Once, when the ship was shifting berths, Bernie Marks on the bow narrowly missed Ash on the dock with the hard "monkey fist" of a heaving line. There was a sharp exchange of words between the two — each bridling at the other's assumption of authority. The only results were some nettled feelings and, since the ship was being set down by the wind and current against a concrete dock, a bent stem, which stayed with *Warfield,* like a crooked nose, to the very end.

The winter was bitter cold. In Europe, it settled in to become the most severe of many years. In the camps, the Jews huddled around the stoves for warmth. Across a frozen Europe, in the broken cities, and along the trails of Aliyah Beth, privation and want aggravated by the intense cold presented UNRRA and the private agencies of mercy with new dimensions of human suffering. On the upper Chesapeake Bay, ice blocked the channel and piled up in rough shapes across windswept reaches.

On *Warfield,* without heat, the cold penetrated. The crew for the most part lived in cheap waterfront hotels. But the man on gangway watch huddled at the open port with an oil heater under the chair he sat on. At night, the snow often sifted into the frigid ship through the shuttered windows. Somehow, repairs went on.

In the midst of the cold, Itzak Aronowitz arrived. One morning, the twenty-odd members of the crew already on board assembled in a room of a small Pratt Street hotel where they were introduced by Danny Shind to the new "chief mate." No one there had any illusions about the identity of the youngster confronting them. The moment that Schlegel as master fulfilled his contract and delivered *Warfield* to Marseilles, Aronowitz would be the Haganah's skipper to run her to Palestine. In the meantime, as ostensible chief mate, he would be for the crew a kind of commanding officer.

His boyish appearance was deceptive. Twenty-two years old, he looked even younger — a slim, thin-faced, blond stripling with a youngster's exuberance. His background, in contrast, was a mature one. Born in Poland of parents who were ardent Zionists, he had gone to sea at the age of sixteen. Almost at the same time, he joined Palyam, the naval branch of Haganah. For a time he studied seamanship and navigation in a maritime college in London. At twenty-one he earned his third mate's ticket in the British merchant marine; he sailed immediately for the Manchester Lines between Britain and Canada. Early in 1946, through his Haganah membership, he met Saul Avigur at the Jewish Agency's headquarters in Great Russell Street near the British Museum. The latter shortly afterwards nominated Aronowitz for command of one of Haganah's ships being readied in the United States.

Through the intercession of Danny Shind in London and the influence of a stockholder in the Atid Navigation Company there, Aronowitz got a berth as extra mate on a British coal carrier bound for New York and Newport News. Shind was waiting on the dock in New York when he arrived and took the newcomer to a house in Brooklyn used discreetly as a training center for young prospective immigrants to Palestine. The next evening, he brought Aronowitz down from New York to Baltimore.

Aronowitz was thunderstruck when he saw his new command. He realized immediately that a ship of its type could never get to Europe, take aboard immigrants, and make it to Palestine without being detected. He felt that Haganah would have to plan on early discovery by vessels of the British blockade force and that the only possibility of success would lie in last-minute evasion and a dash for the beaches.

Nevertheless, he totaled up the advantages. In spite of her

decrepit state, *Warfield* was relatively fast — fourteen knots cruising speed, possibly seventeen knots or better in a short, high-speed run. Her shallow draft would permit her to navigate close inshore where combatant ships of the Royal Navy might not venture. Furthermore, her staterooms and huge open spaces on the main, saloon and gallery decks would accommodate a great number of passengers. Her galley, engineered by the British and the U.S. Navy for the feeding of troops, was an asset. Finally, there was much material about the ship which could be sold in postwar Europe — bathtubs, mirrors, bunks, lamps, navigational gear — all of which could bring a good price as salvage in Mediterranean ports, where the black market flourished. All in all, *Warfield*'s possibilities seemed to outweigh her disabilities.

Difficulties of repairs, logistics, and readiness for sea seemed to plague *Warfield* at every turn.

One of her immediate problems involved registry and flag. The November 2 application of Chinese-American Industrial to the Maritime Commission for transfer of the ship to Weston Trading Company included transfer of her Panamanian registry. Thus, *Warfield* at the start of her career with Haganah was scheduled to fly the flag of Panama. Almost immediately complications developed. On November 4, an advertisement appeared in the New York *Times* which called for support to the American League for a Free Palestine in furthering activities of Palestinian organizations in defiance of the British. This advertisement called to mind several earlier ones. One on April 17 and another on April 19 called for contributions to get Hebrews to Palestine "behind the backs of the British"; still another on October 29 called for a dedicated crusade to establish a Hebrew state in Palestine in spite of the British. All of these advertisements had been sponsored by a committee headed by Ben Hecht, the playwright. This committee represented the efforts in the United States of Irgun Zwai Leumi, the splinter group of Palestinian extremists. Their efforts were bent toward the sailing of S.S. *Avril* renamed *Ben Hecht*, for Palestine. The British, remembering the spurious history of certain ships of Panamanian registry, queried Panama about *Warfield*'s registry. More than that, the British intelligence apparatus, tuned in on the whispered gossip around the waterfront and red-light district of Baltimore, relayed their suspicions concerning *Warfield* to both the Panamanian government and the Department of State. Within a short time, *Warfield*'s Panamanian registry had been withdrawn.

Even before the Maritime Commission had approved the transfer from Chinese-American Industrial to Weston, therefore, the question of her eventual registry had become imperative. Herman Goldman and the apparatus of Weston went to work. By the time the Commission met on December 3 to consider the application for *Warfield*'s transfer, it had in hand an application for Honduran registry and flag. The transfer of *Warfield* was consummated on December 17. However, the matter of registry had not yet been resolved. The arm of British influence was long and strong. Before the Honduran government could be persuaded to issue the registry, the Weston Trading Company had to certify that *President Warfield* would not be used for any illegal commercial trade and would not be used for running the British blockade into Palestine for the purpose of carrying refugees. This certification was made in the form of an affidavit dated January 21, 1947. The fine hand of the British Embassy in pressuring the Honduran Embassy and its consul general in New York could be seen. Even then, one might have surmised that the affidavit containing so specific a statement as Weston's denial of interest in running the blockade would inescapably find its way into the archives of the British Embassy. Nevertheless, with such a document in hand, the Honduran consul general in New York could not refuse to issue the certificate of registry. *Warfield* was granted permission to fly the Honduran flag.

It was almost the end of January. The sailing date was only a few weeks away.

As the first of February arrived, *Warfield* neared her readiness deadline. Stores from the Haganah warehouse flowed aboard, including quantities of canned water (since *Warfield*'s fresh water capacity was not large), life jackets, dried foods, army K rations, messkits, even Dr. Seidel's obstetric kit. Goods for trade had been loaded — even some three million cigarettes — which would bring a good price in the European black market. Her engines were functioning well, and she was ready for trial runs. In the wheelhouse stood a six-hundred-dollar gyrocompass, installed at Captain Ash's insistence, so that the navigators on the final run could escape the tedium of getting azimuths and making up deviation charts. In the radio room, the equipment, at least for the time being, operated. With the boilers fired up, the ship got warm. The crew, now numbering over forty, moved on board from the hotels ashore. And the rat population, at first overwhelming, had been reduced to a minimum, largely due to the night-and-day onslaughts of William Bernstein.

Nothing remained but final preparations and the last word to sail. She compensated her magnetic compasses one day in a howling blizzard and made her test run at a speed of nearly eighteen knots wide open, a fact which gratified Aronowitz. Captain William Schlegel had arrived on board, ready to take her to sea.

Her first scheduled stop was Horta in the Azores for fuel — a six-day run. After that, Marseilles — and Palestine.

The last week of February 1947 had arrived. All that remained were the farewells.

TWELVE

THE SAILING DATE HAD BEEN SET for Tuesday, February 25, 1947.

For the third time in her career, *President Warfield* was girded for sea. A wooden turtleback again covered her forecastle, and her sides were boarded up above the saloon and gallery decks. She seemed a fragile counterpart to the *Warfield* that had sailed from the Bay in 1942 and returned in 1945. This time, her dejected, dismal appearance suggested an air of resignation.

Some of her gear and furnishings had been taken off to make more room for immigrants. The U.S. Navy motor launches stowed in the freight deck from the days of decommissioning in 1945 were removed. Quantities of overstuffed furniture, incredibly still remaining on board from her halcyon days on the Bay, were moved ashore and eventually came to rest in the Hightstown Agricultural Farm, New Jersey, then a training school for Palestine under Histadrut.

Then, in the last days of preparation, there came aboard over ten thousand dollars' worth of surplus stores, readily procurable in Baltimore to fill the storerooms.

Schlegel took the measure of his crew. He seemed particularly suspicious about the meetings that took place without his presence in various staterooms. Some were the planning meetings of Aronowitz and his lieutenants. Others took place — at frequent intervals — in John Grauel's room. He held the key to the liquor locker, and the officers came to his room for access. Schlegel, after his trip on *Ulua*, was apprehensive.

On Sunday, February 16, a ceremony took place on board. It began at one in the afternoon and lasted until three. The entire crew, with the exception of Captain Schlegel and Chief Engineer Crabson, assembled in the after part of the main deck where once Chesapeake revelers had dined in sumptuous comfort. Many Baltimore Zionists — Moses Speert and others instrumental in the movement — came aboard. I. F. Stone, the author of *Underground to Palestine*, was there. Captain Ash arrived. But, most important, Ya'akov Dori, Danny Shind and Rudolph Sonnenborn slipped over the gangway and appeared among the crew.

Each crew member took the Haganah oath. Each was given a sweater and a Hebrew Bible (John Grauel, now a non-Jewish member of Haganah, was thoughtfully given a prayer book of his own faith). Danny Shind presented Itzak Aronowitz with the Haganah flag, the familiar blue Mogen David of Israel. A bottle of champagne appeared — not for consumption at the moment, but for the day in the Mediterranean when the ship would be rechristened, according to custom, with a name appropriate to her mission.

There were only a few words said. Aronowitz responded tersely to the presentation of the flag. Danny Shind introduced Captain Ash as the man who brought about the culmination of their efforts and desires.

"We've learned how to get along with Captain Ash's temper," he said, "but we know also of his valuable work."

Captain Ash responded, "I envy you your opportunity. You are the twentieth-century Maccabees, doing today what they did in the days of the Hasmonaeons. I wish you Godspeed and good sailing."

John Grauel spoke quietly. "You may wonder why a

Christian clergyman should volunteer as a crew member on a ship destined to transport Jews from Europe to Palestine," he said. "Perhaps my presence can best be explained by an incident that took place in Italy during the war. A U.S. Army unit was bivouacked beside a Catholic monastery during heavy bombardment. The day was Friday, the eve of the Jewish Sabbath, and some Jewish soldiers decided to hold the traditional service. To hold such a service, according to ancient law, there must be a minyan, or ten men present. Only nine Jews could be found. Then they saw the statue of Christ in the monastery garden. Remembering that Christ himself was a Jew, they decided that the statue made the minyan and held the service, even as the bombardment continued and salvos landed all around."

No statement could have had more meaning.

The ceremonies ended; the farewells were said. Then began a week of waiting. The crew continued to clean the ship as best they could; they tried out the large stock of phonograph records and games donated by the local Jewish community; they held classes in seamanship and Hebrew history; and they frequented the local YMHA. The more adventurous as usual found the bars of East Baltimore tempting. The last few days were savored, the hours nursed with care.

During the week before departure, Cyril Weinstein married a local Catholic girl. Under Maryland law, the marriage had to be performed by a clergyman. The ceremony took place aboard *Warfield*, and the Reverend John Stanley Grauel officiated.

There was no ceremony when *President Warfield* departed. She slipped away from the snow-covered Pier 5 of Ruckert Terminal in Canton, where she had been taking aboard the last of her provisions, and put Baltimore harbor behind her forever. The day was cold and somewhat blustery, but the waters of the Bay were only slightly ruffled. For the last time, *President Warfield* steamed past her old haunts

President Warfield, *now owned by Haganah, underway for the Atlantic on her departure from Chesapeake Bay, February 1947, before the storm struck*

— Bodkin Point, Sharp's Island, Cove Point, Windmill Point, Point No Point, Wolf Trap, and Thimble Shoals. Once, in passing another ship, she sounded her whistle, the last time it was heard on the Bay.

In the early hours of morning, she cleared the Capes and breasted the first swells of the Atlantic Ocean. Cape Henry Light dropped astern as a periodic glow in the sky. The long rollers coming from the south were deep-troughed and whipped by the wind. *Warfield* began to labor.

During the following day, Thursday the twenty-sixth, the weather rose to a full gale. Fierce, sporadic storms gripped the entire North Atlantic, and winds of sixty miles an hour built up heavy seas over a vast area. To the north, nine crewmen were taken off the sinking fishing schooner *Catherine L. Brown.* Two hundred miles northeast of Bermuda the U.S. Navy salvage tug *Mosopelea* fought for hours to take in tow the freighter *Georgia,* which had lost her propeller in the mountainous seas. Ships were in distress all over the Atlantic. *President Warfield,* seventy-five miles east of Diamond Shoals Lightship, was finding it heavy going.

The U.S. Coast Guard cutter *Cherokee,* off Ocracoke Inlet, was wallowing in the seas, too. Sunset was officially "executed" at 5:57, and Lieutenant Commander J. T. Hagglove, the commanding officer, prepared to go below for a dinner served up in fiddleboards to hold the plates in place. Five minutes later an emergency message from ComFive headquarters came crackling over the radio. *Cherokee* was ordered to proceed at once to the assistance of "S.S. *President Garfield*" (sic), reported in position 35° 40′ north, 74° 00° west, steering northwest at five knots. Hagglove took his meal to the darkened bridge, and *Cherokee* shortly afterwards swung about in quartering seas, headed for a rendezvous with *Warfield.* As far as Hagglove could deduce from the message, the stricken ship must have reversed course and was limping back toward the Chesapeake entrance.

Shortly after midnight, he received by radio the information that the tanker *H. C. Sinclair* was standing by *Warfield*, which now was reported five miles from her earlier position, moving at five knots on course 320. *Sinclair* soon reported that *Warfield* was in danger of engine-room flooding, with a power failure likely at any time. At 2:45 A.M., *Cherokee* sighted the two ships. She relieved *Sinclair* and fell in astern of *Warfield*. At nine o'clock in the morning, Hagglove decided to hail *Warfield* and ascertain her predicament and intentions. He conned his ship to a point abreast of *Warfield*'s bridge. Hagglove noted that she was down by the head and listing to starboard — making heavy weather of it at three or four knots. His own ship was heaving about, but he tried to establish communications with *Warfield*'s bridge by megaphone and blinker light. No one emerged from the wheelhouse. He dropped back astern.

At 2:40 in the afternoon, Friday the twenty-eighth, *Warfield* reached Chesapeake Light and took aboard a pilot. As he went up the jacob's ladder and contacted *Warfield*'s officers, he shouted to *Cherokee* lying close aboard that no further assistance was required. Hagglove, after a sleepless and storm-tossed night, turned *Cherokee*'s bow for Elizabeth City and the refuge of home base. He saw *Warfield* on his starboard beam suddenly surge ahead in a burst of speed and show a remarkably clean wake for Hampton Roads.

Aboard *Warfield* on that fateful evening of February 25, there had been increasing chaos as the evening wore on and the storm increased in intensity. First were the casualties from seasickness — a green crew in heavy seas, with no chance to get their sea legs. They crawled about the ship, many too weak to care for themselves. Soon they were augmented by those who were bruised and battered from being thrown about the pitching hell or from being caught under cascades of stores and gear which tumbled about in a thundering confusion. The interior of the ship turned into a shambles.

Then came the water. It was noticed in a number of places

almost simultaneously. Grauel, in the galley below the main deck aft, saw it accumulating ankle-deep in the storage rooms just forward of where he was working. He seized an axe and cut away the wooden paneling; water seemed to be coming in at the overhead, where the wooden fender joined the main deck. He ran up the ladder to the main deck to sound the alarm.

Almost immediately the cry went up forward. Water was pouring back through the paint locker and storerooms from the chain locker in the bow. The chain locker was flooded. The ship was down by the head and taking water fast.

Sudden panic that the water might reach the boilers seized the engineers. John Crabson, the chief engineer hired by Captain Ash, slipped on the engine-room grating and cracked his ribs. Somehow, he managed to sound the alarm to the bridge. The alarm spread through the ship.

At 11 P.M., the able members of the crew, led by Marks and Aronowitz, set to work to block off the source of the water. They realized too late that before they left port the hawsepipes should have been filled with cement and the cement allowed to set. However, Coast Guard regulations required the anchors to be free on clearing port. No one, of course, had reckoned with the low freeboard of *Warfield* in a seaway; and no one had anticipated a gale. Now the storm-driven swells of the Atlantic were breaking over the bow and filling the port chain locker. Water was filtering aft into other compartments.

Belatedly, the men mixed cement and attempted to seal off the openings. The cement gave way. Shortly after midnight, the starboard chain locker began to fill. Then water flooded aft to the brig — the caged compartment built by the Navy in the exercise of its discipline, which was now used as the crew's "slop chest" for the storage of cigarettes, whiskey, foodstuffs, and other "goodies" calculated to maintain a sailor's morale. With this compartment under water, the whole main deck soon seemed to be awash.

With speed that at times seemed frantic, the men jammed kapok life preservers, blankets, anything, into the hawse-pipes. Near-hysteria sometimes generates humor. John Grauel, sitting on the mountain of stuff to keep it in place against the pressure of the waves from underneath remarked that this was probably the first time that anybody had been goosed by the Atlantic Ocean.

Working in such a pitching confusion was bad enough, but the inflow of water continued.

At 4 A.M., some of the more seasoned seamen lugged a heavy portable steam pump to the main deck forward. They managed to hitch it up to a steam line, with the ship wallowing about and sloshing water bucking their every effort. The pump had too little power to gain suction. As soon as it started, it burned up. The ship's boatswain was injured.

Suddenly, a number of those who were still about the saloon and gallery decks noticed that the wooden paneling and the beams above the steel uprights were behaving strangely — sliding back and forth an inch or two at a time with each roll of the ship. Hard as it was for them to believe, the superstructure seemed to be shifting — the whole wooden house above the hull moving off center with the working of the ship in the storm.

Furthermore, the wooden guard rail was breaking loose from the iron channel that held it in place. Each time the ship dipped in the seas, the water splashed inside the hull through the holes left by the rivets.

On the bridge, Captain Schlegel was overwhelmed by the volley of reports — all indicating that the ship was sinking by the head, that the engine room was in immediate danger of flooding, and that the lives of all hands were endangered by a superstructure which seemed ready to collapse with each sickening wallow of the ship. He immediately slowed the ship to steerageway — a measure he probably should have taken much sooner. Next, he ordered the closing of the watertight doors — also a precautionary measure he might have taken when he left port in heavy weather.

At 11:35 A.M. on February 26, Schlegel, Crabson, and Aronowitz in company crawled around the starboard side up forward to determine the seaworthiness of the ship. Schlegel decided to turn the ship around and head for port. Aronowitz, his mind on commitments in Europe, was reluctant. Schlegel's will as master prevailed.

Turning a ship like *Warfield* about in such a wind and sea was risky, touchy business. Her hull was too long, narrow and shallow for easy maneuverability in a heavy seaway; once in a trough, she would tend to stay there rather than to swing her stern up to the oncoming waves. Her high superstructure made her act like a sailboat running "full and by" before the wind.

Schlegel, trusting no one else, took the wheel himself and eased her around. Three-quarters right wheel — then amidships, as she heeled over — then right rudder again. Slowly, she swung about in a series of giddy arcs, rolling deeply in the trough and pounding heavily with seas abeam. Then, with a burst of spray, she spun around — her stern riding up on the next comber and her bow, heavy with water, cutting low in the trough. She made it around and headed for safety. Making it to port depended on whether the water could be contained and the damage limited.

With the water continuing to rise and the ship down by the head, Schlegel at 5:48 P.M. ordered the sending of an SOS. Coast Guard District Headquarters in Norfolk acknowledged; several other ships in the vicinity reported their positions and intentions to stand by. Then Schlegel sent a message to Captain Weiss, Alcoa's agent in Norfolk, informing him and Captain Ash of his predicament.

Conditions seemed to go from bad to worse. The seas and wind mounted in force, and the superstructure seemed to sway more ominously, sometimes two to four inches at a time in either direction. Schlegel feared that if it collapsed,

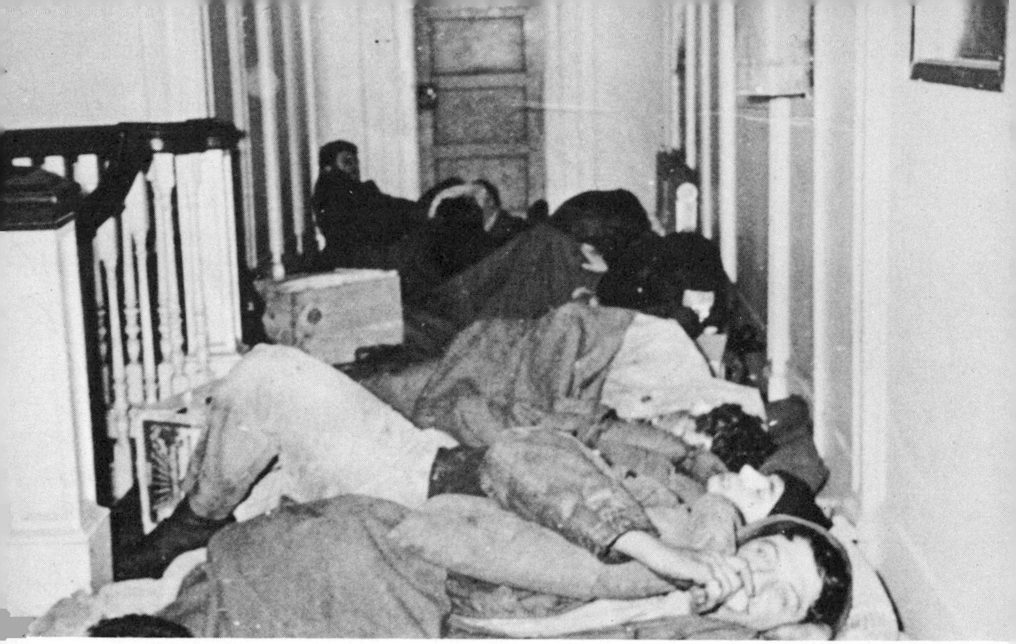

Injured crew members of President Warfield *after the gale, off Diamond Shoals*

Murray Aranoff salvaging crew's stores from the "brig" flooded in the storm, February 26–27, 1947

the life boats would go with it. At 8:00, he sent out a second message on the distress frequency. The Fifth Naval District acknowledged it. At 8:40, Schlegel fired off two distress flares.

By 9:00 P.M. on the twenty-sixth, *Warfield* was under escort. The Coast Guard cutter and other ships were present in her vicinity. But the storm roared about her unabated. In the early hours of the next morning, a tanker passed her close aboard and for a moment gave her a lee from the force of wind and sea. All the loose water in the forward end of the ship seemed to shift at once, and *Warfield* took a violent lurch to port. With engines stopped, *Warfield* hove to and rode the seas, while some shaken engineers investigated for further damage. When it seemed that she was no worse than before, Schlegel rang up to half speed and *Warfield* crept on into a blustery morning.

The seasick and the injured — none seriously, but all believing the worst of their own condition and the fate of the ship — now numbered all but six of the forty-two men on board. Those whose physical anguish seemed to be most severe were placed in cabins on the hurricane deck, preparatory to abandoning ship, should that become necessary. Others in the crew were more nonchalant. Grauel, for example, figuring that the next events were out of his hands, simply found his bunk and slept soundly until the ship was at anchor in Hampton Roads.

Some of the crew were more enterprising. Led by Murray Aronoff, they donned rubber coveralls, — which they promptly nicknamed "Jesus suits" (for walking on water) — and dove into the flooded brig to save what they could of the "goodies."

Warfield weathered the storm. The watertight doors held; the ship's pumps handled the water; the flooding was contained; and the superstructure stayed in place. Under her own power, *Warfield* reached the Chesapeake sea buoy.

At 2:34 P.M., she took aboard pilot Dozier, ordered by

Captain Ash; and at full speed proceeded to outdistance *Cherokee,* sent to rescue her. She came to anchor in the quarantine anchorage of Hampton Roads at 4:30. Crabson and the injured boatswain were put ashore for medical treatment. The next day, she moved to a lay berth at Upton's Dock, halfway between the Naval Operating Base and the city of Norfolk. It was an old, rickety dock, held up by rotten piling. Much of the flooring had fallen through, and picking one's way to the ship was precarious travel.

Captain Ash, at his home in Jamaica, Long Island, had been awakened in the middle of the night by a phone call informing him of the difficulty of *Warfield.* He was flabbergasted. Up to then he thought that she was on her way to her agents in the Azores for fuel, and that he had safely washed his hands of her. Now she was up to her mast in trouble at sea, and he was being asked to come down to Norfolk and sort it out. He wrote an immediate message for transmission by radio giving instructions to Schlegel, still floundering about at sea. It was never received — probably because the off-duty period of the radio operator on *Warfield* coincided with its transmission time — and this was fortunate. In the heat of the moment, instruction could scarcely have been welcome to Schlegel.

Captain Ash, along with Weiss, the agent, boarded *Warfield* in Norfolk. When Ash found out what had really happened to the ship, his temper knew no bounds.

"As far as I'm concerned, I'd get rid of all of you," he exploded. "I put ready-mix cement aboard this ship for you people. What do you think I put cement on her for? You go out to sea and you haven't got sense enough to cement up your chain pipes. Water comes over the bow, fills up the chain locker and forepeak, and puts her down by the head. Why'd you drive her so hard? Don't you know enough to slow down when the seas are up? So she pounds in the seas and breaks loose the wooden guard rail. And more water comes in through the rivet holes. And you nearly sank her!

Do you call that seamanship? What kind of seamen are you?"

Schlegel made excuses. Aronowitz equivocated. Ash ranted until his anger wore itself out.

The tension wore itself out on the crew, also. The ship was a shambles. The galley and storerooms ran with water. The interior looked like a pigpen. Some twelve thousand dollars' worth of supplies were beyond salvage. Captain Ash, with a seaman's love for the orderly, dressed down everyone in sight for the filthy condition of the ship, until at last he was spent.

One member of the crew had a gift for mimicry. Harry Weinsaft, an Austrian who had risen to the rank of major in the U.S. Army, struck a pose that at once resembled the stance of Captain Ash and that of Captain Bligh.

"Aren't we dogs? Aren't we filthy?" he said, his tone an exact imitation of Captain Ash's gravelly voice.

The calm voice of John Grauel prevailed. "You're all missing the point. We're on a mission. We've got a job to do. We'll clean up the ship and get going again. Let's forget what's happened and get at it."

Many others were saying the same thing.

In the weeks that followed, the ship was put to rights. The water was pumped out of the chain lockers; pumps emptied flooded storerooms, and new stocks filled the shelves; and mechanical equipment functioned again. Soon the ship found herself ready to move to the shipyard for further repairs.

Sometimes the old ship seemed jinxed. On the day scheduled for shifting berths, Chief Engineer Crabson, in preparation for departure, tested the main engines. Somehow, with the engines in reverse, the throttle went over too far. The great piston rods of *Warfield*'s engines thrashed, and the propeller bit deep. The ship, under a surge of power, backed down full and shot astern into the channel, carrying the rotten pilings with her at the end of her mooring lines.

But she made it in the end without further mishap to the

Brambleton Yards of the Norfolk Shipbuilding and Drydocking Company. The wood was removed from the guard rail, and the U-shaped metal retainer was plated over completely around the sponson. The main deck was now stoutly girdled in a steel fender. In addition, shoring was installed to brace the superstructure. Heavy 8-by-8-inch timbers were crisscrossed inside the main-deck cargo spaces and through the gallery and saloon decks, in some areas making transit through the cabin space difficult. The idea was to stiffen the housing from further shifting. The repairs completed, the American brokers representing Lloyds inspected the ship and awarded claims of $14,000.

In the meantime, John Grauel attended secret parlor meetings in Norfolk to raise money for repairs and expenses of the voyage. Aronowitz and the Haganah boys were getting increasingly uneasy at the delay and concerned about commitments in the Mediterranean. While the crew enjoyed themselves in the bright lights of Norfolk, they chafed at the wasted moments. They also expressed loudly their worries about the ship and its ability to survive another transatlantic crossing. A few men left the ship; most were determined to try again.

A few new faces appeared. An engineer from American Foreign, the Ginsberg interest, came to take the place of Crabson. Replacements for the few members of the crew who left came from recruitment sources ashore.

No one on board at the time forgot the arrival — and departure — of Sidney Butter. He came limping down the pier one day, old suitcase in hand — a thin, wispy lad, solemn-faced, round-eyed — dressed primly in coat and tie. He said little, except to complain about his feet. And, indeed, his distress was real enough, with both flat feet and fallen arches. That evening, he was placed on night gangway watch. He complained weakly that he couldn't stand up for so long a time. His statement had the ring of truth. Someone found a chair for him to occupy while he "stood" his watch — a disconsolate figure sitting with his knees bent sedately under his chin and his tie still neatly in place, an incongruous figure sitting through the night at the main-deck port of a disheveled old ship at the end of a rotten pier. The next day, the only evidence of Butter was a set of old snapshots and a used tube of toothpaste. He had vanished. His sad appearance and sudden departure quietly amused the crew, and signs appeared around the ship: "Butter Was Here!" He became a legend which was long in dying out.

The delay of *Warfield* in Norfolk provided an opportunity for additional acquisitions. With the money available, some material found in the army surplus stores came aboard. Other items of a nautical character found their way, through the "management" of some Jewish personnel inside the Naval Operating Base, to *Warfield* lying not too far away. The habit of "acquiring" or "liberating" needed materials for the cause was in the process of developing into a fine art. Many sailors had learned the techniques during their wartime naval service; they called it "moonlight requisitioning."

Just before departure, Captain Ash gathered the crew together and delivered a pep talk. His tones were almost fatherly.

"You've been through a great emotional experience," he said. "But now let's get down to brass tacks and stop all the belly-aching. I assure you that this ship is seaworthy in every respect."

Captain Ash's speech and his continued assurances that the ship was watertight only highlighted a serious misunderstanding. On the one hand, the feeling of Captain Ash, at least as perceived by the crew, consisted of his appraisal of the crew as a lot of venturesome and idealistic landlubbers, now reluctant after what had happened to take an old and ailing ship to sea. On the other hand, the vocal members of the crew were trying to make it clear that they would take the ship to sea even if it was a leaky crate. But neither Captain Ash nor the crew comprehended the other's view, largely because so much feeling had been generated between them by the incident of the storm.

Warfield at length departed Norfolk on Thursday, March 20, 1946, for Paulsboro on the Delaware River to take on bunkers. Fuel was short all over the Eastern seaboard, the aftermath of the great coal strike of 1946 when the railroads almost stopped running, the national economy went slack, and everyone watched the diminishing woodpile behind John L. Lewis's house in Alexandria as he defied federal authority. *President Warfield,* caught short in the wake of the fuel crisis, was unable to load oil bunkers in Norfolk. However, Socony, with whom Captain Ash had a working relationship, suggested Paulsboro. The weather being calm, *Warfield* took the outside route around the Capes and moored alongside the Paulsboro fuel dock late on Friday.

On the stretch from Cape Charles to Henlopen and the Delaware breakwater, the ship rolled once again in the swells of the Atlantic. Immediately, her anxious crew members, including Captain Schlegel, Weinsaft, Grauel and others, noticed once again the working of the superstructure, the exaggerated "old wooden streetcar effect" seen by the Navy. The cross-members placed through the ship in Norfolk stiffened the housing but they did not eliminate the sway. Captain Schlegel promptly informed Captain Ash that *Warfield*'s needs were not just fuel but also repairs.

On Saturday morning, *Warfield* moved from Paulsboro to a lay berth at the foot of South Street, Philadelphia. Captain Schlegel ran afoul of the regulation providing that a master of a ship with foreign registry entering port must deposit the ship's papers at the customs house; finding the Philadelphia customs house closed on Saturday, Schlegel went on to his favorite place of entertainment in Baltimore. The ship was subject to a fine of one thousand dollars for the delinquency.

Almost from the moment of arrival in the Delaware, all the worries, frustrations and internal dissension that had been smoldering beneath the surface in the relationships between Schlegel, Captain Ash, the Haganah leadership, and the crew — trouble brewing since Baltimore and more particularly since the storm — broke out into open flame. A highly vocal group demanded that something be done to anchor down the superstructure, and in a midnight session a few key leaders proposed to Schlegel that he take the ship outside territorial waters and, with the ship's crew as a labor force, brace the superstructure with wire cable and turnbuckles. Schlegel refused, stating that the crew were not seamen enough to do the job and the risk was too great in a season of rough weather. Tempers rose, and Schlegel disappeared ashore to find consolation.

Captain Ash cornered the most vocal of the crew, among whom was Harry Weinsaft, and squared himself off for a scrap.

"Now look," he shouted, "this is the last straw! You are either going to sail it or get off — right now. This ship is seaworthy."

"If it's so seaworthy," sneered one of the crew, "why don't you make the trip?"

"I'd love to," answered Ash, "but I have commitments here that I cannot escape. But don't ever accuse me of not wanting to sail on this ship. The classification society and the underwriters state that she is seaworthy. She is fully insured with Lloyds of London. Who are you to say that the ship isn't seaworthy? Now, those of you who have the whole crew stirred up, shut up or get off the ship! I've had it!"

When Schlegel returned to the ship, he was confronted by Captain Ash and the leadership in one of the staterooms. He was peremptorily fired; he retorted that he was only too glad to quit. Schlegel left the ship and entered the Marine Hospital, never again to put to sea in the capacity of a ship's master. There were bitter recriminations on both sides accompanying his departure from *Warfield* — a suit on his part against Ash alleging violation of contract — dark suggestions on the part of the ship's operators that Schlegel, not content with leaking the ship's destination to the press, had been playing footsie with the British.

A new skipper was hired by Captain Ash from the top of the list of the Masters, Mates and Pilots local in New York. Captain Vigo Thompson, a Norwegian-American skipper of the traditional school, was fond enough of his bottle, too, but reserved it for the end of the voyage. He was paid on the order of five thousand dollars to take *Warfield* to Marseilles. His quiet comment when seeing *Warfield* for the first time was, "If it stays afloat, I'll get it over there."

Again, a few of the crew decided not to go any further with *Warfield* and to leave her in Philadelphia. However, other volunteers came aboard, including two engineers. One was Sol Lester, first assistant. The other was Frank Stanzac, who became chief engineer, and a hardworking, hard-driving engineer he proved to be. Born in Poland, he rode *Warfield* to the end of her voyage, he and John Grauel being the only two non-Jews in the crew when the saga reached its climax.

Little by little, the edge wore off the tension, and tempers cooled. The atmosphere aboard *Warfield* settled down once more to determination, easy nonchalance, and resignation. Once again, *Warfield* made ready for sea.

The last of March brought mild weather and the promise of summer. The ship's agent, William De Witt of Lavina Shipping Company, had completed the loading of last-minute stores. All was in readiness for departure at the stroke of noon, on Saturday, March 29, 1947.

Early that morning, Captain Ash had a telephone call from Manuel Funes, the consul general of Honduras in New York. The call did not come precisely as a surprise.

Trouble over the registry had already been brewing. Schlegel just before dismissal had received a telegram from the Honduran Embassy alleging misconduct in stating the ship's destination. He had sent a rather awkwardly worded telegram in reply: "Please take notice that I enjoy the counseling of your government to sail as master of the S.S. *President*

Warfield. The owners instructed me to deliver the vessel at Marseilles, France, and I return to the United States of America. I do not see that I implicated myself according to your message." Quite clearly, the Honduran government had reason to think that the destination was other than Marseilles. In any event, Schlegel did not stay around for the next move from Honduran authorities.

"I've got bad news for you," stated the consul general to Ash on the phone. "Our ambassador in Washington has had strong representations made to him by the British Embassy, and I have instructions to go down to your ship in Philadelphia and remove her Honduran registry — to remove her Honduran flag."

Ash groped for time.

"Look, Funes," he said, "I've always kept my word with you. What train are you going down on? I'll go down with you. Our agents are the Lavina Shipping Company. I don't know where the ship is, but we'll find the pier through the agent. We'll go down together."

As agreed, the consul general and Captain Ash met at the information booth in Penn Station and boarded the 10:30 train for North Philadelphia. They chatted amiably together all the way down. Ash planned the next move.

Since the day was Saturday, he knew that Lavina's office would be closed by the time they arrived in the afternoon. As he expected, he and the consul general stood before the darkened and locked door of the agent's office shortly after one P.M.

"There's an easy way here," said Ash pleasantly. "The ship must be somewhere down near South Street. We'll take a run up and down the waterfront in a taxicab. But, now, look! We're so close to the Bellevue-Stratford. Let's go have some lunch."

They repaired to the bar of the Bellevue-Stratford and drank their lunch, passing the time quite happily.

Then Ash said, "It's getting late. We might as well go and do that disagreeable job."

Before leaving New York, Ash had called De Witt, at Lavina.

"Send a message to the captain," barked Ash, "and tell him I'll give him a bonus for every fifteen minutes sooner than noon he gets the ship underway. Tell him to get his crew on board, get a pilot, and get that ship out!"

In midafternoon, Funes and Ash drove up and down the Philadelphia waterfront in vain.

President Warfield had sailed hastily at 11:10 A.M. and was far down the Delaware River headed for the open sea.

"All right, Funes, I have a little promise to make to you," said Ash, when their futile search came to an end. "This ship sailed from here under the Honduran flag. I'll work it so that when it gets to France, we'll change it to the flag of Panama. Money talks over there, and we'll pay enough. Don't worry about it. When that ship sails from France, she'll be flying another flag."

Ash believed then that he would never again be able to send out a ship under the flag of Honduras.

At sunset, *Warfield* cleared the Delaware capes and headed east for the Azores. Her bow knifed cleanly through the calm seas, and her wake frothed white astern to the land of her birth — forever left behind.

THIRTEEN

PRESIDENT WARFIELD entered Ponta Delgada in the Azores on the morning of April 5, 1947. The Portuguese sailing ship *San Sebastiano* was lying at anchor in the harbor, the cadets at work on her yards. The *Warfield* moored near the end of the long quay which swept in an arc around the harbor. If the wharf rats stirred in the morning heat, they might have recognized the old gray hulk from the time, two years before, when she slipped into the same slot on a night in July.

Warfield had crossed the Atlantic for the third time. Calm seas had been with her most of the way. Once or twice the trade winds freshened and chopped up the sea. Again, as she pitched in the head seas, the old timbers creaked, and she sagged and swayed as before. This time, the crew regarded the groans from the old ship as a joke.

On the way over, the problem of obtaining fuel oil became critical. Before her departure from Philadelphia, Captain Ash had arranged for bunkering through Socony-Vacuum at Horta in the Azores. Horta had been selected rather than Ponta Delgada because it was the nearest port in the Azores on an eastward passage and safely within *Warfield*'s fuel range. The local fuel agent in the Azores was Ben Saude, who operated under a British franchise. The British, frustrated by their lack of success in preventing *Warfield*'s sailing from Philadelphia, were bent on stopping her in the Azores. Ben Saude found himself under heavy fire from both his home office and the Portuguese government. *Warfield* was diverted by radio to Ponta Delgada with the hope that Ben Saude, himself a Jew, would at the last minute find some solution there.

On Saturday morning in Ponta Delgada the solution had not been found. Ben Saude had no approval for the release of the oil, and *Warfield*'s tanks were low. While Aronowitz pondered the next move, the off-watch went ashore and sampled the wine in the local bistros. At four o'clock in the afternoon, there was a false alarm when *Warfield*'s whistle blew to summon the crew back to the ship; they returned merrily to their bottles when they were told the ship would be delayed.

Aronowitz and the leading crew members were busy. They had been tipped off by a Norwegian skipper that oil could be tapped from the concrete tanks and the pipelines right on the pier. When the crew came roistering back aboard in the wee hours of the next morning — hauling the burly cook over the camel's width between the ship and dock by block and tackle — the answer had been found. The guards on the dock had been persuaded by liberal rewards to turn their backs; the oil lines from the ship had been run directly to the outlet pipes on the dock; and oil was pumped quickly on board. Shortly after daybreak, before Ponta Delgada stirred in the morning breeze, *Warfield* was standing out of the harbor entrance, down to her marks with fuel.

A few days later she was lying off Gibraltar, the Rock a shadow on the horizon. She was waiting for darkness to hide her from the Royal Navy. Also, she waited for the winds, which gusted dangerously off the African coast, to die down. Under cover of darkness, she steamed boldly past the Rock.

A signal light challenged her: "What ship is that?" Unlike the Irish sailor many years before who had flashed back: "What Rock is that?" *Warfield* answered with a crisp epithet which invited the challenger to enjoy a very warm hereafter.

She steamed quietly across the Gulf du Lion. On the second morning, she entered Marseilles on a glassy sea in a thick fog. The voyage was practically over, and some of the crew were standing about the wheelhouse in a bright mood — perhaps even a little boisterous. Suddenly, a floating object appeared ahead, practically under the bows. The captain thought it was a floating mine. Startled, Thompson belched a volley of orders. *Warfield* under full rudder turned away. A large wooden box swept past, and Thompson turned his anger first on the box, and then on the levity around the bridge.

Warfield, after picking her way through the World War II wrecks that cluttered the anchorage of Marseilles, moored alongside the still unfinished Quay Grulet, next to the coal piers, far out in the harbor. As she approached, the signalman in the Ship Signal Station telephoned the ship's agent, Ginesta, on the Rue Jean Triquet, with the tidings that the ship was arriving, and, furthermore, that she was the strangest-looking craft he had ever seen.

Waiting on the dock was a very small reception committee — a Ginesta representative, the local Haganah agent, and Joe Baharlia. The first offered administrative services only. The second promptly established the link with the Haganah organization in southern France. The last proved immediately invaluable.

Joe Baharlia was a commanding figure, whose very presence brought respect. His tragic life had deepened a sense of commitment that knew neither bounds nor scruples. His entire family, with the exception of his brother and himself, had been wiped out by the Nazis. Somehow, at the end of the war, the two brothers managed to revive the ship chandler business started many years before in France by the Baharlia family. Their primary attention, however, was devoted to the care of the ships of Haganah coming and going through the port of Marseilles. The business was exceedingly well placed. Joe and his brother pulled wires and extraordinary things happened. The French customs net suddenly developed holes. Supplies and facilities became available when they seemed hopelessly beyond reach. When no legitimate bunkering outfit would provide black oil, Joe found it on the black market in barrels and had it poured into *Warfield*'s tanks via homemade wooden troughs. He was ingenious and unscrupulous for a purpose — a charming man with wit and grace, a quick and clever man with the cold shrewdness of an operator in the international underworld. His contribution to the cause of Haganah could not be calculated.

During the stay in Marseilles, the character of *Warfield* subtly changed. Captain Thompson departed and returned to the States. Itzak Aronowitz, under the Haganah code name of Ike, assumed command of the ship on April 15. Bernie Marks, Bill Bernstein and Cy Weinstein moved up to their assigned billets. The Haganah controls for the forthcoming operation asserted themselves. From time to time, Abe Schwartz, Shmarya Zamaret, Arazi and others appeared, and *Warfield* found herself within the operational network of Aliyah Beth.

Marseilles lent the atmosphere for roistering. Some of the crew proved their worthlessness. One burly cook made endless trouble. Finally, he was dismissed, after it was recognized that he had sold large quantities of ship's coffee in the black market for his own profit. Haganah considered stern punishment — this was a deadly game. But in the end, he was put on a truck and packed out of sight.

John Grauel went to Paris. In a way, his trip was a sojourn before the real one. In another way, he served a useful liaison function between the ship in its stages of preparation and the high command of Haganah in Europe. During his stay in Paris, he was questioned closely about the passenger capacity of *Warfield* by Arazi and other Haganah leaders in their headquarters and in cafe meetings. Arazi, bent on doubling the refugee load on all ships of Aliyah Beth in order to accomplish his "flooding" concept, hoped that *Warfield* could carry ten thousand passengers.

Grauel was accompanied during these meetings by Shulamet Arlossoroff, the daughter of Chaim Arlossoroff, former political department head of the Jewish Agency. He had been murdered in 1933 on the beach at Tel Aviv, and the *Ulua* had been renamed for him. The daughter was a key figure in the Paris headquarters of Mossad le Aliyah Beth.

These were days of fear in Paris. Extremists of the Stern Gang had threatened the life of Ernest Bevin in London; envelopes containing magnesium which exploded when opened had been delivered to the Colonial Office; Rabbi Baruch Korff, co-chairman of the American Political Action Committee, was making dark threats about "bombing" London. Much of the extremism which seemed to threaten the hierarchy of the British Government seemed traceable to Paris. Fear existed, too, that Jewish reprisals against the British in Paris might begin. The Sûreté and the British intelligence were actively in search of the Jewish underground. To them, there was no measurable difference between Haganah, Irgun, and the Stern Gang.

Before he left, Grauel had to obtain a visa for Palestine. This was one of the initial reasons for his trip to Paris. It required a visit to the British Embassy. When he discovered that the British Embassy and the adjacent streets were surrounded by gendarmes and plainclothesmen, he dressed in his clerical garb as a Methodist minister. Then he walked past the lion-guarded gate of the Embassy, accepting the salutes of the guards and the greetings of the British secret service.

He presented himself to the secretary in charge of visas and stated that he wished to enter Palestine as a tourist.

"It's a sticky time, you know," vouchsafed the official. "If you're shot, we'll have to explain to your government. Do you really mean to go?"

But Grauel insisted that he always wanted to see the shrines, that he would take care. The official murmured approval. Grauel paid the money for the necessary cables to obtain the approval of the Palestine police. Then he left the Embassy in the same way, nodding pastorally to the guards as he passed.

One morning Shulamet called Grauel from the Hotel Florida and said, "Don't talk! I'll meet you at the Place de la Concorde."

When Grauel got there, Shulamet warned him, "Everything is blown up. All Israelis are suspect, and everyone with them is considered to be part of the Jewish underground. The secret police is searching everywhere. You must leave."

However, with the scare still on, Grauel decided to join eight other members of Haganah at the opera. There they were — nine in a row at a performance of *Thaïs* — while the area of the Paris Opera and the streets of Paris swarmed with secret police looking for the Jewish underground.

A week later in Marseilles, he picked up the visa at the British consulate — again in clerical garb. The consul greeted him, "Doctor, we've been waiting for you. Here is your visa." With it firmly in hand, Grauel returned to his hotel room, changed back to his khakis, and resumed his role in Haganah.

By the time Grauel returned to Marseilles, *Warfield* had departed for Portovenere near La Spezia, Italy. He found himself placed aboard *Hatikvah,* the old *Tradewinds* formerly used as a training ship at Kings Point and outfitted after *Warfield* in Baltimore by Captain Ash. *Hatikvah* was to take him from Port de Bouc near Marseilles to La Spezia to join up with *Warfield.* Grauel was literally dumped aboard *Hatikvah* by the Haganah agents in Marseilles. She had been run out of Lisbon by the Portuguese police; now the French were behind her; and she had to sail within the hour.

President Warfield had cleared Marseilles under a cloud of trouble. Part of the difficulty began when in maneuvering away from the dock she rammed stern-end into the French packet *Providence* and ripped up some twenty feet of her railing and housing. Furthermore, she had accumulated some thirty million francs' worth of fines, levied by the French for alleged violations of sanitary and port regulations. A subsequent ship, *Northland*, was detained by the French authorities on the grounds of *Warfield*'s nonpayment of these fines. The departure of *Warfield* left a wake of problems for others to sort out.

British intelligence kept *Warfield* under constant surveillance. While she lingered in Marseilles, they took pictures of her from every angle, and the agents who took the pictures for the British promptly sold copies to *Warfield*'s crew. Nevertheless, little by little, the British accumulated evidence to confirm the character of *Warfield*'s mission. This evidence they transmitted via the Foreign Office to the British Embassy in Washington. The accumulation resulted in a demarche dated April 27 to the U.S. Department of State declaring that *Warfield*, sold by the Maritime Commission as a responsible agent of the U.S. government, was now destined to carry illegal immigrants to Palestine.

The routes of Aliyah Beth led into southern France. They also led into Italy. Ships readying for the assault phase of the operation had to be kept on the move to disguise their final port of embarkation and their immediate intentions. *President Warfield* accordingly had to move to an area of readiness, an area used for embarkation by immigrant ships in the past. If her identity as a prospective immigrant ship could not be hidden, her movements at least could be made as disconcerting and elusive as possible.

With surveillance in Marseilles making her stay there untenable, *Warfield* put to sea. Where next to go was at first undecided by her Haganah masters. The island of Monte Cristo was considered. Then she was ordered to head northeast into the Gulf of Genoa. Meanwhile the leadership of Aliyah Beth debated. Arriving off Genoa, *Warfield* hove to, awaiting orders from the leadership to enter port. Ashore, the leaders in Milan had misgivings — Genoa was untried and probably risky as a place for unobserved embarkation; there were mines still unlocated in the harbor; and the apparatus ashore for movement and loading was not in readiness. After a few hours, *Warfield* received abrupt orders to steam southeast, along the coast of Italy.

In the end, Portovenere was chosen as the spot for *Warfield* to lie in wait. It was near the headquarters of Aliyah Beth in Milan. It was accessible to the means of supply, and Haganah had operated successfully in Italy for some time. Furthermore, Ada Sereni could be depended upon to handle the ship as she had all the others she had readied for the cause. If all went well, *Warfield* might even load her passengers there, but this was a matter for later and careful judgment.

As the month of May began, *Warfield* let go her anchor off the quay of the picturesque little town and swung her stern to the beach for mooring by cable. Behind her, the pastel-colored houses of the town rose in tiers up the slopes. To the right of the town, facing the sea, reared up a sheer wall of rock. From this promontory, Shelley had contemplated the Gulf of Spezia in 1821, during the summer before he died. Now from this cliff, a British intelligence agent watched *Warfield* below. Each day he drove up in his car and looked her over through binoculars. The crew of *Warfield* peered back at the agent through binoculars. On the agent's staff, in the very house of Shelley which the agent occupied, an operator of Haganah, placed there by Arazi, spied on the workings of British intelligence.

What had stirred the British from the beginning and now alarmed them even more was the size of *Warfield* in comparison to the little tubs that had previously served Aliyah Beth. Obviously, this ship, as a former passenger vessel, could be crammed, Mossad-style, with many thousands of immigrants. Moreover, from a study of her times of departure and arrival at various ports and from known data from her days in the British merchant marine, a naval intelligence analyst could conclude that she was relatively fast. All of these factors boded ill. They seemed to bear out the conclusions of Whitehall that the Zionists were bent on breaking the British back in Palestine with a deluge of immigrants. Instructions went out to all British military units, intelligence services, and diplomatic missions in Europe: *Warfield* must be kept from sailing at all costs.

British diplomacy went to work on the Italian government. Within a few days after *Warfield*'s arrival in Portovenere, an Italian Navy cable tender (like a gunboat) came coasting into the harbor and dropped anchor across *Warfield*'s bows. Unless the Italian ship moved, *Warfield* was trapped. In Milan and elsewhere in Italy, the leadership of Mossad le Aliyah Beth pondered the next step. For the time being, until the overland movement of immigrants southward to the Mediterranean triggered *Warfield*'s mission, the best tactic in the game was to sit tight, to continue the game of cat-and-mouse.

For seven weeks, *Warfield* lay in Portovenere with the Italian gunboat across her chain. The crew did what work they found convenient to do. Some preparatory measures were accomplished, but not enough to excite undue attention. Outside ladders were taken down; some surplus equipment was removed and quietly sold ashore; and, in view of the number of passengers to be carried, an inclining experiment was conducted to determine the ship's stability.

Some of the natives of Portovenere were hired as workmen and performed valiantly for their employer. In fact, they were shocked at the American custom of stopping work in midmorning and midafternoon for coffee. However, in an amazingly short time, they not only found the breaks acceptable but were even informing the Americans when the coffee breaks were due. These workmen certainly became aware of *Warfield*'s mission; every barmaid and prostitute in town knew the ship's purpose, too. Moreover, among them were

Bluff above Portovenere, Italy. The bow of President Warfield *appears on left below hill*

Sol Lester, engineer of President Warfield, *on the bluff above Portovenere*

paid informers, sometimes for both sides and at the same time.

In Portovenere, a number of the Haganah leaders in Europe came to visit, slipping aboard at times when they were unobserved. The old black Packard bearing Ada Sereni often negotiated the narrow streets of Portovenere to the quayside, and her short, dignified, black-clad figure became familiar to the crew.

One by one special Haganah agents to accompany the ship on her run into Palestine came aboard to stay. One, of course, had been aboard since Baltimore. This was Ike — Itzak Aronowitz — who was now the navigating skipper and ship's master. At Portovenere, the new ship's commander to take charge of the entire operation came aboard. Josi Harel — former Hamburger — under the code name of Amnon, had a position on board comparable to an admiral, not replacing the ship's captain but overseeing the mission. Josi, as he came to be known, was a tall, square-jawed young man of twenty-nine — lean, levelheaded, and experienced in Haganah operations. Enav Azriel, code name Barak, became the communications officer, trained not only as a radioman but also as a specialist in Haganah's Hebrew code and the communications network which linked up the ship with the Aliyah Beth apparatus in Europe and Palestine. He was twenty-one. Micha, whose real name was Perlson, used the names of Gad and later Peri. His job was defense. There were others: Miri, who stayed with the refugees, even after they left *Warfield*, and a young girl, Sima, a nurse.

The American members of the crew looked apprehensively at this collection of youngsters on whose judgment and skill their very lives depended. These Palestinians had the raw courage, surely. But their very youth impugned the depth of experience and capacity for sound decision which might be desperately required. On the other hand, the Palestinians looked skeptically at the American crew. Haganah required discipline, and the undisciplined behavior of these Americans left them aghast.

A new American crew member appeared. Arthur Stanley Ritzer, a veteran of Guadalcanal, who had come over on *Ulua* in the engineer gang and fetched up in Milan after *Yacob Mildaran* broke down at sea, was available for assignment to *Warfield*. His roistering in Marseilles and a recent illness were scarcely clues for reassignment, and Ada Sereni turned to the ship's officers for advice: "What will we do with him?" No one had an immediate answer. John Grauel had one possible solution. As the only cook left on board, he needed help — and in the days to come, even more help. Ritzer by general agreement became a cook.

The Haganah leadership certainly had reason to question its own judgment in not having an all-Palestinian crew. The Americans were a rip-roaring lot and expected to spend their off-duty time in the local bars and around the girls.

The Palestinians considered the behavior of the Americans dangerous to the cause and wanted them to stay aboard to work, thereby not adding to the security problem by their presence ashore.

Seeing the Palestinians enjoying themselves with shore privileges which they assumed as part of their status but denied to the Americans, a good portion of the American crew abruptly asserted their independence and marched resolutely ashore. In effect, they were AWOL. To the leadership, accustomed to the harsh discipline of Haganah, this behavior constituted insubordination. Shortly afterward, many of the Americans found themselves in Milan before the Haganah equivalent of a court-martial.

The leadership threatened to send them home.

"Go ahead and send us home!" they answered. "We are only volunteers anyhow. Do anything you want to do!"

A day of sullen silence followed. Then one of the Americans found a soccer ball. None of the Americans had ever played the rough-and-tumble game of European soccer, but, expecting nothing more than to be thrown out of Haganah on AWOL charges, they turned to the sport with a fervor that surprised and fascinated the Palestinians. Little by little the Palestinians were drawn into matches. A spirit of competition blossomed. Slowly, some of the old vigor and comradeship returned. Campfires at night, a songfest or two helped, and the wounds seemed to heal.

In a few days, the Americans were returned to the ship in Portovenere. There, the leadership and the crew set about as best they could to keep alive the spirit rejuvenated at Milan. Campfires had succeeded in bridging the chasm at Milan, and they were held again, this time on the rough and rocky beach behind the ship. The crew soon found themselves feeding the whole town in nightly picnics. Accordions and guitars appeared, and the hills of Portovenere rang with music, Italian, American, Jewish style.

Elsewhere, the Haganah leadership planned the next move of *President Warfield*. The decisions were being coordinated in the old villa in Milan used by Ada Sereni and others of the Mossad. The conferences would often be held at dinner, in a room filled with massive Florentine furniture. Ada, in a quiet way, presided at the head of the table. One word from her was usually decisive.

At length, the decision was reached that the refugee buildup should be coordinated with a large-scale move from southern France, and that *Warfield* shortly should make a dash for freedom.

Careful plans were made for a day in the last week of June. One afternoon, the port captain of Portovenere received an official-looking letter bearing the crest of the Italian Admiralty. The letter ordered him to move the gunboat away from *Warfield*'s bows. He pondered over the order with nagging doubts. Finally, he reached for the telephone to call the office in Rome that had issued the order. In early 1947, the Italian telephone system was still struggling to repair the damages of the war. A long-distance call from La Spezia to

Rome could take many frustrating hours. As the hours ticked away, and the phone connection to Rome was not progressing very satisfactorily, the port captain was filled with apprehension. If the orders were spurious, he would be in great jeopardy with his superiors if he released *Warfield* without checking on the authenticity of the letter. On the other hand, if the orders were bona fide and he failed to carry them out immediately as they specified, he would be in still greater difficulty. He rationalized. Since he had made the effort to check and the telephone system was at fault, perhaps the better choice would be to order the gunboat out of the way and release *Warfield*. Having mentally excused his way out of the dilemma, he gave the necessary instructions. The Italian gunboat picked up her anchors and moved across the harbor.

Warfield was ready to move instantly. The fine hand of Ada Sereni could be perceived somewhere in the generation of orders bearing the official crest. Whether any member of the Italian Admiralty ever saw the orders was another matter. The very dilemma of the Italian port captain and the telephone impasse had been anticipated.

Warfield took in her stern lines from the quay, picked up her anchor, and steamed at full speed into the open sea.

Shortly afterward, the port captain got through to Rome. He spluttered incoherently when he had his answer. He ran down the quay wall, flailing the air with his arms like a windmill and hailing the gunboat. Somehow he made himself understood, and the gunboat in a cloud of smoke and a white wake headed in pursuit of *Warfield*, nearly hull-down on the horizon.

The chase lasted into the night. The old cable tender was not fast for a warship, and *Warfield* was showing her speed. Furthermore, the pursuit itself was half-hearted. The Italian commander of the gunboat knew very well that in this instance he had no jurisdiction on the high seas, but he was acting to satisfy the conscience of his superiors.

A squall descended at the opportune moment. *Warfield* turned off her running light and disappeared into it, shaking off her pursuer. By the next morning, she was inside French territorial waters in the vicinity of Toulon.

President Warfield moved into the picturesque little harbor of Port-de-Bouc, near Marseilles. Here the readying of the ship for her assault mission began in earnest. Bulkheads were ripped out. Five thousand bunks were rigged in the open spaces and around the criss-crossed shoring — shelf-type bunks, four or five high, with eighteen inches of space per person, modeled after prison camps for maximum use of space. The great U.S. Navy kettles in the galley were prepared. Life rafts to hold up to a total of five thousand persons were rigged. What had been the sunroom aft on the gallery deck became a hospital. Only two bathtubs remained on board: one for the skipper, the other for the chief engineer. Finally, *Warfield* was scrubbed from stem to stern.

The work was heavy and the crewmen were busy. On the Fourth of July, a number of the Americans asked for the day off to celebrate. Ike and the other Palestinians could not understand the strange reasoning of the Americans wanting time off when time was a critical commodity. The Americans informed Ike that they regarded Independence Day as he, a socialist, regarded May Day. Pondering this explanation, Ike offered a half-day holiday. Whereupon the Americans barricaded themselves in the galley and proceeded to get drunk.

On off-duty hours, they stormed once again to the bars of Marseilles. They hopped aboard the night freight passing through Port-de-Bouc at seven each evening and stayed to the small hours of the morning. They caroused, they wenched, and occasionally they fought. One member of the crew quarreled with a British officer in a café one night; a fight started; and the crewman left the officer cold on the floor.

The underground went to work to convert *Warfield*'s negotiable fixtures and cargo into money. Bathtubs, lamps, navigation equipment, all sorts of hardware brought extravagant sums on the black market of the Marseilles waterfront. American cigarettes sold at the equivalent of $2.50 per package. Currency exchanges and check cashing at discount for tourists whose countries of origin restricted the export of funds but whose borders were penetrable by Aliyah Beth for recovery of payment proved profitable. The profits entered the accounts of the Mossad.

In spite of brawling ashore, the crew of *Warfield* found itself knit together. Departure day approached. The test was near.

The British were watching, too. Their agents seemed ubiquitous and obvious. On occasions, members of the crew, having been followed for hours, would go right up to one of the British agents and invite him to join them at dinner. Every move on the ship and by her crew on shore was reported immediately to Whitehall. To both the British government and the Zionist hierarchy, *Warfield* was becoming a symbol — an embodiment of the test of will, of courage, and of compassion that was yet to come.

At dusk on Wednesday, July 9, *President Warfield,* on signal from Mossad headquarters, quietly slipped out of Port-de-Bouc and skirted the French coast on a westerly heading. She was darkened except for her running lights.

Part Six

Victory in Defeat

FOURTEEN

THE COAST OF FRANCE between Marseilles and the Spanish border in mid-July 1947 basked in the summer heat and the first real prosperity since the war began in 1939. Vacationers had returned to spend money. The villas were again occupied by the wealthy. The idyllic sense of repose seemed undisturbed by the political and economic ferment of postwar Europe. To the holiday-makers and the fun-seekers in the hotels and the prosperous residents of the villas, the Jewish refugees in the putrid camps and the back roads of Europe were another world away.

In fact, the refugees were right beside them — hidden in a number of coastal villas acquired by Mossad le Aliyah Beth from among those formerly owned by French collaborators. Here, behind high walls and sheltering parks, the apparatus of Haganah had performed many of its missions — collecting arms and stores, training refugees for duty in its ranks, and sheltering immigrants as they collected for transportation on the ships to Palestine.

Here, on the night of July 9, 1947, were over forty-five hundred men, women, and children, who had traveled the land route of Aliyah Beth from Poland and Germany, across France to the Mediterranean. Overwhelmingly these were Jews from the countries of Eastern Europe and Germany.

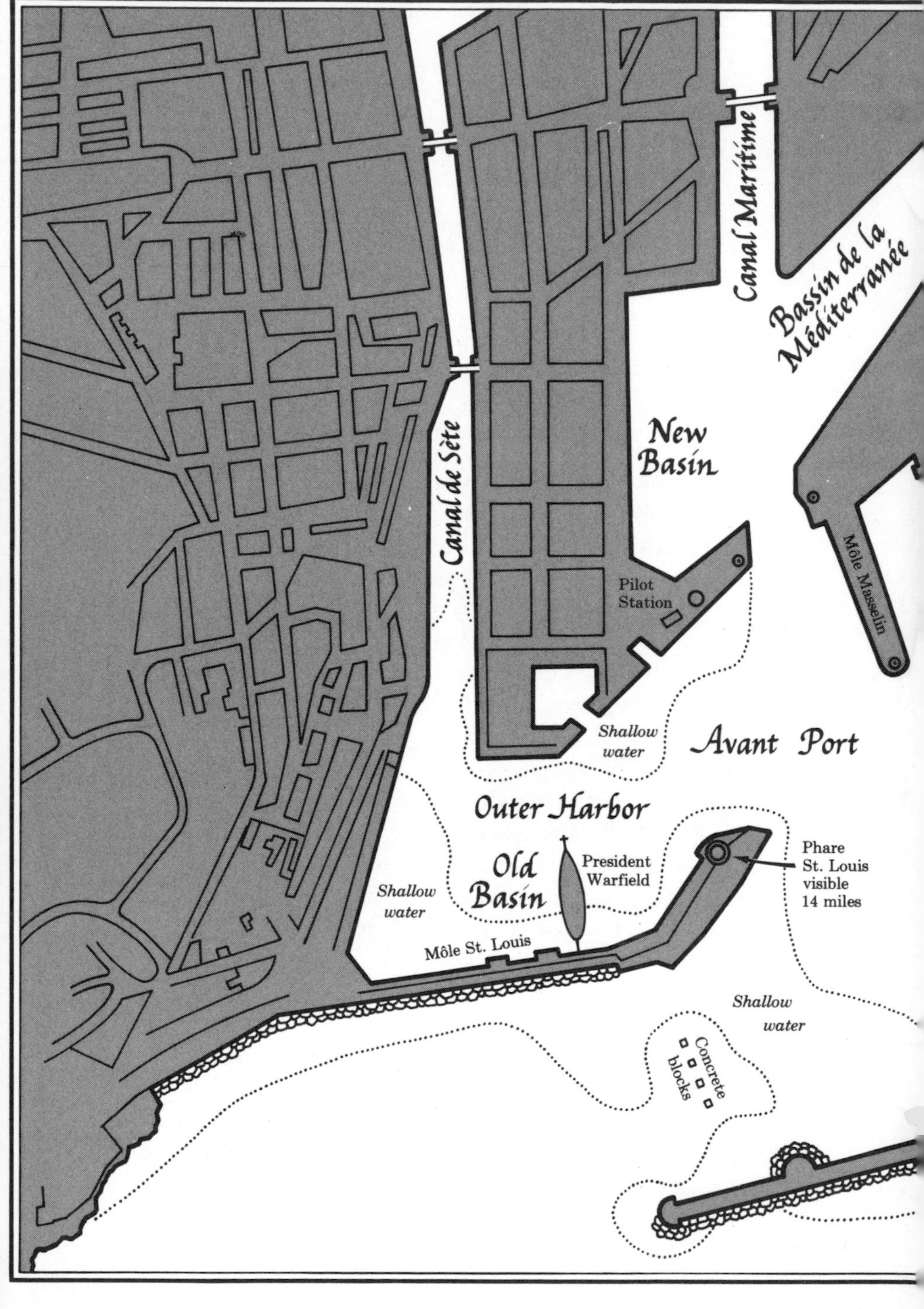

Canal Maritime
Bassin de la Méditerranée
Canal de Sète
New Basin
Môle Masselin
Pilot Station
Shallow water
Avant Port
Outer Harbor
Old Basin
President Warfield
Phare St. Louis visible 14 miles
Shallow water
Môle St. Louis
Shallow water
Concrete blocks

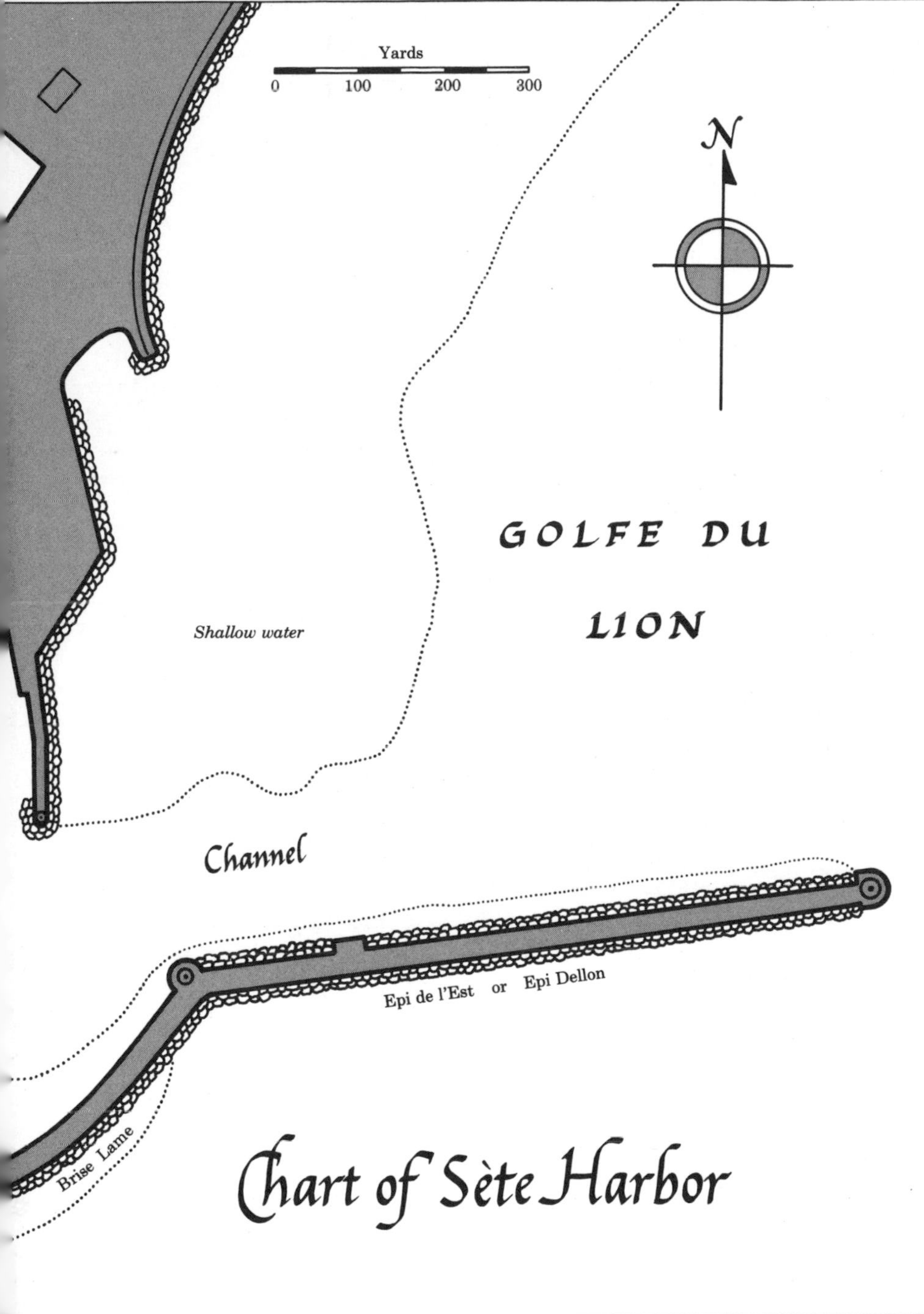

Yards
0
100
200
300
N
GOLFE DU LION
Shallow water
Channel
Epi de l'Est or Epi Dellon
Brise Lame
Chart of Sète Harbor

But their numbers included others. There was a group from Morocco. A number of youngsters from England had enlisted to get to Palestine. A variety of languages rose in a babel. Here were the old and the young; the lighthearted, the ill, and the pregnant. There were the Orthodox and the Conservative; the political moderates; and the socialists. Here were the gentle and subdued; there, the rabble-rousers and the firebrands. They all gathered their meager knapsacks and awaited orders.

Their fate rested in the hands of Aliyah Beth and its leaders. It rested, too, in the shadowy hulk approaching the coast not far away.

President Warfield, her gray hull merging with the pall of evening, picked up a pilot off the outer breakwater of Sète. This old French city rose up the hillside above the harbor, which had been cut up in an intricate maze of breakwaters, canals and basins. Lights twinkled in the busy port, up the slopes, and around the coast. Far across the Gulf of Lion lay Marseilles.

At bare steerageway, *Warfield* picked her way through the confusion of ships, canal barges, fishing boats, and small craft cluttering the walls of the breakwaters and basins that made up, like a labyrinth, the harbor of this tight, congested port. For this small harbor, *Warfield* was a large ship, and her three hundred feet of length and nearly sixty feet of beam barely squeezed between the concrete seawalls and quays and shipping. Entering from the east, she skirted the long seaward breakwater on her port side; then she turned hard to starboard to enter the Avant Port, or Outer Harbor. Almost immediately, in the space of her own ship length, she had to swing through an arc of 120 degrees to the left to round the jetty where stood the St. Louis Light and to enter the Ancien Bassin. Here she was to moor, her stern to the Mole St. Louis and her bow anchors out forward in the basin. To reach her moorings, she had to stop, and without headway pivot 90 degrees to the right, and then back into her slot. Here, with the aid of a tug and the skill of a harbor pilot, she came at last to rest, her anchor in the narrow Ancien Bassin, one stern line aft to the long concrete mole. From her taffrail, one could look across the mole to the dark water of the Mediterranean beyond. Steps and ramps from the road along the top of the mole led down to the dock at the stern of the ship. Barges were moved in by tug and moored along both sides of *Warfield*.

The city beyond the harbor darkened and lay quiet. On the end of the mole to the right of *Warfield* flashed the St. Louis Light, a brilliant white arc visible to seaward for fourteen miles. Along the mole and also across the basin against the quay in front of *Warfield* was concentrated a bewildering conglomeration of barges and little ships of every description, narrowing the channel and making passage through it difficult. The space from *Warfield*'s bow to the opposite side of the basin, thus constricted, was no more than her own length and perhaps less. *Warfield* found herself locked in by seawalls, quays, breakwaters, and an entangling mass of boats. Without tug and pilot to twist her in the narrow confines of the port and set her head to the open seas, she was a virtual prisoner.

During the small hours of the morning, the Haganah apparatus began to function. A bleary-eyed crew, worn after three or four sleepless nights, prepared to receive the human cargo. On shore, some seventy trucks, assembled in the area from the clandestine motor pools of Aliyah Beth, moved to the villas and loaded with refugees. Transportation to quayside was as systematic as a military movement; the immigrants were organized into groups; they had orders to move by groups from the trucks, past the French customs authorities where they displayed their spurious Colombian visas, and from the barges alongside into the ship from the side ports. All night long, the trucks rumbled over the coast roads and through the cobblestone streets of Sète.

Daylight came — a blue sea and a red sun. Half of the

refugees were on board. Shmarya Zamaret, the local commander of Aliyah Beth in southern France and an American, was deeply worried. If the ship could sail now, all might be well. Every moment of daylight loading increased the danger.

Now the passports, hastily prepared for only about two thousand persons, were running out. They were being collected on board the ship and smuggled back ashore for the refugees who followed. The French officials, fully aware of what was happening, glanced only perfunctorily at the spurious documents with the Colombian visas so ostentatiously displayed.

In the tension of the forenoon, the line of trucks and refugees seemed endlessly long and conspicuous. Just before twelve, the last of the passengers boarded. The barges alongside were moved away. *Warfield* had steam up and was preparing to sail. Given an hour, the ship could clear.

Shmarya's fears were well grounded. The network of British surveillance was too tight for *Warfield* to disappear for long; too much was at stake for the British not to find her quickly. Even as she entered Sète in the dark hours of the previous evening, she had been observed. The news of her discovery was on the desks of the watch officers in Whitehall within minutes. During the bright morning hours, a plane flew just outside the three-mile limit at slow speed, obviously observing and photographing the loading.

On the morning of Thursday, July 10, Ernest Bevin, the British Foreign Secretary, was in conference in Paris. The meeting in the Quai d'Orsay with Georges Bidault, French Foreign Minister, had the air of urgency about it. The week before, the Soviet Union had thrown down the gauntlet of economic nationalism in the face of the Marshall Plan and stalked out of a conference, its East European satellites trailing behind, to leave Britain and France to pick up the pieces of European recovery. Now Britain and France were determined to find a way for the remaining sixteen nations, interested in Secretary Marshall's offer of extensive U.S.

President Warfield (Exodus 1947) *loading refugees at Sète, France, July 10, 1947*

Warfield *fills with refugees at Sète*

assistance, to benefit collectively. On the forthcoming Saturday, the sixteen nations were to vote on the establishment of the Committee of European Economic Cooperation. In preparation for this vote, the Paris meeting on Thursday was critical.

During the meeting, a clerk entered the conference room and whispered briefly to Bevin and his aides. Bevin interrupted the meeting and informed Bidault that reports indicated *Warfield* was completing her loading in Sète and would be sailing shortly. Flatly, he declared that the situation constituted an affront to His Majesty's Government and that *Warfield* must not be permitted to sail.

In spite of French reluctance to stand in the way of the refugees, Bidault felt under the circumstances that he had no room for maneuver in the present confrontation with Bevin. He issued immediate orders for the detention of *President Warfield* in Sète.

Unnoticed, one of the French secretaries in the room slipped outside. In a matter of minutes, the Haganah leaders near *Warfield* learned by phone from Saul Avigur in Mossad headquarters in Paris that orders *Warfield* would receive in the next instant from the French port officials in Sète would come from the highest authority in the French government at British instigation. The secretary in the conference room, who had hastily phoned Bidault's decision to Saul Avigur, was a link in the Haganah chain.

The orders immediately shouted by the harbor police to the ship were explicit: "Halt! This ship is not permitted to sail."

Without tug, pilot, and permission to clear, *Warfield* seemed doomed to rot in the inner basin of Sète. Furthermore, Haganah agents ashore learned that the French planned to move her the next day up the Canal Maritime beyond a low drawbridge which when closed behind her would completely block her escape.

Warfield's decks and cabins swarmed with over forty-five hundred refugees, sweltering in the humid afternoon heat.

For some hours, Josi, Ike, Bernie Marks, Bill Bernstein and some others had been deliberating on what to do if the situation should become critical. In early afternoon, a group of the Haganah team ashore formed a delegation to plead with the French authorities. They hiked to the local prefecture and to the office of the Service Maritime; they were courteously but firmly shown a deaf ear. In Paris, Saul Avigur brought to bear the full weight of the Mossad's political machine to persuade the French government and the British authorities to relent. His efforts were proving increasingly futile.

Shmarya Zamaret decided to try the power of money. He approached the young French pilot who had brought the ship into Sète and offered him approximately ten thousand dollars in francs to take the *Warfield* through the breakwater in the dead of night. The sum looked astronomical to the pilot, even in the face of possible reprisal from officialdom. He accepted the offer and agreed to come aboard *Warfield* at two in the morning.

Tension settled ominously as the evening wore on.

At the appointed time — in the small hours of the morning — *Warfield* was again ready to sail. Steam was ready to pop the safety valves; the crew stood at their stations; and on the bridge, the officers searched the dark streets and the harbor for some sign of life. Nothing stirred.

The pilot failed to appear.

A desperate plan had already taken shape in the minds of the principals on board, to be implemented if the pilot did not come. Harel sent for Grauel — still the cook — and gave him instructions to prepare a meal, and quickly. The French police, on guard on the quay beside *Warfield's* stern lines and gangway, were invited aboard. They were royally wined and dined, and then presented with gifts. An hour or so later, they were ushered ashore, reeling merrily and clutching their packages.

While the banquet was in progress, Bernie Marks in his shorts lowered himself from the guard rail into the black, filthy harbor water and swam to the mole. Moving along the edge of the concrete, he reached the stern line and the bollard which held it. He slipped the bights from the bollard until a single wire held *Warfield*'s stern to the mole.

Bernie was brought up short by the sudden realization that he was being watched close at hand by a French gendarme. Apprehensively, he studied the gendarme for the next move. The Frenchman suddenly shrugged his shoulders and gestured. His meaning was clear: why hadn't Bernie simply asked him to throw off the lines — why swim so far?

As soon as Bernie regained the deck of *Warfield* and the merrymaking guards reeled ashore, an axe was applied to the wire cable. A cut stern wire left hanging on the bollard would certainly exonerate the French guards from any complicity in *Warfield*'s escape. Strand by strand, the wire was cut, blunting the axe in the process. It parted suddenly and dropped under the stern.

Immediately, Ike on the bridge gave the engine order to move *Warfield* ahead. Almost instantly, the propeller kicked over — and just as quickly, stopped. The wire cable, which had just been cut, had wrapped itself around the screw.

A shaken Ike and his lieutenants on the bridge held a quick consultation by voice tube with the engine room. The engines were rocked slowly back and forth — not enough to move the ship — but enough to dislodge the wire. Presently, the engine room jubilantly reported that the engines were running free; the propeller was clear.

But getting to sea in the gloom of the little, twisted harbor was another matter. *Warfield*, a single-screw ship, had first to rotate herself to starboard by 90 degrees with little or no headway, since the quay crowded with small boats lay directly ahead of her, and with little or no sternway, since the mole lay behind her, equally crowded. Then, she had to maneuver within a space of two ship lengths to accomplish a second turn to starboard of more than 120 degrees, with a quay wall directly ahead during the turn, small boats clustered under her port bow and stern, and the shallow water close to the St. Louis Light along her starboard side. Once pivoted and moving ahead, she would find herself headed directly for the outer breakwater, less than three ship lengths from the bow — thereby requiring a sharp swing to port of 120 degrees, again with little headway. With tugs to shove her around the turns, the maneuvers with a ship of *Warfield*'s size would have been difficult enough. Without them, and without even the guidance of a local pilot who knew the harbor in the dark, the task appeared to be virtually impossible.

Ike's experience as a shipmaster was confined to *Warfield;* she was his first command. As a third mate, the opportunity to handle a heavy ship had been virtually nonexistent. Ike had courage, but he confronted an exasperating job that required infinite skill and a "feel" for shiphandling that came with long experience.

Warfield managed to clear her berth at the mole and at once found her bow dangerously close to the quay on the far side. Engines astern, she backed down; then, with small craft bouncing under her counter from her wash, she went ahead. She pivoted painfully, slowly. Under hard right rudder and full power, she surged forward and immediately collided with the concrete seawall on her port bow. She bumped along the concrete on her guard rail. Ike backed down full to get clear. *Warfield* kicked white water under her stern, gathered sternway and plowed stern first into the shallows at the end of Mole St. Louis. She shuddered to a halt in the mud. The engines stopped.

The officers were close to panic. Ike looked ashen. By now, it was broad daylight, and the ship sat in plain view, aground in the outer harbor.

The only hope rested in the power of *Warfield*'s engines. Ike remembered her trial run in Baltimore, and the reserve above her rated horsepower, evidenced in the performance of the massive reciprocating machinery. The engineers began to kick the engines ahead, then to build up the revolutions. At 105 RPM, the engines were designed to develop about 2,600 indicated horsepower. This time, the engineers built up the turns still farther — 110, then 115 RPM. *Warfield* quivered from stem to stern, and the water boiled up in great muddy blotches under her counter. In normal circumstances, such a procedure would have been suicidal to a ship. This was an act of desperation.

Almost imperceptibly, the ship moved. Miraculously, she pivoted — her bow swinging to the right, as her propeller dug into the mud astern. She stirred again — and then again — and inched her bow far around to starboard.

Then abruptly she surged forward. She was free! And her bow pointed to the open Mediterranean. Literally, she had walked from dry land to sea.

As she gathered way to clear the breakwater, out from the harbor came the black pilot boat, its blue flag streaming in the breeze. The pilot pointed ahead from *Warfield*'s starboard side, indicating the channel past the breakwater to the open sea. Here was the young pilot prepared to collect his bribe, now that the risk was past. He was peremptorily waved away by the men on *Warfield*'s bridge.

Ike, Harel and the other officers were jubilant. They had made it. In spite of all obstacles — in spite of Ernest Bevin and all the efforts of the British — they had made it.

Their jubilation was short-lived.

There hove into view the stocky lines of a British man-of-war, the sloop H.M.S. *Mermaid* (1,400 tons). The swiftness of her arrival made it clear that she had been lying in wait outside French territorial waters. She ran down *Warfield*'s side at a distance of several hundred yards and looked the old ship over with care.

Warfield, shortly afterward, stopped dead in the water to permit Bernie Marks and Ben Foreman to put together some wooden planking to hold the cement in place in the hawsepipes, the lesson learned earlier. The resulting planking and cement curiously resembled a coffin, and some wit in the crew marked in the wet cement the words, "Here Lies Butter." The *Mermaid,* closing the bow of *Warfield,* hailed to ask if something was wrong. *Warfield*'s crew gave her a genial wave, and she dropped astern. One of the British officers took careful note of the sign about Butter and reserved what seemed to him to be a very curious bit of information for a later day. *Warfield* picked up speed and headed south, with *Mermaid* trailing behind. A Lancaster plane flew over and observed her closely. There was no question of evasion now. *Warfield* in the open Mediterranean was under surveillance by the Royal Navy.

The refugees, exhausted from nights and days of continuous ordeal, huddled below during the escape from port. Many of them thought that the jolting of the ship and its quivering were normal. Packed together in tiers of bunks in the open spaces from main to gallery decks — or three families together in each of some sixty staterooms — they slept soundly, the first sleep for many days. They slept, curled up on the tubular life preservers that served as pillows at night.

Daylight and heat and the ship's loudspeaker aroused them. Josi Harel on the public address system spoke briefly. First, he announced that the ship, manned by an American crew, was under Haganah command. Second, he stressed that the difficult days at sea on a crowded ship would require the ultimate in self-discipline and organization. And, finally, he stated that the ship had the honor of being escorted by the British Navy.

Breakfast followed — double rations for the first day — of cocoa, cheese, and crackers, with grape juice and eggs for the children.

In the dangerously overcrowded conditions — 2,500 on the main deck, 2,000 on the saloon and gallery decks, the crew on the hurricane deck — organization was vitally important. Masses of people meant weight, a constantly shifting weight, affecting ship stability. Consequently, movement in groups from side to side or end to end was restricted, and the rules were enforced. On board were some members of the Hashomer Hatzair (Young Guardians), a pioneering left-wing socialist group, who had learned discipline the hard way. They were detailed as police to control traffic throughout the ship.

A commissary detail helped in the galley, where the great Navy kettles heated up barley soup for distribution in buckets. In addition, the members of the detail carried fresh fruit and dried rations to various parts of the ship for issue to the passengers. Movement of the refugees to stand in line might have proved dangerous. Pemmican — a dried mixture of beef, suet, raisins, and sugar — was a principal staple. When the sea turned choppy a few days later, it proved disastrous in its cathartic effect.

The hygiene and sanitation detail could not keep up with the consequences. Pemmican, the heat, and the Mediterranean swell combined to start an epidemic of diarrhea of seemingly catastrophic proportions. More than two hundred people were continually standing in line to use the trough-type toilets. When they overflowed, the stench approached the unbearable.

Water was always short and had to be carefully rationed. Most of the immigrants carried their own bottles, and the cans of water carried as stores supplemented the supply. The ship's fresh water tanks could not carry enough for bathing. Only the ship's officers, berthed in hurricane-deck staterooms, could enjoy the luxury of an occasional respite from the sweat and grime that surrounded them.

The passengers were organized troopship style. Everyone, except infants and expectant mothers, had duties to perform.

In addition to police, galley and sanitation duties, there were other assignments: holding classes in Hebrew and in the vocations of a new life ahead, serving in the secretariat, even turning out a handwritten newspaper for shipboard distribution.

President Warfield became a community in itself, a microcosm of the Jewish exodus. There were laborers, artisans, teachers, physicians, scientists, crackpots, and thugs. There were the old and infirm, the adolescents, and the very young. Refugees numbered 4,515; of these, 1,282 were women and 655 were children; 1,017 were adolescents. Many of the children were orphans, assembled by the agents of Haganah from hiding places, Catholic refuges, and crèches all over Europe. Most of the passengers had known the Nazi concentration camps; many were verterans of the wartime underground; nearly all had passed through the DP camps of Landsberg, Fedalfing, Linderfels, Indersdorf or Dornstadt. Here and there could be seen the numbered tattoos of Dachau and Buchenwald. Some still carried the yellow star, no longer as a label but now as an honored symbol.

Among the crew and the passengers were the social and political cross-sections of Zionism — the formerly prosperous and influential, the middle-of-the-road socialists of Mapai and the left-wingers of Hashomer Hatzair, the orthodox conservatives of Mizrahi and the critical rightists of Aliya Hadasha. Diversity in origin, political flavor, language, and appearance characterized the sweltering mass of humanity which turned the decks into a veritable anthill of activity. They were united, however, by a profound sense of common purpose, which converted an exodus into an odyssey to the Promised Land.

Isaac Perlov, a poet on board, spent his time converting the odyssey into heroic verse in Hebrew.

Light moments happened, spontaneously. Passengers sang softly on the top deck under the Mediterranean stars. Or the crew entertained them with sea stories and skits. The Americans suddenly found that the roistering was behind them, and a new note of gentleness replaced their rough behavior. The refugees touched them as they passed with small gestures of gratitude. A measure of compassion swept the crew. John Grauel, with a little gold cross on a chain about his neck, moved about with a quiet word and a smile. To many, he seemed like an omen of good luck.

On Wednesday the sixteenth, a women died in childbirth. The child, a boy, lived. Silence settled over the ship. Josi wanted to take the body on to Palestine for burial, but the physician's diagnosis of septicemia ruled out keeping the body on board.

At sunset, *Warfield* came to a stop. In an evening ceremony, the body, wrapped in a handwoven flag of Zion, was lowered into the sea. Scripture was read from the Hebrew prayer book; a short speech consecrated the crew to the tasks ahead; the death was entered in the log. *Warfield,* her solemn duty completed, picked up speed again and steamed away to the east.

Bill Bernstein, stricken with emotion, told his closest friends, including Bernie Marks, that he was the one who should have died, that his death would have made good propaganda for the cause. To Bernstein, the events of the moment were epic and deeply moving. This was a heroic crusade for him, and history, even in its ironic course, was being written. On the bulkhead of his stateroom was a motto in Gothic letters: "Men who recently fought for freedom are fighting men fighting for freedom." For Bill Bernstein, freedom was worth the last extreme, and *Warfield,* gathering way in the solemnity of evening, was its symbol.

Within twelve hours of leaving Sète, Barak was able to establish radio communications with the secret radio station of Haganah hidden in the villa outside Milan. Shortly afterwards, he established the all-important link with Mossad le Aliyah Beth headquarters in Tel Aviv and with the illegal broadcasting unit, Kol Israel — the Voice of Israel.

On the twelfth, *Warfield* reported her position: time 1315, 38° 29′ North, 17° 41′ East, speed 11.5 knots, course 130, sea calm. Haganah headquarters asked for information on the number of passengers and "workers"; and the number of lifeboats. Amnon (Harel) reported on the fourteenth: exact number of passengers 4,515, "workers" 36; four boats for 37 people each; two big "barges"; forty-three small "barges" holding 25 people each; ten rubber boats for 10 people each — all in good condition. He declined to identify the "workers" for fear of compromise.

The British escort shadowing *Warfield* grew in size. *Mermaid* cruised along in *Warfield*'s wake. Then other ships appeared from Malta and Haifa, relieving each other in turn. The minesweepers *Providence* (Lieutenant W. G. Messinger) and *Rowena* (Lieutenant-Commander D. A. Dunbar-Nasmith, D.S.C.) appeared. Shadowing turned into close surveillance.

On the fifteenth, H.M.S. *Ajax*, accompanied by the destroyer *Childers*, came over the horizon and rapidly closed on *Warfield*. The cruiser's 550-foot length, sleek in her greenish-gray paint, impressive from her gun mounts to the ranks of white-clad sailors lining her upper decks, brought the refugees to the decks in awed attention. The historic power of the Royal Navy was on display. An officer on the bridge turned an electric amplifier toward *Warfield* and spoke rapidly in German.

Ike picked up a megaphone and shouted back, "You'll have to speak in English. We're not the *Graf Spee!*"

Shortly after noon on the sixteenth, three destroyers joined the interception force. Early the next morning, a frigate appeared. The ships took station on *Warfield* like a task force maneuvering on a guide ship.

Amnon reported the presence of the large British task force to Haganah headquarters. There could be no doubt. The battle had been joined. The prestige and power of Britain stood against them. At sea, the might of the Royal

Navy — a cruiser, four destroyers, a frigate, and two minesweepers in task force — surrounded an ancient steamer bearing on its teeming decks a human message in despair and hope.

Amnon radioed headquarters: "Instruct as to our Hebrew name. Immigrants suggest '*Mordecai Anilevitz*' or '*Roosevelt.*' Escorts suggest '*Ha'meri Ha'ivri* [Jewish Protest].' "

The answer was succinct and dramatic: "Your name has been decided to read in Hebrew '*Yetziat Eiropah Tashaz* [*Exodus 1947*].' "

FIFTEEN

AT NOON ON JULY 16, *President Warfield* was some 125 miles south of Crete on course 125, cruising at a speed of 10.2 knots. The sea was choppy, and the ship was rolling uncomfortably.

The distress of the passengers at the motion of the ship had tempted Ike to reduce speed several days before. Siegel, a seaman in the crew, noticed *Warfield*'s old complaint and told John Grauel that the superstructure was shifting again. Grauel informed Ike, who in an understandably bad temper, snapped, "Everybody's telling me how to run my ship." But he came down from the bridge to see for himself and shortly afterwards reduced *Warfield*'s speed by several knots. Still, she swayed uncertainly back and forth, with a motion exaggerated by the weight of people on her upper decks. If the weather freshened, she would have to slow even more.

About one o'clock, the destroyers *Chequers, Chieftain* and *Charity* joined the formation at high speed. *Chequers* flew the pennant of the Captain First Destroyer Flotilla, commander of the task force. A flutter of signal flags appeared at the halyards on *Chequers* and were repeated throughout the formation. One by one, the destroyers swung into column formation astern of *Warfield,* while *Ajax* remained on the flank.

The destroyer column moved past *Warfield*. From the bridge of each destroyer, officers studied the old ship with infinite care — her wheelhouse, upper decks, construction, and measurements. The rail of each warship was manned by natty, white-uniformed sailors spaced at exact intervals. It was a display of naval precision — of men-of-war slicing through the seas. Grudgingly, the officers of *Warfield* admitted their admiration.

The last ship delivered a warning by megaphone: "You are suspected of going to Palestine with illegal immigrants. It is forbidden. If you enter Palestinian waters, we will have to board and arrest you. Please do not resist. We have superior forces here and in Palestine. If it becomes necessary, we will use force to board you, but you will have medical attention."

Warfield signaled back, "Thank you."

The next day saw the performance repeated. *Cardigan Bay*, a frigate which had joined at eight in the morning, completed the task force. As the destroyers and frigate "passed in review," with the officers studying their quarry and the sailors manning the rail, Ike, Josi, Marks, Bernstein, Grauel and some others lined up on *Warfield*'s bridge and rendered the stiff-armed salute of the Royal Navy. *Warfield*'s public address system blared forth with Elgar's "Pomp and Circumstance." The sarcasm was not lost on the British commander.

In the Mossad headquarters in Tel Aviv, the high command of Aliyah Beth planned for the crisis that by now seemed inevitable. Their calculations were based on a number of factors. One was the known speed of *Warfield*, which if pushed to the limit, might make a quick dash at seventeen knots or better from just outside Palestinian territorial waters to the beaches. Second was the shallow draft of the ship, which would permit her to navigate close inshore where the British destroyers could not go. Also, the ship because of this draft could beach herself near enough the breakers, so that rescue teams could reach the refugees quickly. Finally, the planners reckoned on the reluctance of the British to attack the ship on the high seas or to open fire on a ship heavily laden with defenseless women and children.

Instructions, based on these calculations, were radioed to *Warfield* on Wednesday, the sixteenth. The ship was to beach herself at Tel Aviv between six and seven o'clock in the evening of Thursday, July 17, at a point south of a red brick building on the beach which had once been Haganah headquarters. *Warfield* was to make her approach from the south, staying six miles offshore as she moved north toward the landing site. Thus, she would be outside the three-mile limit, yet close enough to make a dash for it and unload within an hour on the beaches. All boats and life rafts were to be used to get passengers ashore, as soon as the ship grounded. Passengers who could swim were to jump and start for the beach on their own. Life belts were to be distributed, and ropes were to be stretched quickly from ship to shore to aid debarkation.

In the event the British stopped the ship on the high seas, unarmed opposition was to be used. If the British naval forces demanded that the *Warfield* go to Haifa, the officers of the *Warfield* were to comply. Communications were to be continued until the ship was overpowered, and codes were to be hidden if a safe place could be found on board.

If the British escorted the ship into Haifa, the Aliyah Beth agents on board — so sorely wanted by British intelligence — were to be hidden about the ship with enough food and water to hold them until they could be rescued. They were to stay in hiding until Haganah people in the guise of laborers came aboard to clean the ship after debarkation of the immigrants had been completed. When the Haganah "laborers" sang in Hebrew as a signal, the agents were to come out of hiding and go through the British guards at Haifa as laborers themselves. One of the agent "escorts" should continue with the immigrants to Cyprus.

Although not relayed to *Warfield,* the Aliyah Beth leadership was preparing to mount a major action at the landing site. Plans called for the assembly of some thirty thousand armed men at the beachhead to meet the refugees struggling in the surf. Haganah itself was prepared to alert a hundred thousand men by word of mouth in less than half an hour; if necessary, this force would storm the area and create diversionary incidents, in addition, all over Palestine.

The leadership tensed for a major crisis. There were few who did not realize that if armed force of this magnitude were employed the action could precipitate a state of virtual civil war in Palestine from which there could be no retreat. In the precarious balance, it could bring on a worldwide crisis at once — and it could destroy the entire Zionist effort in one stroke. Here was a situation of unprecedented danger — for Zionists, for Britain, for the Middle East, for the world.

On board *Warfield,* the leadership tensed for the crisis, too. Their calculations coincided with those of the Mossad high command, except for several particulars. One was a question concerning British reluctance to open fire, if all other measures of stopping *Warfield* failed. The second was a doubt concerning British unwillingness to pursue *Warfield* into shallow water. The third was a question whether *Warfield* in the increasingly choppy sea could make the beachhead rendezvous on time.

Messages went back and forth on the sixteenth between *Warfield* and Mossad headquarters with changes and refinements in plan. The worsening weather caused the ship to slow down. The hour of beaching was altered to midnight on Thursday, then changed again to 11:00 P.M. on Friday, the eighteenth. *Warfield* proposed a new beaching site where the beach gradient would allow the ship to get closer to shore — a position opposite the beginning of Nardan Street to the north of Tel Aviv. Mossad headquarters had a change of heart about the feasibility of a frontal landing on the beaches of Tel Aviv and changed the landing site to a point just south of Bat-Yam, several miles below Tel Aviv. Final plans were confirmed for a landing at that site at 2300 hours (11:00 P.M.) local time on Friday. Mossad leaders acknowledged to *Warfield* that the plans involved many dangers.

At three in the afternoon of the sixteenth, *Warfield* reported her position at 32° 37′ North, 27° 13′ East, on course 125, speed 10.2 knots. She was headed straight for the Egyptian coast at Rashid, the Rosetta Mouth, distance approximately 160 miles.

Amnon and Ike had several purposes in running south toward the Egyptian coast. One was to get in position to approach the landing site at Bat-Yam from the south. The second was to waste time, in order to arrive at the beachhead at the appointed time. The third was to deceive the British into believing that the landing site was at Rafah, right beside the Egyptian-Palestinian border. The fourth was to give maximum publicity to *Warfield*'s plight by transiting the shipping approaches to the busy port of Alexandria. All afternoon, the ships of the world came over the horizon and passed the strange task force — the cruiser *Ajax* and six destroyer-type men-of-war flying the white ensign of the Royal Navy, clustered about an old, dilapidated steamer black with humanity flying the flag of Honduras. *Warfield* exchanged calls by blinker with each freighter and passenger ship that would answer her.

There was a fifth reason for running toward the Egyptian coast. It was to test the willingness of the British to risk their ships in shallow water. Just beyond the Rosetta Mouth the water shoaled to form the Damietta Banks with depths of three fathoms or less. In the small hours of the morning, *Warfield* crossed the three-fathom line and inched her keel toward the sandy bottom. Her naval escort stopped short and dropped astern — then spread out in a long screen to seaward. Wary skippers on the destroyers were not ready to jeopardize their careers by taking their ships into dangerous waters, even when they had the technical right to close in on *Warfield* and board her within territorial waters.

Warfield turned about and headed away from the dangerous coast. In the darkness, the running lights of her escort quickly reappeared, and the weird convoy was underway as before.

All through that day and the next, preparations speeded on *Warfield* for the impending engagement. Boats, life rafts, life preservers, and manila lines were readied for the landing operation, should *Warfield* succeed in eluding her pursuers at the crucial moment.

On Thursday afternoon, the seventeenth, there was a meeting of the principal members of the crew in the wardroom on the hurricane deck. Two urgent problems had to be met. One was the defense of the ship if the British attempted to board. The other concerned the security arrangements for the underground Haganah agents on board, if the British captured the ship and took it to Haifa. These were not matters of planning, because the plans had existed for some time; these were sealed orders which were now being opened for execution. Amnon, as the ranking Haganah officer on board, made the decisions.

During the course of the grim discussion, a kind of macabre humor prevailed.

"Someone is sure to get killed," someone quipped. "Who's it to be?"

"Maybe Ritzer," another suggested. "He was in the Marines."

"How about John Grauel? He's a Gentile."

"No," said Bill Bernstein quietly. "It'll probably be me." The conversation suddenly died.

The defenses of the ship were readied for the expected boarding by the British. No matter how they discussed the alternatives, the crew could perceive nothing left to the British but an attempt to stop the ship before it approached the coast of Palestine. If the British found it unpalatable to open fire, their only remaining choice was to board and seize control.

Accordingly, the crew went to work in earnest to rig the ship against boarding. Wire mesh was spread around the promenade deck and across exterior openings through which the British might jump. There were some seamen in the crew like Bernie Marks who protested that the wire mesh not only prevented the British from gaining a foothold but also trapped forty-five hundred people below decks — defenseless women and children who could find themselves with no way of escape if *Warfield* caught fire, capsized or sank. But the precautionary voice was stilled in the urgency of preparation for battle. The wire was rigged at great labor and no little risk on the part of the crew.

Oil pipes were run from the engine room to jet fuel oil upon the decks at the moment of boarding and make the gaining of a foothold on the slippery canvas difficult. Similarly, steam lines were rigged around the side to play live steam over the areas where boarding might be attempted. Finally, open deck areas up forward were planked up, and sandbags were piled inside the wheelhouse to stop any bullets or flying objects from entering. The passengers themselves had been searched for firearms, and *Warfield* — crew and human cargo alike — lacked the means of firing a single shot. Nevertheless, she was ready for the immediate contingency.

Ike moved about the ship with a fierce gleam in his eye, directing the preparations as though he were getting ready to fight the ship like a man-of-war.

To the extent possible, *Warfield* was ready. Her bridge would be protected from small-arms fire. Wire mesh and decks rendered slippery with oil would make boarding difficult, if not impossible. Live steam would create a quick diversion. If the attempt to board did not take place until the ship was in Palestinian territorial waters, then such a diversion might be just enough to let *Warfield* elude her pursuers in the approach to shallow water and effect the beaching. The chance of success was slim, but it was worth the try.

Four hiding places for the special Haganah agents — wanted by the British — were prepared. In this task, the skill and ingenuity of Nat Nadler showed itself. One hiding place was under the wheelhouse floor; the wheelhouse itself was two feet higher than the rest of the housing on the hurricane deck to provide visibility fore and aft; in the chartroom, just aft of the wheelhouse was a false bookcase and, behind it, a small door opening to the space under the deck of the wheelhouse. Unfortunately, on test, it proved to be too hot and untenable. Other hiding places were rigged about the ship — one aft in the tool room on the main deck — others behind the paneling on the saloon deck, or in the ballast at the bottom of the ship. The spaces were equipped with water, dried food, and toilet paper, all of which unfortunately disappeared among the refugees who, prying into everything, did not comprehend the significance of their find.

Forty-one people were to be hidden in these spaces. Amnon, Ike, Barak, and Micha obviously had to be included; they had prices on their heads. Others, too American in appearance and lacking papers, were added. Lots were drawn among the crew for the remaining spaces. Miri and Sima, less well known to the British, were assigned to mingle with the refugees and share their fate, whatever it might be. John Grauel, who had much to do with these preparations and arrangements, had the safeguard of his official British visa and his status as a correspondent for the *Churchman*.

Final plans were made for the safeguarding of the ship's documents. Codebooks, orders, and logbooks, sketchy as they were, were to be smuggled, at the last possible moment, down deep in the hull of the ship and secreted in the gravel ballast.

Preparations for every contingency seemed complete. Whether they would work, when the time came, remained to be seen.

To the British the situation was painful. In the operations plot in the Admiralty the dilemma of the task force escorting *Warfield* in the eastern Mediterranean was all too clear. Every course of action open to it carried unacceptable implications. Firing on the ship to stop her on the high seas would almost certainly result in heavy loss of life. She was precariously loaded, and any fall of shot in the hull would either capsize her or sink her; the casualties would be staggering. The Royal Navy was not prepared to accept the onus of such a slaughter. For that matter, the Foreign Office and even the Foreign Secretary had little relish for it. The legality of stopping a ship of another flag on the high seas in peacetime was open to debate, although international law had never denied the right of a state in self-defense to use its public vessels to seize a private ship flying the flag of another state if that ship was being used by insurgents or rebels as a means of attack upon the state. The question turned on the nature of the immigrants or the crew as insurgents. Then, too, the right to search a ship for validation of its registry was recognized in international law. The question turned on the grounds for suspecting the validity of the registry. On humanitarian and legal grounds, any attempt to stop the ship on the high seas seemed distasteful in Whitehall.

On the other hand, could the ship be allowed to enter territorial waters before apprehension? With her speed, draft, and maneuverability, she could probably beach herself and begin unloading. With so many refugees involved, the Jewish organization would do no less than the maximum to organize its people on the beach in such numbers and possibly armed strength that a major battle would follow. The danger of an explosion that would tear Palestine apart was all too real. The British were less militarily and economically prepared for a complete upheaval in the Middle East than they were for damage to their international prestige which might follow any action on the high seas. Overwhelmingly in the balance was the status of negotiations, being conducted by the United Nations Special Committee of Inquiry on Palestine (UNSCOP), which could take Britain forever off the painful hook of its Mandate.

With its position becoming more and more untenable in Palestine and its petulance increasing at the intransigence and truculence of Arab and Jew alike, Britain was nearing the point of painful decision in a mood of exasperation, frustration and irrationality. For the British, the sands of time were running out.

The instructions from the Admiralty to the task force commander in *Chequers* were precise: Stop *Warfield* at all costs.

There seemed to be few alternatives for Captain R. D. Watson, O.B.E., Captain First Destroyer Flotilla, who was entrusted with the operation. *Warfield* had to be brought to a halt before she could make her dash for the beaches. As his staff estimated it, *Warfield*'s intention was to beach near the Palestinian-Egyptian border. Estimated time of arrival was dawn on Friday morning. By that time, *Warfield* had to be stopped, by boarding and direct capture, if necessary.

The forces available to Captain Watson were considerable. In addition to his own ship, *Chequers*, he had the destroyers *Chieftain* (Commander D. H. R. Bromley, D.S.C.), *Charity* (Lieutenant A. H. L. Harvey, D.S.C.) and *Childers* (Lieutenant-Commander M. C. Morris), the frigate *Cardigan Bay* (Captain G. K. Collette), the minesweepers *Providence* (Lieutenant W. G. Messinger) and *Rowena* (Lieutenant-Commander D. A. Dunbar-Nasmith, D.S.C.), and the light 6-inch cruiser *Ajax* (Captain S. B. DeCourcy-Ireland) with a small unit of Royal Marines embarked.

Captain Watson's calculation of the problem confronting him and his selection of possible courses of action were based on three considerations: the dictates of humanity where unarmed refugees, particularly women and children, were concerned; the likelihood of achieving initial surprise in any forthcoming interception; and the overriding requirement to bring *Warfield* to a halt within a safe distance.

The characteristics of *Warfield* — her size, her high superstructure with few openings, and many areas both below decks and topside where defenses could be effective — entered into his calculations. If *Warfield* had to be boarded, the boarding parties undoubtedly would be facing something new — a difficult scramble up the sides of a high superstructure and resistance of a magnitude not heretofore encountered.

One other consideration entered the calculation. To Captain Watson and his staff on *Chequers*, the run of *Warfield* into the shoals off Damietta smacked of poor navigation. Perhaps, if the Jewish navigators had no better idea of their position at that time, they might have no proof of their later position — inside or outside of territorial waters. The place to strike, therefore, would be at a point where legal equivocation might be possible, yet the chances of *Warfield*'s escape would be impossible.

Acting upon what he knew of *Warfield* from studying her while alongside and earlier reconnaissance reports, and making his decision from the necessities of stopping the ship, gaining surprise, and saving life, Captain Watson selected his course of action.

During the morning of the seventeenth, the destroyers of the task force moved to positions where their preparations for the forthcoming action were concealed from *President Warfield*. *Cardigan Bay* took station two miles ahead of the formation. *Chequers* maneuvered alongside *Ajax* and the two captains discussed the possible employment of the cruiser and her marine contingent. Just before noon, *Ajax*, *Chieftain*, and *Childers* proceeded ahead, and marine and naval personnel were transferred from *Ajax* by boat to each of the destroyers. About five o'clock, the destroyers and *Cardigan Bay* took station ahead and *Chequers* transferred orders to each of them by heaving line. Preparations by the British were now complete. Orders awaited execution. At eight o'clock, the ships assumed a night cruising disposition and blacked out shortly afterward. Only an occasional flicker of phosphorescence revealed their presence in the darkness.

Beginning at nine o'clock and continuing every hour thereafter, one of the destroyers moved near *Warfield* and surveyed her decks with care. On one visit, *Chequers* took note of the fact that the upper decks seemed crowded with masses of refugees, while the lower decks seemed clear. Captain Watson weighed the effect of this intelligence upon the prospects for achieving surprise.

On board *Warfield,* the day had been strenuous. The crew had struggled throughout the long, hot day to complete the defensive preparations. Many of them had gone for several days and nights without sleep. Exhausted, they turned to their bunks for rest. The ship slept — refugees stacked high on their tiers of bunks below, many children and young people lying about the open decks for air.

Midnight came. Bill Bernstein relieved the watch in the wheelhouse. William Millman, the tall ex-sailor from Boston, took the wheel. The ship was rolling slowly in the swell. Below decks, the engines throbbed patiently. A taffrail log whined at the stern, recording the ship's mileage for the navigator. It was a dark night — damp with a slight mist. The decks and railings reeked with water. All about, there was an eerie quietness.

Two hours passed. Bernstein made his taffrail log entries. Ike stepped from his cabin to the wheelhouse. *Warfield* was now twenty-three miles off the coast, and the captain's place was on the bridge when the ship was approaching land. In another hour and a half, *Warfield* would be changing course to the north as she skirted territorial waters and headed for the landing site. Ike and Bernstein were uneasy. The critical time was drawing near. The clock struck five bells (2:30 A.M.).

Suddenly, the whole sky seemed to light up in a brilliant, dazzling blue.

From every side, the searchlights of the destroyers and *Ajax* caught *Warfield* and illuminated her starkly from end to end.

Ike and Bernstein stood stunned. Then Bernstein leaped for the whistle. *Warfield*'s great wail sounded like the shriek of an animal caught by beasts of prey.

The battle was on.

SIXTEEN

THE SHIP'S WHISTLE SCREAMED IN LONG, DRAWN-OUT BLASTS.

Ike stood ashen-faced at the wheelhouse door staring out into the blinding glare of the searchlights. Bernstein hung on the whistle.

On the upper decks, the youngsters roused themselves and ran up to the top of the hurricane deck housing to see the destroyers on both sides. People shouted and ran about. There was sudden panic and confusion. Below decks, the refugees awakened and stirred uneasily at the noise, confused by what was happening and waiting for orders.

The crew came running. Some went down to the refugees to tell them to prepare for trouble. Others broke through the crowds and reached the upper decks.

A destroyer closed in on *Warfield* and came up opposite her bridge. A loudspeaker announced that *Warfield* was now in the territorial waters of Palestine, that she must stop her engines, and prepare to be towed into Haifa.

A livid Ike screamed back at the destroyer, "You're a —— —— liar!" and preceded the noun with a string of abuse that only a strong seaman could understand. He turned back to the wheelhouse and gave orders to Millman at the wheel to bring the ship about and reverse course. *Warfield* started to turn on her heel to head westward.

The searchlights held her in their blinding brightness. Everyone on the destroyers and on the upper decks of *Warfield* now witnessed for the first time the Mogen David, the white and blue flag of Israel, flying from the staffs fore and aft.

The big wooden boards, which port and starboard abaft the bridge wings had carried the name *President Warfield* in gold had been flipped over, and on the reverse side appeared a new name: *Haganah Ship — Exodus 1947*.

John Grauel, standing on the wing of the bridge, felt a surge of excitement and pride. Cy Weinstein was standing behind Grauel. As Weinstein remembered the moment, Grauel with his blond hair nearly to his shoulders looked like a stallion smelling a forest fire.

Before *Exodus* completed her turn, there was a sharp sound, like shots. The British had strings of firecrackers which they lit off to simulate gunfire. But Weinstein, nevertheless, hit the deck for protection. Up on the top of the hurricane-deck housing, some youngsters were rigging a painted canvas. On the canvas was a drawing of a woman holding a baby and the inscription: "England, this is your enemy."

On the voice radio a message was being sent from *Exodus* to the task force commander. It stated that there were 4,500 men, women and children on board *Exodus* who would never recognize a law forbidding Jews from entering their country and that they would never go voluntarily to a concentration camp, even a British one. It added that any attempt to stop the ship would be a violation of international law and act of piracy for which the British would have to answer before the United Nations.

Suddenly there was a sharp lurch — then shortly afterwards a second one. A sound of breaking timbers came from below. The destroyers *Chieftain* to starboard and *Childers* to port had rammed themselves alongside *Exodus* amidships.

Drawbridges were lowered from the signal bridges of the

destroyers to the upper decks of *Exodus*. They fitted with remarkable precision, reflecting the careful observation and labor of the previous day. Sailors and marines under command of Lieutenant K. P. Challow of *Childers* and Lieutenant R. J. G. MacPherson of *Chieftain* came over the precarious boarding platforms to *Exodus*.

The boarding party raced for the bridge and wheelhouse. Dressed in combat uniforms, with helmets and heavy leather protector belts, they carried steel-tipped truncheons. Some carried side arms. Except for officers, whose helmets displayed a stripe, it was almost impossible to distinguish between sailors and khaki-clad marines. Fistfights broke out when the boarding party met some of the crew and passengers, and a melee on the hurricane deck quickly developed. Gunfire — simulated, from firecrackers, and real, from machine guns — came from the destroyers.

The suddenness of the boarding caught the crew unprepared. The steam hoses and oil lines had snapped under the impact of the ramming destroyers, and not enough of the crew were on the upper decks to oppose the boarding party. Quickly, the British gained the forward part of the bridge and broke into the wheelhouse. There was a sharp struggle. The men on watch, including Bernstein and Millman, were forced out.

Bill Bernstein, ejected from the wheelhouse, grabbed a fire extinguisher to squirt as a weapon and charged back in. A marine clubbed him with his truncheon on the side of the head.

Some crew members about to enter the wheelhouse grabbed Bernstein as he fell and dragged him through the chartroom into the captain's cabin beyond. As they placed him on the captain's bed, the door behind them shut and locked. They made their exit through the louvered window, which dropped behind them and also locked. Bill Bernstein was locked inside — unconscious and mortally injured. He was to stay there alone for nearly three hours, unattended.

Big Bill Millman, also ejected from the wheelhouse, ran back up the starboard side of the hurricane deck and threw open the wheelhouse door. He reached in, grabbed a British sailor by the seat of the pants and the belt, and tried to drag him out on deck. Another British sailor aimed his pistol at point-blank range and shot Millman in the jaw. He fell back across the bridge, blood spurting from his face. Eli Kalm took him aft to the first aid station.

Murray Aronoff ran up to the bridge waving a pistol he had just captured from a British sailor and fired it into the wheelhouse. No one was hit. He had raced about, organizing the force he had earlier recruited among the Moroccan refugees, which had become known among the crew as Murray's Moroccans (some called it Murray's Marauders). They were at the center of the developing fray. Murray himself was shortly afterward wounded in the head.

Ike, with the aid of some crew members who got to the bridge, tried to force his way back into the wheelhouse. The British inside kept opening the door and throwing out containers of tear gas. Ike tried throwing them back. Someone seized an axe and chopped through the roof of the wheelhouse. Ike and the others reached in the life rafts close by and found the emergency smoke markers. These they lobbed inside the wheelhouse. The area reeked with the fumes. At the sight of the man with the axe, the British directed small arms fire from the destroyer alongside.

Boarding operations were not going very well for the British. From the very start, the maneuverability of *Exodus* and radical course and speed changes ordered by Ike and Bill Bernstein had raised havoc. When *Childers* and *Chieftain* initially closed at the sides of *Exodus*, Ike rang down to stop. The two destroyers overshot. By the time they could turn around and make a second approach, the advantage of surprise and synchronization of boarding had been lost. Except for a brief period when the British had actual control of the steering, the movements of *Exodus* were so radical and so skillfully timed that destroyers found it extremely difficult to maneuver alongside and, once there, to hang on for long.

The destroyers repeatedly attempted alongside operations. In the face of fierce opposition from *Exodus,* only a few sailors and marines succeeded in boarding. In a thirty-minute period from 3:00 to 3:30 A.M., *Childers* succeeded in getting across three officers and twenty men. Her skipper, Lieutenant-Commander Morris, then reported to Captain Watson in *Chequers* that her boarding platform had carried away and that her plating had been damaged. The destroyer *Charity* relieved her on the port side of *Exodus. Charity* got over only one officer and four men before she reported that she had suffered severe damage and was unfit for continued boarding operations. On the starboard side of *Exodus, Chieftain* succeeded in putting over only three officers and six men in over an hour of attempted boardings. Damaged, she was relieved by *Chequers,* who got over three men. In nearly two hours of operations, the British succeeded in putting on *Exodus* a total of forty men. But all four destroyers suffered damage.

The early boarding parties ran into difficulties. One group was besieged in the wheelhouse, and some of the boarders elsewhere on *Exodus* found themselves in trouble. Some of the crew, together with a dozen refugees, had cornered three marines on the hurricane deck, laid open the cheek of one of them with a swift blow and frightened the other two into submission. John Grauel, coming from the starboard side to check his cabin for the personal belongings entrusted to him by the crew, stumbled on the party of British and their captors.

"Whatta ya know! We've captured some British. What'll we do with them?" the boys asked enthusiastically. The British marines, youngsters themselves, looked terrified.

"Put them in my cabin," answered Grauel. And he threw a few shirts at the injured marine. "Here, laddie, tear these up and use them for bandages."

Grauel spotted a responsible youngster he had seen around the ship, and with another refugee, placed him in charge. "You stand by the door; nobody is to come in and nobody is to get out," Grauel ordered in Yiddish. Three uniformed members of the British armed forces remained for several hours guarded by two unarmed youngsters fresh from the DP camps of Europe.

The prisoners made good use of their confinement. Under Grauel's bunk was a case of cognac entrusted by Josi to Grauel for delivery to Dr. Chaim Weizmann in Palestine. Josi in the past had been Weizmann's special Haganah guard and his good friend. Somehow the marines located the cognac. When they were released some hours later, they were delightfully merry. They had unearthed enough about Grauel in poring through his possessions to call him padre, and they were loud in their praise of the ship's hospitality.

The failure of the first boarding party led the British to renewed efforts to stop *Exodus* and to gain control of the ship. The destroyers tried to remain against her side. The evasive maneuvering of *Exodus* led to repeated rammings, tearing out the wooden side of the saloon deck for over two hundred feet on the port side. She looked like a shattered box. *Exodus* shook with the impact of each collision. The steel plate, welded over the guard rail in Norfolk after the storm, saved her. The plating held under the impact, and the damage to the sides of the destroyers was extensive. Without the steel guard rail, the hull plates of *Exodus* might have started, resulting in extensive flooding, even sinking. As it was, the rivet holes opened once again, some plates on the port side buckled, and water began to collect in the bilges. The pumps managed to keep pace with the water.

As dawn approached, the waves of successive boardings had put forty British on the decks of *Exodus*. Heavy fighting continued to erupt all over the decks. The crew and refugees fought with whatever they could find to throw — cans of corned beef, smoke canisters from the life rafts, fire extinguishers, fruit, and bare fists. They tore out the railing on the grand staircase in the main saloon and used the balusters for clubs. At one point the British rushed aft and cut away several lifeboats from their davits, for fear that the refugees would drop them on the decks of the destroyers. Unwittingly, they inspired the crew of *Exodus*, who proceeded to release the pelican hooks on the huge life rafts, stored upright on frames at the ship's rail, just as the destroyers came alongside. A life raft crashing down on a destroyer's bridge, taking everything in its path, could cause massive damage.

Some of the boarders swung from destroyers to *Exodus* on lines thrown over the gap between the ships or on the remnants of the boarding platforms. Three who had vaulted across in this fashion were thrown summarily in the water as they reached the deck of *Exodus*. They narrowly escaped death between the grinding hulls, but emerged unscathed astern to be picked up by other destroyers. The emergency lights on their life jackets saved them. Some months later, one of the marines met one of the men who had thrown him overboard; there was mutual recognition, but the marine fortunately could not recall where it was they had previously met.

The battle lasted for over two hours. British sailors and marines surged over the upper decks — groups of young refugees and crewmen met them in hand-to-hand fighting. Josi was everywhere in the thick of it. Destroyers would slip alongside in the semidarkness, and showers of tear gas would envelop the ship. The British would put on their masks; the Jews would fight for their breath.

Grauel was caught alone in a heavy discharge of tear gas and only with great difficulty made his way off the open deck into the center passage of the officers' quarters. Choking and gasping for breath, he was astounded to see dozens of small children coming up the ladder led by a young girl. The youngsters were in distress from the gas, and Grauel knew immediately that he had to find water to wash out their eyes. He sought the small galley near the wardroom. The door seemed to jam. He pushed his way through and found the little room packed with Moroccan refugees, hiding from the battle.

Grauel's overwrought temper exploded. He grabbed them one by one and literally kicked them out on deck. "Go fight!" he yelled.

The water pipe was broken. But Grauel saw the coffee urn on the small galley stove. With cotton and coffee, he swabbed out the eyes of the children, until their pain subsided.

Early in the battle, with the wheelhouse in British hands, Ike and Cyril Weinstein had made their way through the frightened refugees below decks to the steering engine over the rudder post aft on the main deck. Cyril quickly uncoupled the drum with the cable leading to the wheelhouse. The steam steering engine could now be operated by hand from the after steering position on the main deck, and the wheel on the bridge was useless. Steering from back aft above the rudder post itself, however, required some endurance; Cyril Weinstein with his powerful frame was able to provide it. On the bridge, the British suddenly found that they had lost the means of steering the ship.

Cy Weinstein began to maneuver with skill and daring. The British, unable to control *Exodus* and unable to seize it completely with the men they had been able to put aboard, were left with the choice of opening fire — and such action against women and children was not an acceptable alternative — or of repeatedly attempting to board. The continuing approaches of the destroyers alongside, therefore, were designed to reinforce the small contingent already on the top decks of *Exodus*. But each time a British ship approached the side of *Exodus,* Cy threw over the rudder and crossed the bow of the oncoming ship. Each time, the sharp prow rammed into the steel guard rail of the old boat. And each time, it was the guard rail that saved her. The steel plating added to it in Norfolk stood firm again and again against successive collisions. But each British ship, thrown off by the maneuver, raked down the side of *Exodus*, breaking in the wooden superstructure with sides of steel.

For the British, each attempt to get alongside was a maddening and dangerous experience. For Cy and Ike, maneuvering was a last desperate gamble. The beaches were far away.

Sometime about daybreak the British used small-arms fire on deck. There were sharp bursts. Isolated shots rang out here and there. Hirsh Yakubovich, a fifteen-year-old orphan from the DP camp at Indersdorf, died of gunshot wounds when, peering through the slats of a life raft, he startled a jumpy marine into opening fire. Mordecai Baumstein of the camp at Bad Reichenall was shot in the stomach during the fighting and died an hour later.

Bill Bernstein still lay mortally wounded and alone in the captain's cabin.

Grauel was swabbing out the last of the children's eyes with coffee when the machine-gun bursts rang out. Glass in the ports shattered. He shouted, "Hit the deck!" in English. His own demonstration was enough, and all the youngsters crouched beside him. Then he crawled through the door to investigate.

In the passageway outside the wardroom were a half-dozen British sailors and marines standing with pistols leveled. Grauel groped to his feet, displayed his armband with the American flag on it and announced that he was an American correspondent. The officer in charge immediately asked Grauel how the fighting could be brought to a halt.

Suddenly, the passageway door flew open. There stood Aronoff in a state of hysterical fury. He had an axe in his hand.

"You're killing women and children!" he screamed at the British. Forgetting Grauel, the British leveled their pistols at

Aronoff. Just then, Eli Kalm, another crew member, started up the ladder from the deck below, calling to Aronoff to quiet down. The British immediately turned their weapons in his direction. Grauel shouted, "Eli, stay where you are!"

The British officer, Lieutenant R. J. G. MacPherson, in charge of all boarding parties, kept his head. Fortunately, the British had the foresight to send responsible men in charge — like Lieutenant K. P. Challow and Lieutenant A. Stein from *Childers*, Lieutenant G. Pearse from *Charity* and Lieutenant MacPherson from *Chieftain*. As a result, bloodshed was far less than it might have been, and the passengers themselves were generally not molested.

MacPherson turned to Grauel. "How can we halt the fighting? Why don't you stop your action against us, and we will stop against you."

Grauel's answer, "I'll see what I can do," was more of a rejoinder to save Aronoff than an offer to mediate.

Grauel moved quickly to a window that looked forward on the hurricane deck to the wheelhouse. Here the fighting had returned and had reached its height. The British were flailing about with clubs; the crewmen were throwing everything they could find — nuts, bolts, canned goods, potatoes, stair railings, gravel ballast, anything portable. With missiles sailing through the air in all directions, Grauel found it dangerous to stick his head out. He recognized Perlson.

"Micha! Stop! Don't throw anything!" he shouted. Then he emerged cautiously through the deckhouse door to the open deck. Josi appeared suddenly, then Bernie Marks, and finally Ike. There was a rapid conversation concerning surrender.

The idea that the ship would have to be surrendered, unpalatable as it was, had been accepted by Marks some time beforehand after an inspection of the superstructure. During most of the battle, he had been on the hurricane deck. But when it seemed to him that the British attempts at boarding were not only falling short of getting men on the deck of

Exodus but, more importantly, were taking a heavy toll in damage to the old ship's sides, he had picked his way aft and down to the cabin areas below. The sight that had confronted him was appalling. The wooden sides at the promenade-deck level were splintered open; timbers and bulkheading were hanging broken and shredded. Bernie decided then and there that the lives of several thousand defenseless people could not be jeopardized any further.

He had tried to get back to the hurricane deck through the main cabin staircase, but the British held the spaces at the top. Then he had threaded his way through the mass of refugees to the after deck and had run into Josi. Bernie stated flatly that the ship would have to be surrendered. Josi was tight-lipped, tense. Together, they had sought out Ike and had held a hasty conference.

Ike was flushed with the fever of battle. He refused at first to consider surrender, arguing that the ship could be fought or beached or, failing in its mission, sailed back to France or Italy. But Josi and Marks were now convinced that they had no right to endanger the lives of the passengers any further. The situation seemed hopeless. Ike's disappointment was acute. The decision was made that Bernie Marks would take over as captain, with the eventual objective of prosecuting the British in a court of law on charges of piracy on the high seas.

Josi and Marks, followed by Ike, picked their way through the fighting on the hurricane deck.

Ike, still reluctant, whispered to Grauel, "Don't let the ship go! Tell Josi, don't surrender the ship. We are still in control aft."

But Josi had already made the decision. With a shrug as the signal to the others he disappeared abruptly.

Lieutenant MacPherson appeared as Bernie made his way forward to the bridge. They stopped short and faced each other.

"I will take the ship into Haifa," Bernie said quietly.

MacPherson interpreted his statement as the act of surrender by the officer in command. Together they entered the wheelhouse.

Marks rang up stop on the engine-room telegraph and reached Cy Weinstein on the telephone to after steering. Steering control was restored to the bridge. Weinstein shortly afterward joined Bernie and the British in the wheelhouse.

It was broad daylight, 5:15 in the morning. *Exodus 1947* lay at rest, dipping her battered hulk drearily in the morning seas.

A British sailor leaped to the top of the wheelhouse and began to signal by semaphore. On the bridge of *Chequers* the appearance of the British signalman on *Exodus* came as a great relief. For some time nothing had been heard of the boarding parties on board *Exodus* and Captain Watson was convinced that they had been overpowered. With the other destroyers unfit for further boarding operations, Captain Watson was preparing to take *Chequers* alongside to starboard for another attempt. He had already asked *Ajax* to stand off *Exodus*'s port beam to prevent a turn in that direction, and he was readying his boarding party for the forthcoming action. The news from MacPherson that resistance had died out on *Exodus* and that the master of the ship was willing to take her into Haifa came as a welcome relief from the prospects of a last desperate measure.

The message from MacPherson stated, also, that medical attention was urgently needed. At 5:40 *Chequers* went alongside *Exodus* dead in the water and transferred Surgeon-Lieutenant D. C. S. Bett and a sick-berth attendant. Shortly afterwards, *Childers* closed and added her sick-berth attendant to the medical team on *Exodus*. No additional British personnel were then transferred, in deference to Lieutenant MacPherson's view that the ship could be controlled with the men on board.

Exodus was ordered to proceed at best possible speed for

THE MORNING AFTER THE BATTLE

Refugees amid barbed wire, potatoes, and debris on deck—the remnants of their spirited defense the night before

The British close in on Exodus. *The boat contains a boarding party from* H.M.S. Ajax.

H.M.S. Childers (R-91), *British destroyer, alongside. Note marine and naval personnel in boarding rig.*

Refugees and British sailors share the deck

Two of those injured in the battle

Haifa, directing her course to pass thirty miles off Tel Aviv. British personnel manned the wheel. In the engine room, the regular crew continued to answer orders from the bridge, even when they wondered why they should do so, now that the ship was under British control. But the British officers had been firmly informed by Marks that the crew would be ordered to shut down the engine room if the British started below, and that the British would be well advised to refrain from going below the hurricane deck and to let the crew mingle with the people and lower the tension. The British agreed.

Surgeon-Lieutenant Bett turned to his medical duties. His attentions to Yakubovich and Baumstein were brief. There was nothing anyone could do. But there were one hundred and forty-six people with injuries — club and gunshot wounds. Twenty-eight — ten men, seventeen women, and one child — were seriously injured and required hospitalization as soon as the ship could reach port. Three members of the forty-man boarding party of the British were badly pummeled in the fighting and needed medical attention — Able Seaman Davies of *Chieftain* and Able Seaman Feltham of *Childers* each with a fractured scapula, and Stoker Mechanic Moreton of *Chequers* with head injuries and a lacerated ear.

In the captain's cabin lay William Bernstein. By now members of the crew had discovered him. Abe Lippschitz, the pharmacist's mate, found Bernstein's plight perplexing; while there was a contusion on the side of his head, there was no break in the skin and no bleeding. Bernstein remained unconscious, fighting for breath, nostrils pulled in against his septum. He spoke only one word, "Doctor." Abe bandaged his head; Grauel later removed the bandage as unnecessary. The British surgeon examined Bernstein and decided to let him remain where he was until he could be hospitalized in Haifa, fearing that any jostling around in removal by boat to *Ajax* would prove immediately fatal.

Marks got the ship underway for Haifa. He was shortly relieved by an officer of the Palestine police who took the conn. Grauel, Marks and Ike lingered in the chartroom, where some of the British officers were standing. Suddenly Ike glanced across the chartroom and realized with dismay that the chart showing the incriminating plot of *Warfield*'s entrance into the territorial waters off Damietta was in partial view on the chart table. He nodded imperatively at Grauel, who, perceiving the situation, quietly walked over to the chart table, extricated the chart from the others, and tore it up, right under the noses of the British. They failed to question what he was doing. Ike shortly afterward disappeared. Like Josi, Barak and thirty-eight others, he literally melted into the woodwork.

At one in the afternoon, Lieutenant MacPherson signaled to *Chequers* that he would need forty additional hands to maintain control on entering port and to handle lines. *Exodus* was ordered to stop. A boat was lowered and transferred about twenty white-clad men each from *Chieftain*, *Childers*, and *Providence* to the decks of *Exodus*. *Ajax* hove to and transferred some men by whaler.

At the same time, large containers of tea and quantities of white bread, sandwiched with "corn-willy" (corned beef), came aboard. The British sailors wolfed down the fare with relish. The children on board looked at them hungrily. It was a moment of thoughtlessness and poignancy.

Bernie Marks wandered back to his stateroom. In a locker over his bunk was the bottle of champagne presented to the ship in Baltimore for the moment of christening as *Exodus 1947*. The British had found it. The bottle was partly empty. Bernie finished it without ceremony. *Exodus* had already been christened in the fire of battle.

Cyril Weinstein must have found liquid reinforcement somewhere. On the bridge, he badgered the British, even urged them to mutiny. The British laughed at him.

The old ship, crushed and battered, with her sides hanging

in shreds, limped toward Haifa. Her short masts fore and aft still carried the white flag with the blue star, stirred now and then by a light breeze. On the bridge, there was crisp formality between the crew and the British officers. One of them flatly stated that if the ship had not been halted, the next phase of the British plan was to have *Ajax* stop dead, close aboard, in her path. The bow-on collision of *Exodus* against the armored side of the cruiser could very easily have stove in the light plating of the old river boat and sunk her.

On either side of *Exodus* were the destroyers of the Royal Navy. Some showed obvious signs of the battle — heavily dented side plating, tangled bridge wings, the debris where the heavy life rafts had come crashing down. Ahead steamed *Ajax*, the white ensign streaming proudly from her mast.

Toward afternoon, a ridge of land showed faintly on the starboard bow. The upperdecks of *Exodus* were packed with refugees, crowding every inch of space and looking ahead toward the land.

Here was the fulfillment of two thousand years of history — of ambition, prayer and hope. Here was Eretz Israel — to them, the Promised Land and the land of promise.

They were praying in the tradition of their people from ages past.

SEVENTEEN

FRIDAY AFTERNOON, JULY 18. The beginning of the Jewish Sabbath. All over Haifa movement ceased. Shops closed. Shutters went up. The sidewalks emptied, and the city died. The only sounds in the street were the marching feet of British military power.

As the quiet of the Sabbath settled, the Jews of the Yishuv contemplated the fate of the refugees on *Exodus* approaching the shores of Palestine. As early as Thursday morning, the Yishuv had known that the ship was coming. Handbills had been distributed throughout Palestine. On Thursday night at 10 P.M., Kol Israel had broadcast: "World, listen to the immigrant ship of the Jewish resistance movement, the Haganah ship *Exodus 1947*, which is approaching the shores of Palestine." There had followed a twenty-five-minute program in Hebrew, English and French, including the story of the ship, a youth's chorus, a message addressed to the United Nations Committee by Grauel, and "Hatikvah," the Hebrew hymn of hope.

Grauel's message to the United Nations Committee, which he himself delivered, was as follows:

"Gentlemen, at this time we make intercessions to you at assemblies in Eretz Israel. We request, in truth we demand, that you hear together testimony from the four thousand five

Above: The Mogen David, later to become the flag of Israel, whips in the breeze from the mast. Below: Royal Marines on deck.

Exodus *bears 4,500 refugees on her decks. They are looking at Eretz Israel, the Promised Land they hope to enter. A British destroyer follows.*

hundred Jews who are coming to Palestine in a few hours aboard the Haganah *Exodus 1947*. We remind you that no commission was called together to witness the death of six million Jews in Europe. This is your opportunity to fulfill the requirements of your declared justice in these matters. Witness if you will the heartache, the sorrow, the suffering and the utter brutality inflicted upon our people by the British. They have acted as the Nazis acted. They club and beat and shoot down in cold blood our women and children. These British are imprisoning our people in the same type camps in Cyprus as they suffered in Hitler's Europe. You have declared yourselves to guarantee equal opportunity to all who seek freedom. Their witness is, in truth, to the very thing that the United Nations had pledged itself to destroy."

During the small hours of the morning, the Yishuv was electrified with the broadcasts from *Exodus*. At 2:50 A.M., a message announced: "We are being attacked. Shots and tear-gas bombs are being hurled at us without warning." At 5:15, "The sailors who captured our bridge are now our prisoners. We have disarmed them and thrown their guns into the sea." And later: "Water is pouring into the engine room. Destroyers are around us and planes are over our heads. The number of British prisoners has reached thirty. We are in danger of drowning. We shall sail full speed for Haifa to save our people." Then came the news of the surrender of the ship and its impending arrival in Haifa under escort.

Shortly before 4:00 P.M., the *Exodus* rounded the Haifa breakwater and crept up to the long pier. She was led by *Childers* and followed closely by *Providence*. *Ajax* and the remaining escorts lay to off the entrance. A tug moved up to the starboard bow of the old gray boat and nudged her toward the pier. A launch carried her hawser to the bollards. Her shattered port side, with much of its superstructure hanging in a confusion of broken wood and tattered tiers of bunks, touched the dock.

Her decks were black with refugees, packed together on

Exodus *entering Haifa, her decks loaded with refugees and her side broken in*

Alongside the dock on arrival. At extreme left, the boards showing the ship's new name: Haganah Ship—Exodus 1947. *On the dock (center, behind the officer in the white uniform) is the United Nations observer, Justice Emil Sandstrom.*

the upper deck house and peering out through the windows and broken side. As *Exodus* moored to the dock, they sang "Hatikvah."

Underwater explosions thudded in close succession near the ship. The charges were fired by the British to discourage the refugees from attempting escape by diving into the water and to guard against sabotage from underwater swimmers.

On the dock was a large gantry crane. Beside it stood a large contingent of officials, mostly in the khaki of the British Army. Two men in civilian dress standing slightly forward of the rest were conspicuous. Wearing a straw hat was Justice Emil Sandstrom, chairman of the United Nations Special Committee of Inquiry on Palestine (UNSCOP); and Vladimir Simitch, a Yugoslav delegate, stood out sharply from the crowd in a white suit.

Tied up on the opposite side of the pier was the *Ocean Vigour*, a British transport. Over her forward hatch was a wire cage. Alongside at another berth were two more transports, *Runnymede Park* and *Empire Rival*, similarly equipped with wire cages. These three transports had been used by the British to ship illegal immigrants to the camps in Cyprus.

The press had been restricted to an area far down the pier from *Exodus*, behind a fence, where they could observe but not be near enough to question the refugees or their British captors.

The Royal Navy and Marines had completed the assigned task of bringing *Exodus* under guard into Haifa. Their officers and men who had ridden the ship into port left civilly enough, some merrily waving goodbye to Americans whose liquor they had drunk. The responsibility now rested on the Palestinian police and the British Army.

Bernie Marks and Cyril Weinstein, as the ostensible leading officers of *Exodus*, were put under arrest and placed under guard in a waiting car. Ritzer, whose declarations about the importance of his position on board had made him conspicuous, was arrested and escorted to the car also.

Grauel was standing on the port wing of the bridge with Eli Kalm and Lennie Sklar with a bandage around his head; Sklar's skull had been cracked but he was ambulant. The three of them had stood, almost in a trance, watching the pathetic scene as the ship docked. Someone touched Grauel's arm and handed him the Jewish prayer book of the American armed forces. Instinctively, Grauel knew what it meant. He turned to the prayer for the dying and moved quickly to the captain's cabin. To his amazement, Bernstein was not there. He had been moved by litter seconds before, down the starboard side and through the ship to a military ambulance. Yakubovich, dead and stinking in the heat, was carried off in the same way, his body uncovered. Grauel in anger shouted to the British on the pier that this behavior was despicable.

Three British officers spotted Grauel. "Newspaperman, come down — now!" they ordered. Grauel went down through the ship. The refugees reached out to touch him as he passed. "Give 'em hell, John," an American crewman said, as he emerged on the dock. He was escorted to the car containing Marks, Weinstein, and Ritzer, and driven to the police station on the Haifa docks. The station was heavily guarded and surrounded by great rolls of barbed wire. Charges were placed. Marks, Weinstein, and Ritzer were confined in the Haifa jail to await trial. Grauel, surrendering his passport and visa, was placed in the Savoy Hotel, where he was in virtual confinement without papers, pending deportation. With the aid of Haganah and some American newspapermen, however, he slipped out. That night from another hotel he telephoned (at some risk, since the British were looking for him) and learned that Bernstein had died in the hospital, never once regaining consciousness. Wrapped in an American flag, he was buried on July 20 in Martyr's Row in Haifa Cemetery, along with the two others who had lost their lives on *Exodus*. Marks, Weinstein, and

Ritzer were released from jail long enough to serve as pallbearers. Fifteen thousand persons in Haifa turned out for the funeral.

When he walked off *Exodus,* Grauel had in his possession a number of the personal belongings of the crew — a watch of one crewman, a rosary bought in Rome by Bernstein to be sent to a Catholic friend in San Francisco. Also, he had the ship's money — a total of $4,500 to be used for defraying the ship's expenses — now to be turned back to the general funds of Haganah.

As the car containing Marks, Weinstein, Ritzer and Grauel sped down the dock, they heard a loudspeaker blare, "Please come peacefully off your ship. The commanding officer . . ." The words trailed off.

Evacuation of *Exodus* began.

Gangways were run into the cargo ports and later to the upper decks. Corpsmen rushed stretchers aboard. Slowly the refugees came down — the destitute, the frightened, the aged, the children — singly, then in groups. They filed across the dock to processing stations, where their hand baggage was searched and sharp objects removed; where they filled out tags for their bags too heavy to handle; and where they were subjected to body search and delousing. The wounded were examined on the spot — some treated, others sent to the hospital. They filed across thirty feet of the soil of Palestine, took a quick look at Mount Carmel, and boarded the British transport. Night came, and the ghastly operation seemed even more unreal under the harsh lights of the pier. By nine o'clock, *Ocean Vigour* had loaded and backed clear. *Runnymede Park,* taking her place, was filled during the early hours of the morning. *Empire Rival,* the last to load, cleared the dock by six. The refugees, unwilling at first to remain in the stifling holds, crowded the wire cages on deck for a last look at Eretz Israel, firm in the belief that they would be back in a short time. After all, the baggage tags all said Cyprus.

Eli Kalm, crew member, beside the grave of William Bernstein in Martyr's Row, Haifa, 1949

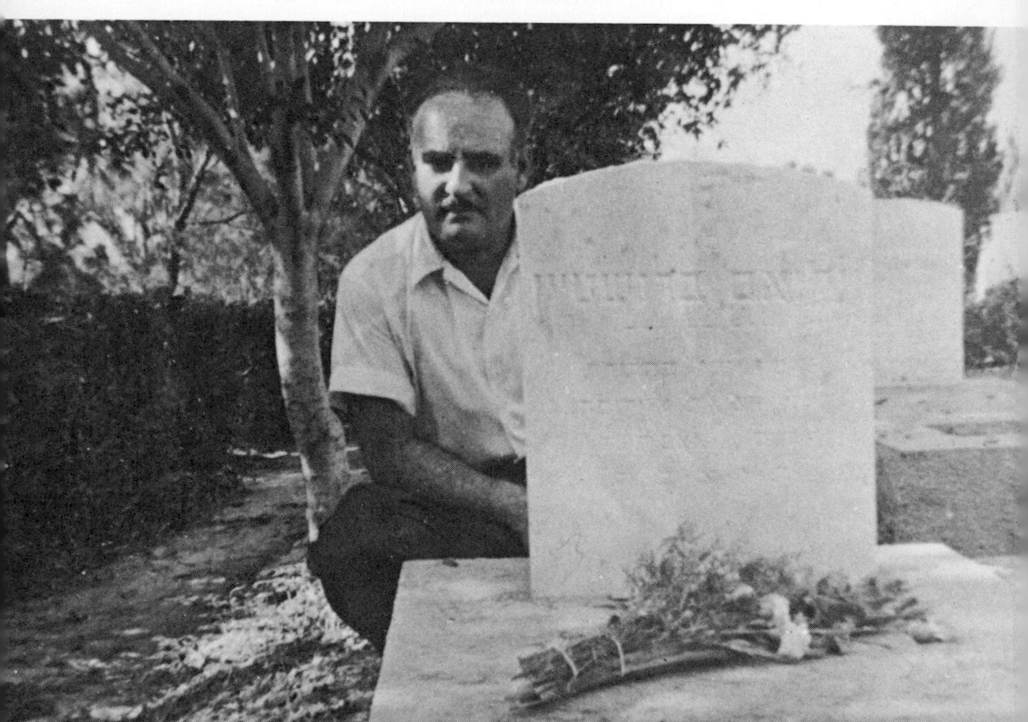

Exodus lay alone at the dock. Her boilers were cold, and life aboard had ceased. A few British soldiers stood guard on the pier. Another night came, casting an eerie spell over the deserted dock and the ghostlike hulk.

In the morning, a work detail of men assigned by the Jewish Agency came down the dock to clean the ship. At the insistence of the British — who wanted no part of the stinking hulks — the Jewish Agency had the assignment of sending men aboard to disinfect and clean them. The guards on the dock, without any instructions, never bothered to count the workmen. Invariably, the workmen were agents of Haganah.

The detail in groups boarded *Exodus* and spread out through the ship. Several sang or whistled the song of the Palmach. This was the signal. Out of the hiding places came the forty-one, including Ike and Amnon. Without food for several days and cramped by the narrow space between the paneling, they were weak and tired. Nevertheless, they quickly changed to work clothes provided by the Haganah men, and each shouldered a bag of rubbish. Then they filed off the ship right under the noses of the British guards. Amnon badly frightened the others when he stumbled under the weight of his pack, but he carried off an act of making it seem an accident. The suspicions of the British guards were not aroused. That night, Ike walked into John Grauel's hotel room in Jerusalem.

The Haganah leadership convened a court of inquiry. Some of the crew members, including Ike, contended that the ship had been surrendered too hastily — that physical control of the ship still remained with the crew in after-steering, and that the British, even the second boarding party, were getting the worst of it. On the other hand, the overwhelming odds presented by *Ajax* and the destroyers were obvious, and the safety of thousands of defenseless people certainly had been at stake. Josi's decision was upheld.

Marks, Weinstein, and Ritzer were released after a few

Exodus *moored at the breakwater in Haifa. The extensive damage to the superstructure from repeated rammings by British destroyers is visible.*

days from the Haifa jail on £1,000 bail posted by Shapiro, later attorney general for Israel; but they still could not move around in Palestine without identification papers. Robert MacFee, the American consul general in Jerusalem, filed a request for their deportation. The British seemed intent on trying Marks as the responsible officer, on the charge of aiding and abetting illegal immigration. They interrogated him at length. They recalled the writing on the coffin-like planking and cement off Sète and wanted to know who Butter was. They asked about the movements of the ship in France and Italy, about people in the United States, like Captain Ash and Skieve Skidell — they even badgered him with stories of Jewish shopkeepers who fleeced their customers. Bernie answered that he, too, had met up with fleecing — from British shopkeepers during the war. Coolly, he fed to the British only the information which he knew they already possessed.

In the meantime, the ship's log and the taffrail log had been recovered by Haganah agents from the gravel ballast in the bottom of *Exodus*. The officers of *Exodus* had kept it deliberately sketchy, but navigational data was dutifully recorded. Here was evidence that the British courts would find difficulty in refuting — the last entries by Bernstein, showing the day's run as recorded by the taffrail log and the ship's position at the time of attack. With Bernstein dead, there could be no question of alteration. The dead man was an unchallengeable witness. The British elected to drop the charges. Marks, Weinstein, and Ritzer were deported.

In the meantime, the whole world began to stir as the refugees from *Exodus* started out on yet another tragic odyssey.

When, two days after departure from Haifa, *Ocean Vigour*, *Runnymede Park*, and *Empire Rival* with their escorts failed to show up in Cyprus, suspicions arose that the intentions of the British government were not to adhere to the old pattern of internment. Anxiety mounted throughout the entire Zionist world. In the immediate wake of the *Exodus* seizure, the fate of the refugees held the center of the world's headlines.

Bevin, supported by Attlee, found that he confronted a monumental dilemma — in his government, in Palestine, with the Arab world, with the United States; indeed, it seemed, with the whole world. A British cabinet crisis ensued.

The Foreign Secretary, sustained by the Prime Minister, lashed out in a burst of irrational anger at the escape of *Exodus* and its refugees from Europe and at the now obvious Jewish policy of engulfing Palestine in illegal immigrants. His speech brought down the wrath of Lieutenant-General Sir Alan Cunningham, the High Commissioner of Palestine, who declared that Britain could not cope with the repercussions in a seething Palestine of any acts of reprisal which might be undertaken against the Jewish refugees.

Bevin, nevertheless, set forth a course of action designed to punish the transgression of the Jews and, simultaneously, to deter the Zionists from their plans to flood Palestine with refugees at the beaches. His course of action — no less than to return the refugees to their port of origin — would have the added benefit, in his view, of taxing France (and any other accessory country) with implicit negligence in letting the refugees cross her territory and use her ports in the face of British protest. Perhaps the French, thus confronted with the unpalatable evidence of their failure, could be persuaded to accept more responsibility for alleviating the international troubles that nagged Britain from every side.

Beset as she was in Palestine with countrywide insurrection, Britain could not, in Bevin's view, do less than stop the illegal immigration which threatened to destroy the Mandate in a war of Arabs and Jews. Britain was not strong enough to contain such a war, and France, Italy, and the United States were doing nothing to head it off; in fact, they were abetting it by actively assisting the Jews. Bevin was determined to make an international example of the *Exodus* case. He thought his action might awake the world to Britain's suffering.

Bevin won his case. Once started on his course of action, he found that there was no turning back.

The three transports escorted by H.M.S. *Cardigan Bay* and two corvettes reached Port-de-Bouc on July 28. They anchored outside the territorial waters beyond the breakwater. The voyage across the Mediterranean at the height of summer had been insufferable in the fetid holds of the transports. When the refugees realized they were not going to Cyprus, there had been a violent upsurge of anger. A hunger strike lasted through an entire day.

France refused to use force to put the refugees on French soil. Instead, she extended hospitality. Premier Ramadier announced that the refugees would be able to settle in France provisionally if they wished until they found a refuge, and he did not preclude the possibility that they might settle permanently in France if they requested it. But the French firmly declined to exercise coercion. The decision came after a stormy session of the French cabinet in which Bidault, wanting to keep peace with Britain, proposed to drive the refugees off the ships. Following a strong and rather petulant complaint from the British that the French refusal had put Britain in a difficult position, M. Pierre Bourdan, Minister of Information, said that in international law no state had the right to enforce the embarkation of nationals of any other state on its soil. French-British relations, in spite of the moderation of Premier Ramadier and the accommodation of Monsieur Bidault, developed a decided chill.

The *Exodus* refugees, encouraged by Haganah agents on board and some who circled the ships in small boats and called to them with loudspeakers, refused to leave the British transports. Only about sixty of the sick and aged, who felt that the limit of their endurance had been reached, went ashore. The remainder were defiant. They forced out of the portholes of *Empire Rival* a flag of bedsheets, saying: "A Nous La Palestine: Liberté, Egalité, Fraternité. We Thank France but Tell England to Get Us Out of Here." At the masthead of the same ship they ran up the flag of Zion — the very flag that had been presented to Ike in Baltimore and later stained with blood as it covered the dead Yakubovich.

The three ships remained at anchor in Port-de-Bouc for over three weeks, while the British fervently hoped that the heat and the latrine-scented holds would drive the refugees ashore. The British now recognized that they had committed a monstrous blunder. Their position in Palestine, already precarious, was rapidly becoming untenable under the weight of world opinion, increasingly hostile over the *Exodus* affair.

But there was no room for maneuver. The Jews at this point would accept nothing less than a turnaround of the ships and legal entry of the whole *Exodus* group into Palestine. Arab response would be rebellion. France would not help the British out of their dilemma by forcing the refugees off the ships on French soil. Colombia, whose "passports" the refugees held, was not hospitable. No preparations had been made elsewhere in Britain's colonial empire to receive the forced immigration of so large a group, and the Jews would not go to such a destination anyhow. The refugees now refused even to go to Cyprus. Trapped, the Labor government made a hasty and incredibly vindictive decision.

On August 21, the Jewish Agency was informed by the Colonial Office that unless the refugees left the ships by 6 P.M. on August 22 they would be taken back to Europe and deported into the British Zone of Germany.

The ultimatum shocked the world. Nothing the British could say — that they were justified in their decision, or that the treatment of the *Exodus* refugees in Germany would be humanitarian — could erase the fundamental fact, that the Jews were being returned involuntarily to the soil they hated — to the land of Auschwitz, Buchenwald, and Dachau.

In vain did General Sir Alan Cunningham, High Commissioner in Palestine, and others in the British hierarchy plead that the government was off on an irrevocable and dangerous course. In vain did Mr. D. N. Pritt, K.C., use a writ of habeas corpus for six persons on board as an excuse to hold up the ships in Gibraltar and to postpone the implementation of the government's decision.

The ships sailed from Port-de-Bouc twenty minutes after the ultimatum expired; they stopped briefly at Gibraltar for fuel. Some of the merchant crew tried to get off. In spite of protests and attempted legal action and a universally hostile press, the three transports cleared Gibraltar and turned toward the North Atlantic. A few days later they were in the Bay of Biscay with a seasick human cargo in the holds, bound for Germany.

At Hamburg, the British made elaborate preparations. A train route from the docks across Germany to two camps near the border of the British and Soviet zones was kept secret to guard against sabotage. The dock area itself was cordoned off, and press representatives were confined to a square roped off at quayside. Elaborate security plans were drawn up. Six medical teams stood by in attendance, making explicit the expectation of violence.

The British made haste to explain that no firearms or other lethal weapons would be used in debarkation; however, they made the error of saying too much in explanation. They added that three degrees of compulsion were available if the refugees refused to leave the ships voluntarily: first, manhandling; second, ships' hosepipes; and three, tear gas. Troops were to be called in as a last resort. These added details, which the British could have omitted in their press releases, brought a storm of world disapproval. The British, believing that their statement expressed humane and practical alternatives, were left in a state of disbelief at the censure they incurred.

The British military government in Germany let another cat out of the bag. Major-General W. H. A. Bishop, Deputy

Chief of Staff on the Central Commission, announced on August 29, that the returning refugees would be put through two weeks of screening by intelligence officers to determine their bona fides as Nazi victims and to isolate the Haganah ringleaders among them. Ration cards would be issued only to those who submitted to interrogation. The general added that if the refugees resisted debarkation, the military would be called upon to accomplish the task. Again, a totally unnecessary statement brought worldwide castigation.

The British government made a last bid for France to accept what the British felt was her responsibility. The idea was that the ships would dock at Le Havre for a last try at debarking the refugees on French soil. The French declined to deal with any suggested "second-chance" arrival of the transports in northern France; they coldly announced that no preparations had been possible. The French government at that point was in no mood to reopen the wounds of Port-de-Bouc. In Ramadier's view, the Attlee government, having made its bed, should lie in it.

The last impulsive gesture of the British was to deliver a virtual ultimatum to the various Jewish relief organizations in the British Zone of Germany that they were to aid the refugees on arrival or suffer revision of their charters. However, the administrators of these organizations adopted the view that Britain should bear the consequences of its actions and, further, if they were to lend assistance the refugees themselves would regard the workers of the organizations as collaborators of the British. The Jewish relief organizations, also, left the British to take their bitter medicine.

There seemed to be no escape for the British from the glare of world publicity.

Escorted by the destroyers *Burghead Bay*, *Finisterre* and *Tremadoc Bay*, the three transports transited the Straits of Dover on September 4. The convoy shortly afterward ran into a fog. Its arrival, scheduled for the quiet of Sunday, was delayed until Monday, September 8. Hamburg had not awakened when the ships arrived.

Ocean Vigour docked before dawn. At first light, an invitation to the refugees to leave the ship peacefully was called out; the refugees asked for a few moments to consider it. Some of them stated their defiance. However, their spokesmen announced they would come ashore. Debarkation proceeded quietly. The refugees came straggling down the gangplank to the dock, then along corridors of cloth-covered chicken wire to board the trains. The windows of the passenger cars were covered with wire mesh.

Twenty-five hundred troops stood in formation in an adjacent area, ready with clubs and tear gas. On the outboard side of transport, patrol boats searched around the piling for saboteurs. The refugees continued to file off — silent, weary and dejected. As the morning wore on, the tenseness of the British tended to diminish. "Operation Oasis," as they called it, seemed to be going peacefully. Two-thirds of the 1,406 refugees left quietly. The remainder decided at one point to stage a sitdown strike. After a period of unsuccessful persuasion, British troops charged aboard armed with clubs and dragged the last of the refugees off bodily.

Empire Rival unloaded on Tuesday without protest from her 1,420 passengers. Shortly afterward, the British had reason to understand the disposition of the refugees to leave quickly. The rumor persisted that a bomb had been placed in the hold to explode ten hours after the refugees activated it. A naval demolition team went aboard and found a homemade canister bomb, which was exploded on the grounds of a nearby depot. The explosion blew out over a hundred windows in an adjoining barracks. The bomb had been smuggled aboard by Haganah agents in Port-de-Bouc; at the last minute, the activation had been muffed in Hamburg, and the bomb failed to go off on schedule. The charge was enough to have carried *Empire Rival* to the bottom.

Runnymede Park, towed to the pier at 10 A.M. by a tug

named *Fair Play*, was the last to dock. She had 1,485 refugees aboard. British officials invited them ashore for a hot meal. They announced they would not leave voluntarily. They were led by Mordecai Rosman, a middle-aged Jew who had served with an underground unit in Poland. The refugees had removed the starboard ladders from the holds, thereby restricting movement off the ship and making access by British troops more difficult. An ultimatum by the British to leave the ship peacefully was ignored by the passengers. Three hundred paratroopers and military police forced their way aboard. Soldiers sprayed the holds with fire hoses. A wild battle broke out; Jews hurled crates, cans, everything movable; soldiers laid about with their clubs. Rosman was cracked on the head and dragged up the ladder. After a pitched battle that lasted nearly two hours, the Jews who had not already been dragged ashore left quietly.

In the two camps at Poppendorf and Amstau, the Jews attempted a hunger strike and a sitdown demonstration. Both were abandoned when they accomplished nothing.

But the Jews succeeded in defeating their questioners when the British interrogation began. To questions on their country of birth or citizenship, they responded "Palestine!" Their names came from the books of the Bible. Not one person admitted his identity or gave away the identity of another. Baffled, British intelligence gave up.

The winter at Poppendorf and Amstau settled in. In November, the refugees began to disappear. Some few arranged to travel on a monthly quota. For others, the long road of Aliyah Beth beckoned once again.

Back in Port-de-Bouc, when Britain delivered its ultimatum to the immigrants packed in the three transports, the Palmach agents on board had made a promise to the refugees — and sealed it in a contract. They painstakingly stamped out forty-five hundred certificates, signed by them and bearing the seal of the Palmach — the olive branch and the sword. To make the seal, they confiscated Sima's shoe —

she was the Haganah nurse on *Exodus* — and carefully carved its heel to make the imprint. On September 7, 1948, a telegram from the vicinity of Poppendorf reached Mossad's headquarters in Paris. The message was dramatically simple: "We have sent off the last of the *Exodus* passengers from Germany . . . We have kept our promise."

In Haifa, *Exodus 1947* was dragged off to the graveyard of rotting craft of all description which symbolized the history of Aliyah Beth. There she sat, moored to a buoy inside the breakwater, with her bow pointed to Mount Carmel.

She was mute testimony to the best and the worst in the human spirit — to man's tragic balance between altruism and hatred. She was a symbol of sentiment, at once the most noble and debasing of human emotions, imbuing men with fervor for causes outside themselves but perverting their loyalties into bitter conflict. She was a driven thing — spent with the force of human passion. She had seen passion turn to blood — and blood into compassion.

Her decks had seen the unwanted find strength in each other — and in the strength, to build a nation.

EIGHTEEN

In the wake of the Exodus affair the Labor government in Britain continued to feel the thunder of abusive world opinion. The Labor government all along thought it had the moral argument on its side. Its appeal for assistance from other countries in maintaining peace in the Middle East had been turned aside in platitudes. The United States, while willing to participate in decision-delaying commissions of investigation in Palestine, was unwilling to commit its armed forces, even in demonstrations, to bring the contenders in the strife-torn Mandate to heel. The United States government — if the glimmering of a policy could be perceived — was swinging rapidly toward a pro-Zionist course under the weight of political and financial pressure at home. Furthermore, the large sums of money needed for illegal immigration were coming from private American contributions. Britain's pleas to the French and Italian governments to help control the flood of Jewish refugees across their borders to Palestine had been shrugged off. The feeling in these countries was too liberal and anti-British on this score to expect much help.

Yet, in the Labor government's view, the deluge of illegal immigration into Palestine could lead only to severe aggravation of a situation already at the breaking point. The flood could lead only to more bloodshed and to open war. The Arabs were adamant that no external agency, financed from America, should determine the population, economy, and future of Palestine which, in their view, they had occupied for nearly two thousand years. To them, the flood of Jews only made the war more certain and immediate. Single-handedly, Britain could not keep the peace in the Middle East, nor indeed could she fight a war there if it should break out. Her only choice was to pinch off trouble at the source — to stem the flood by deterrence.

Attlee and Bevin both believed that the storm that engulfed them in the wake of the *Exodus* affair would blow over. Their miscalculation stemmed from their inability at such close range to examine their own motives, and from their misunderstanding of the nature of the reaction. On the first count, they failed to perceive that the usual British penchant for balance and fair play was notably absent in their "firm policy" toward the *Exodus* passengers and that an element of vindictiveness, of anti-Semitism, had entered. On the second count, they failed to recognize that worldwide animosity had been aroused, not by logical reasoning on the relative merits of the British case, but by the heat of emotion.

The emotional factor was overwhelming, born of compassion for the downtrodden and the aged, the hopeless and the very young, who had suffered much and were to suffer more, stirred by the pluck of a wooden ship standing off the task force of a mighty navy, and deepened by a sense of guilt for past omissions and present commissions which surpassed all rational calculation.

The press of the world excoriated the British. Editorials were direct and left little doubt that the overwhelming sentiment found the British decision not to put the refugees ashore at once in Cyprus, where they would then have gone willingly, but to return them to a hated Germany, an inhumane and conscienceless toying with the pitiful remnants of the ghettoes and concentration camps of Europe. The press pointed out that any moral claim the British might have had in their decision on the grounds that the camps in Cyprus were not ready to receive the *Exodus* cargo was negated by the admission of eleven hundred immigrants to these same camps less than a fortnight later. The British perseverance in an irrational and inhumane move was universally denounced.

The British had more to face than the denunciation of the press. In Palestine, insurrection and terrorism rose to new heights. Haganah, which had tried to maintain some control over the Irgun and Stern gangs, found now that restraint had little justification and less effect. A vicious cycle of violence, reprisal and counterreprisal began. The hanging and garrotting of two British sergeants at Nathanya in reprisal for the execution of some Irgun terrorists by the British triggered a wave of unprecedented agitation and violence. The Jews were in temper close to full-scale revolt, and the Jewish Agency was hard put to hold the reins. Jerusalem looked like a battlefield; tracer bullets and flares lighted the sky, machine guns barked, and heavy explosions shook the earth. Countrywide strikes, ambushes, and perpetration of atrocities brought the Mandate to the edge of war.

The Labor government found itself under heavy attack from the opposition at home. Winston Churchill from Blenheim Palace castigated the leadership for bungling. One of his statements denounced the government for its "omission to inform the United Nations that Britain could no longer bear the burdens of 'insult and injustice' in Palestine" — a precise statement of the ambiguity surrounding Britain's predicament. Pride stood in Britain's way in acknowledging what the Suez crisis of 1956 was to make explicit; she no longer had the requisite power to be effective in the Middle East, and she could no longer carry the weight of a mandate whose troubles she herself had initiated thirty years before.

The *Exodus* affair divided the British government; many of the cabinet were left with grave doubts and misgivings; and the opposition had been handed a weapon which it could use with trenchant force.

In the British armed forces, deep division appeared, harking back to the days in 1945 when sailors and soldiers had gone on hunger strike in protest to the government's restrictive immigration policy against the Jews.

In France, the cabinet found itself in sharp debate. Georges Bidault, who had been close to yielding to the pressure of Bevin and Alfred Duff Cooper, the British ambassador, suffered attack from the Minister of the Interior and his supporters, who resented what they characterized as British interference. The Communists led the Assembly in passing a resolution demanding the French government "urgently to inform the British government of the emotion aroused by this tragic affair and of French hopes for the earliest possible solution in conformity with the duty of humanity." British-French relations reached a new point of strain over the *Exodus* affair. The French press grew shrill in abuse directed at the British.

In the United States, the reaction was spontaneous and sweeping, not only among Zionists but also in other circles as well. Twenty thousand people gathered on July 25 in Madison Square, New York, to pay tribute to William Bernstein. A high platform facing Madison Avenue and Seventy-fourth Street was decked with pictures of the mate on *Exodus* captioned: "Fought for his country, died for his people." Other placards denounced the British government. Leading Zionists who were present had nothing charitable to say about the British decision.

The American press was denunciatory, and little sympathy was shown for the British actions. The weight of Zionist pressure was brought to bear on Congress and the administration. Former Governor Herbert Lehman in New York asserted that the British action was "a terrible blot on the history of a great country . . . a betrayal not only of Jews but of humanity itself, which [had] shocked the conscience of the world." The Committee of International Law and Relations of the National Lawyers Guild in an appeal to President Truman declared that "the brutality employed by the British government shocked the conscience of civilized humanity." Will Rogers, Jr., former congressman from California, added that what had occurred was "a shock to world morality" and a blow to British prestige. A congressional committee composed of Representative James A. Fulton (Pennsylvania), Representative Jacob Javits (New York), and Representative Frank Chelf (Kentucky) started out for Germany to investigate the condition of the *Exodus* refugees. Secretary of State Marshall, at President Truman's direction, dispatched a message to Foreign Secretary Bevin urging the British seriously to consider their decision. Furthermore, Robert Lovett, the Under Secretary of State, called in the British ambassador, Lord Inverchapel, and expressed the misgivings of the United States government.

A Senate resolution drafted by Senator Morse called on the Secretary of State to inform the British government that the behavior of the British Army in Palestine was that of an army of occupation. Morse added that the Jews in Palestine were sustaining some of the grievances which led colonial America to take up arms. Senator Glenn T. Taylor added: "England will lose more of her young men, of her honor and her prestige — and all in the name of what? Can oil be so dear and British honor so cheap?"

But beneath the clamor of condemnation one could hear other voices speaking different words.

Not all of world criticism was directed at the British. The *Exodus* affair deepened the cleavage between the Zionists and non-Zionist Jews everywhere. The American Council for Judaism, a strongly anti-Zionist minority of Jews mostly of German background, denounced the *Exodus* incident as a propaganda stunt designed to draw around Zionism, at a crucial point in its history, the sympathies of the world. It warned American Jewry against the dangers of a dual allegiance which might lead to conflict of interest and loyalty. A leader of the Council, Rabbi Morris S. Lazaron, emeritus rabbi of the Baltimore Madison Avenue congregation, assailed the "Zionist extremism" which had led to the *Exodus* tragedy:

"*Exodus* is the last in a long story of Zionist extremist hypocrisy, unscrupulous propaganda and exploitation of our brothers' misery . . . Compromise with the Zionists who insisted upon a Jewish state has produced only greater tragedy among our brethren in Palestine and elsewhere, and division and strife in American Jewry . . . World opinion has been shocked and horrified by the *Exodus* episode. To have returned these poor remnants to Germany is almost inexcusable cruelty. It is a sad spectacle which reflects on England's glorious name, but any other nation caught in such a situation might have been guilty of the same thing . . . While she was beset by perilous troubles at home and abroad, the Jewish nationalists began a barrage of ridicule, abuse and vituperation all over the world . . . Moderate Jewish elements desired to cooperate with England, but the need of the refugees still living in the camps, the encouragement given the extremists by Zionist elements here and abroad were too much for them . . . Then came the *Exodus* incident. The miserable people on these ships did not act spontaneously . . . They were instructed to make martyrs of themselves by men who used their pitiful helplessness to create a situation which would evoke world sympathy for Zionist ends. That is the terrible truth of this episode . . . Not propaganda or power, not the trappings of statehood, not terror will save the driven remnant of Israel or redeem the Jewries of the world, but Torah, our religious teaching, is our salvation and the salvation of the world. 'To your tents, oh, Israel!' "*

* Baltimore *Sunday Sun*, September 15, 1947.

Other attacks on the Zionists came from sources less emotionally charged with the depths of division within American Jewry. Some sharp criticism of the Zionists' role in the *Exodus* affair came on legal grounds. A number of responsible observers in the press noted the fact that the UN General Assembly on May 18, 1947, having assumed jurisdiction of the Palestine question and having created a committee of inquiry of eleven nations to propose a solution, had called upon "all governments and all peoples" to observe a truce during the inquiry and to refrain from taking actions which might prejudice an early solution. In spite of this resolution, these observers noted, the *Exodus* affair had occurred within two months. The Zionists could be blamed for recklessness and international irresponsibility, scarcely compatible with their professions of support for the United Nations.

In France, a Foreign Office spokesman said that the *Exodus* passengers were the victims of a fraud: "Everybody in this case has been the victims of a fraud. These unfortunate refugees set out on their journey on false promises and traveled under terribly unhygienic conditions. They were the victims of a racket."

Still other belated attacks were directed at the nations of the world that had turned their backs — with platitudes — upon the plight of the Jews and kept their doors firmly closed. The editorialists for the first time were bold enough to make explicit a distasteful fact — that the nomadic Jews made homeless by the war were not wanted by the settled populations of the world. There was an element of truth in Ernest Bevin's cynical assertion a year before that the agitation of Americans to put one hundred thousand Jews into Palestine "was because they did not want too many of them in New York." The critics were brazen enough to level the finger at many countries — European, Latin American, African — for duplicity in their statements of welcome; and to assert that if these countries had adopted a more generous attitude, many of the passengers of *Exodus* would even at the moment be on the way to becoming useful citizens.

Countries were divided from their allies; Jews were divided from Jews; political opinion chose up sides; governments split; and the tide of conflict ran deep. All the welled-up passions poured out — compassion, hatred, loyalty, and pride.

The *Exodus* affair brought the climax to an unacknowledged war. In the glare of world attention focused upon Palestine, any proposals under the United Nations which fell short of providing an independent Jewish state could scarcely have been considered. A majority within the General Assembly began to coalesce. When the majority became firm, it rejected the minority UNSCOP report advocating federalism and accepted the majority report calling for partition. On November 29, 1947, the General Assembly voted for partition and for the establishment of an independent Jewish state.

The Zionists were overjoyed. At the same time, they were skeptical. After all, the history of the past half-century had been one of broken promises and forgotten obligations.

Pending the vote of the General Assembly and its actual implementation, the Mossad in particular was unwilling to put any faith in the prospects for British relinquishment of the Mandate and for the emergence of a new Jewish state in Palestine. There was good reason to trust no one. The Jewish state had to be wrested from the British, if necessary. And the weapon was the continued deluge of illegal immigration.

Intelligence sources of the British were aware that Danny Shind in the United States had purchased two larger and faster ships, *Pan York* and *Pan Crescent*. Lloyds reported that they were owned by a F. & B. Shipping Company, a new name for the Weston Trading Company. The new firm was directed by Nathan Cohen, who had been associated with *Warfield* before her departure from Philadelphia. Other sources all over Europe noted that the flow of refugees was swelling ominously. The arrival of two ships like *Pan Cres-*

cent and *Pan York*, together capable of moving on the order of sixteen thousand people, boded ill.

Pan York arrived in Marseilles; *Pan Crescent* went in for repairs at Venice. The British watched both with care. To allay suspicion, the Mossad sent *York* on a commercial run to Morocco and Rouen. For a time the Jewish Agency counseled caution. It wanted Mossad to desist from an immediate operation to keep from compromising the meetings of the UN General Assembly. The moderate attitude was short-lived. *Pan Crescent* in Venice was damaged by an explosion on board. Mossad attributed the bomb to British agents among the Italian workmen and decided that a war so declared had to be fought to the finish.

Both ships, pursued by the Royal Navy, headed for the Black Sea to take on refugees at the Rumanian port of Constanza. Barred by the Montreux Convention and the formalities required for transiting the Dardanelles, the naval escorts stopped and set up a patrol to await the return of the ships from the Black Sea. British diplomatic pressure was applied on the Communist Foreign Minister of Rumania, Anna Pauker. Any anti-Zionist tendencies of Madame Pauker that may have led her to hold the ships in Constanza were certainly overruled by Moscow, which quickly perceived the advantages of fishing in the troubled waters of British discomfiture in Palestine.

Over fifteen thousand refugees, coming through Rumania by train, boarded the two ships. Immediately, the British perceived a nexus between Soviet endorsement of the plan to partition Palestine and their acquiescence in the shipment of refugees. What better way could they have for introducing thousands of Communists into Palestine and the Middle East? British press releases had something new for speculation — Communist penetration in Asia via Jewish immigration.

Preparing and loading the ships took weeks. In mid-December, the British tried a last-minute measure to stop them.

Through the British ambassador in Washington, President Truman was persuaded to instruct the American delegation at the United Nations to intercede with Moshe Sharett, leader of the Jewish Agency's delegation. Sharett was told of British evidence that the ships contained Communists headed for Palestine; he was told, too, that continued American support might depend on canceling the sailing of the ships. Ben-Gurion ordered the sailings stopped.

Mossad, for the first time, disobeyed. It refused to accede to Ben-Gurion's order.

The ships sailed on Christmas Day, 1947, under the command of Josi Harel, the former commandant of *Exodus*. *Pan York* was now named *Independence*; *Pan Crescent* was called *Ingathering of Exiles*. They passed through the Bosporus, where the Turks declined to stop them, and found their British escorts waiting as expected in the Aegean. At once, the dilemma of the British became apparent. These refugees, fifteen thousand strong, could not go back to a port of origin, since warships could not legally escort them through the straits; they could not go to Germany, after the furor raised by the *Exodus* affair; areas in the Commonwealth or colonies were unacceptable unless the refugees were unloaded by force; no other country was ready to take them, nor did the refugees voluntarily accept deportation to the ends of the earth; and they could not go to Palestine. There was no choice left but Cyprus.

The British perceived this, and so did the Mossad leadership. The cruiser *Mauritius* steamed alongside *Independence* and addressed the "leader" with a request that he take the ships to Cyprus. Josi announced that if the British wished to force them to go to Cyprus, they would not resist. The ships entered Cyprus on New Year's Day, 1948.

The British were finished and they knew it. Already the Mandatory Power was preparing to withdraw.

The withdrawal was not dignified. Along with opening its frontiers to the Arab Liberation Army, opposing the UN's

Exodus *in the distance at the breakwater in Haifa, March 1, 1951*

recommendations for the opening of a seaport to land immigrants in large numbers, and tightening its blockade, it indulged in a diplomatic and propaganda campaign against Mossad le Aliyah Beth.

Some of the campaign had started earlier and was now intensified. Honduras found itself indirectly the subject of a letter circulated in the United Nations by the British on the subject of illegal immigration and the object of strong representations by the British ambassador at Tegucigalpa. As a result the Honduran government canceled the rights of ships to fly the Honduran flag between Marseilles and Palestine if engaged in the illegal traffic of Jewish immigrants, and, furthermore, relinquished certain of its sovereign rights by permitting British interception of ships flying the Honduran flag on the high seas. Britain filed the same complaint with Panama, in view of the fact that twelve ships, including *Paducah, Northland, Pan York,* and *Pan Crescent,* all of which had followed *Exodus,* had flown Panamanian flags. Panama demanded authentic proof that the alleged irregularities coincided with her prohibitions against ships of Panamanian registry engaging "in contraband or illicit commerce." British attempts to coerce Panama into peremptory cancellation of the registry of specified ships signally failed.

The British next directed their attention to the sources of support for Aliyah Beth in the United States. News releases disclosed the means by which funds had been raised and ships bought. Because of this unwanted publicity, the attention of the United States administration was brought to focus on these activities, and the Federal Bureau of Investigation began to develop some dossiers on the matter. The allegation that Mossad le Aliyah Beth had been instrumental in bringing Communists into the Middle East took time to wither. If some Communists and leftist sympathizers rode *Exodus, Pan York, Pan Crescent,* and other Mossad ships of American origin, they were there only as a small part of the refugees fleeing Eastern Europe and not as an organized group placed aboard as a conspiracy to infiltrate the Middle East. In due course, American authorities found little evidence to sustain the British allegations.

The fact that the British government had lost its capacity for objectivity with regard to Palestine and was submerged in its own emotional involvement was exhibited by the allegation of the Foreign Office that two hundred children (age twelve to fourteen) on *Exodus* had been kidnapped from their parents in Hungary. The spokesman stated that these children were victims of "strikingly inhuman" Marxist-Zionist organizations, like Hashomer Haztair, which took them off ostensibly to summer camps in Bavaria, but instead to illegal ships bound for Palestine. The allegations, when challenged, were never documented, never proved, never withdrawn. The insensitivity of the Mandatory Power, as the reins of power slipped away, was clearly demonstrated.

The denouement had been reached.

The British announced the termination of the Mandate on May 15, 1948. The Jewish Provisional National Council issued its declaration of independence on May 14. Simultaneously, it announced the creation of the State of Israel.

Exodus in the State of Israel was a national symbol. On her decks, the turning battle had been fought. On her staffs the Mogen David had flown, even when the battle turned to defeat.

She was remembered in Israel. Not because she had lost the battle. But because she had won the war.

Epilogue

EXODUS WAS NOT JUST A SHIP. She was an epic. In the annals and traditions of Israel, she deserved an honored place. To her belonged the respect owed to a national symbol, the veneration due another *Constitution.*

In 1951, the mayor of Haifa announced that she was to become "a floating museum, a symbol of the desperate attempts by Jewish refugees to find asylum in the Holy Land." The idea was postponed in the preoccupation of the new country with a war of defense.

On August 26, 1952, the ship caught fire. In spite of valiant efforts of harbor craft in Haifa to save her, she burned to the waterline. The hulk was towed out of the shipping area and abandoned on Shemen Beach. Those who knew where to look could see her resting on the sandy bottom, her main deck awash, with jagged edges of steel from the remains of her engines and steel sides protruding above the water.

On August 23, 1964, an attempt was made by an Italian firm to salvage her for scrap. A team of twelve cut the hull in half, for fear that it would divide if it were raised in one piece. When the pumps from the salvage vessel were applied, the bow section righted itself and appeared above water. Suddenly, without warning, it broke loose and sank again.

Exodus *burning in Haifa*, August 26, 1952

Captain Itzak Aronowitz, skipper of Exodus, *watches the attempted salvage of the hulk, August 23, 1964*

The old hulk, broken in two and submerged, remains on the bottom of Shemen Beach near Haifa. Ike Aronowitz, her last skipper, watched her come to the surface and sink for the last time.

Her life was a study in irony.

She came to life as the pride of the Chesapeake, the queen of the Bay. Yet her romantic youth was an anachronism in a world that had passed her by. She was outmoded when she was born, a vestigial remain of an era that had gone forever.

She was named for a man who, for all his pretensions, had little claim to fame. She represented an era and a tradition that he truly admired. Yet in her moment of trial and triumph, his name was expunged from her side, and a new name made her famous.

She was the pride of the Bay, yet her proudest moment came when she was ignominious, battered, and cast aside.

The name of Warfield was equated with a duchess. Yet S. Davies Warfield had all but rejected his niece and ward, and Wallis Warfield never knew the ship she might have launched. *Warfield* was destined to sail under the British flag. After Edward VIII of England had abdicated his throne for Wallis Warfield, the British of their own accord would scarcely have given the name of *Warfield* to a ship flying the Union Jack. Yet the British flag had flown from *Warfield*'s staff in the desperate days of the war at sea and during her brief moment of glory on the North Atlantic.

She sailed, in fact, under four flags — American, British, Honduran, and Israeli. The British flag, under which she staved off the Nazi U-boats in World War II, became the enemy flag when the new flag of Israel rose to her masts. She carried at the time the victims of Nazi persecution. The flower of British youth had been sacrificed to destroy Nazi persecution and protect the victims. But the victims became, by a strange distortion, Britain's enemy.

Warfield became the hunted hare, and the British became

the hounds in a grim game of war. Yet there was no war, and the bitterness of conflict surrounded only the fate of thousands of defenseless people that she sheltered in her hold.

She symbolized the aspirations of a people — the prayers of long generations. Yet she was a moving testimonial to the profound hatred that brought them together.

She was boarded and captured and escorted ignominiously into port by her captors. Yet she won, and her captors lost.

She belongs to Israel. In time, her rust will mingle with the sands of Israel's soil.

There are those who will remember the glare of searchlights stabbing out of a Mediterranean night, a mortal struggle in the wheelhouse, and the shuddering impact of rammings from both sides. They will remember, too, the smile of a shipmate who lies in Martyr's Row. And the sound of "Hatikvah," sung by four thousand voices on a tragic eve of Sabbath.

There are those who will remember a storm at sea — "Her whole house shifted, and I thought it would go right in the ocean" in a high-pitched voice, answered by a gravelly Brooklyn growl: "You go out to sea and you haven't got sense enough to cement up your chain pipes . . . what kind of seamen are you?"

There are those who will remember the shrapnel on her decks, the sound of her whistle around the bend on the Seine, and the surprising comforts of an old ship in the combat zone. "Her top three decks are made of wood, And her hull is made of tin. A credit to our Navy is This Grand Old Hulk We're In!"

There are those who will remember the icy fear of an unseen enemy, lurking in the depths of the sea, and the horror of sister ships upending in the fiery finish of torpedoing. The only comfort was the steady pulse of her engines, carrying them away to safety.

And there are those who will remember mellow summer

evenings on the Bay, with the wind a caress — and soft music and gaiety and lilting laughter. "Carry Me Back to Ole Virginny . . ."

How does one remember a ship?

Appendix

Some of the details of the specifications of *President Warfield* included in the contract dated August 22, 1927, with Pusey and Jones were as follows: Sale price $850,000 in gold coin or equivalent. Overall length 330′; extreme beam 58′; when loaded with 650 tons deadweight to have a draft of 15′6″ and to make 18.5 statute miles per hour, with one 4-cylinder, triple expansion, reciprocating engine developing 2600 I.H.P at 105 RPM — normal cruising speed 17 statute miles per hour. Licensed for 400 passengers. Crew of 58 to include captain, two mates, chief engineer, two assistant engineers, purser, assistant purser, mail clerk, two quartermasters, two watchmen, two lookouts, three oilers, nine firemen, three coal passers, ten seamen, three cooks, twelve waiters, steward, and attendant for newsstand.

Lower deck: fresh water tanks (adequate for short hauls on the Bay), coal bunkers (later replaced with oil tanks when the ship became an oil burner); engineers' workshops outboard of propeller shaft. Aft: storerooms; sleeping quarters for waiters and stewards; crew's pantry and galley; officers' messrooms; sleeping rooms for second-class passengers. Midships: freight compartment for general stores; refrigeration storage. Forward: quarters for oilers, cooks, seamen and firemen; chain locker enclosed in steel with hawsepipes at main deck level.

Main deck: (called the freight deck by steamboatmen). Stern: warping capstan; above the rudder a steam steering engine, operated by cables from the steering wheel in the pilot house. Aft: dining saloon, smoking room, and barbershop. Forward: freight deck for automobiles and other cargo in transit.

Saloon, gallery, and hurricane decks: 171 staterooms for first-class passengers, each with hot and cold running water and 38 with private baths; staterooms on the hurricane deck with doors to the open deck. Aft on gallery deck: glass-enclosed palm room. Forward on hurricane deck: semicircular pilot house with eleven windows forward, the whole structure raised two feet higher than remainder of housing on hurricane deck to permit view astern through window mounted on after bulkhead; side doors to bridge wings; four-foot steering wheel, engine room telegraph and compass binnacle of brass, 8-day Chelsea clock, upholstered seat on after bulkhead in pilot house. Captain's office and stateroom connected by door to pilot house, the office containing large cabinet and rolltop desk surmounted by Chelsea clock. Deck officers' staterooms aft of captain's cabin with center passageway and stairway to gallery deck.

Smokestack thirty feet high, black with red band, rising from top of hurricane deck house. Flagpoles fore and aft of stack to carry white burgee and Old Bay Line house flag. Staffs at bow and stern to carry Union Jack and National Ensign.

Quality prescribed: "all steel work to be tight, steel to steel, and no foreign substance to be used anywhere . . . No defective material to be used. Lumber to be well seasoned."

Bibliography

For information on the personnel of Haganah and the operations of Aliyah Beth, the author has depended to some extent on certain books, the authors of which were themselves either participants in these undertakings or observers of them from close at hand. These writings, therefore, are primary sources. Gratefully, the author acknowledges his debt to Bracha Habas, Julius Haber, Jon and David Kimche, Munya Mardor, Leo W. Schwartz, and Robert St. John, whose books are listed in the bibliography. Their information, integrated with material derived from independent unwritten sources and evaluated against this data, constitutes the backbone of the background of illegal immigration before which *Exodus* is portrayed.

In addition, the author depended heavily on the day-today reporting by the wire services and newspaper correspondents from 1928 through 1948, when events occurred involving *President Warfield* or *Exodus*. His debt, therefore, to the New York *Times*, the Baltimore *Sun*, and to their contributing agencies is very great. The newspaper articles listed especially in the bibliography were particularly interesting or informative.

For certain background information on the Old Bay Line and the early days of *President Warfield*, the author found the writings of Alexander C. Brown, Robert H. Burgess, and H. Graham Wood very valuable.

Books — Fiction

Levin, Beatrice. *Eyewitness to Exodus*. Chicago: Hardbook Paperbook Books, 1962.

Uris, Leon. *Exodus*. New York: Doubleday, 1958.

Books — Nonfiction

Begin, Menachim. *The Revolt: Story of the Irgun.* New York: Schumann, 1951.

Braynard, Frank O. "An Ocean Odyssey," in *Lives of the Liners.* New York: Cornell Maritime Press, 1947, pp. 188–195.

Brown, Alexander C. *Steam Packets on the Chesapeake: A History of the Old Bay Line Since 1840.* Cambridge, Maryland: Cornell Maritime Press, 1961.

———. *The Old Bay Line.* Issued under auspices of the Mariners' Museum, Newport News, Virginia, and the Baltimore Steam Packet Company. Richmond: Dietz Brothers, 1940.

Burgess, Robert H., and H. Graham Wood. *Steamboats out of Baltimore.* Cambridge, Maryland: Tidewater Publishers, 1968.

Chambers, Frank P. *This Age of Conflict: The Western World — 1914 to the Present.* New York: Harcourt, Brace and World, 3rd edition, 1962.

Crossman, Richard. *Palestine Mission: A Personal Record.* New York: Harper, 1947.

Crum, Bartley C. *Behind the Silken Curtain.* New York: Simon and Schuster, 1947.

Dunner, Joseph. *The Republic of Israel: Its History and Its Promise.* New York: McGraw-Hill, 1950.

Esco Foundation for Palestine. *Palestine: A Study of Jewish, Arab, and British Policies.* 2 volumes. New Haven: Yale University Press, 1947.

Gruber, Ruth. *Destination Palestine: The Story of the Haganah Ship Exodus 1947.* New York: Current Books, Inc., A. A. Wyn, 1948.

Habas, Bracha. *The Gate Breakers.* Translated from the Hebrew by David Segal. New York: Herzl Press, Sharon Books, 1963.

Haber, Julius. *The Odyssey of an American Zionist: Fifty Years of Zionist History.* New York: Twayne Publishers, 1956.

Halperin, Samuel. *The Political World of American Zionism.* Detroit: Wayne State University Press, 1961.

Hurewitz, Jacob Colman. *The Struggle for Palestine.* New York: W. W. Norton, 1950.

Joseph, Bernard. *British Rule in Palestine.* Washington: Public Affairs Press, 1948.

Kimche, Jon and David. *The Secret Roads: The "Illegal" Migration of a People, 1938–1948.* London: Secker and Warburg, 1954.

Lenczowski, George. *The Middle East in World Affairs.* 3rd edition. Ithaca: Cornell University Press, 1962.

Litvinoff, Barnet. *To the House of Their Fathers: A History of Zionism.* New York: Praeger, 1965.

Lloyd George, David. *Memoirs of the Peace Conference.* Vol. 2. New Haven: Yale University Press, 1939.

———. *War Memoirs, Vol. I, 1914–1915.* Boston: Little, Brown, 1933.

Manuel, Frank E. *The Realities of American-Palestine Relations.* Washington: Public Affairs Press, 1949.

Mardor, Munya M. *Haganah.* (Edited by D. R. Elston; forward by David Ben-Gurion.) New York: New American Library, 1964.

Sachar, Howard M. *The Course of Modern Jewish History*. Cleveland: World Publishing Company, 1958.
St. John, Robert. *Ben-Gurion: The Biography of an Extraordinary Man*. Garden City: Doubleday, 1959.
Schwartz, Leo W. *The Redeemers: A Saga of the Years 1945–1952*. New York: Farrar, Straus and Young, 1953.
Stein, Leonard. *The Balfour Declaration*. New York: Simon and Schuster, 1961.
Stevens, Richard P. *American Zionism and U.S. Foreign Policy, 1942–1947*. New York: Pageant Press, 1962.
Stone, I. F. *Underground to Palestine*. New York: Boni and Gaer, 1946.
Wischnitzer, Mark. *To Dwell in Safety: The Story of Jewish Immigration Since 1800*. Philadelphia: Jewish Publication Society of America, 1948.

Articles in Magazines and Journals

Anonymous. "Convoy Maniac." *Log Line*, Winter 1948 (Vol. 3, No. 4), pp. 22–24.
———. "Ocean Odyssey: 'Skimming Dishes' Atlantic Battle with U-boat Pack." *Shipping World*, June 13, 1945, pp. 663–665.
———. (Item on the wartime history of the *President Warfield*.) *Steamboat Bill of Facts*. Journal of the Steamboat Historical Society of America, No. 17, Flushing, New York, August 1945.
———. "They Called it the 'Honeymoon Fleet' Convoy." *Sea Breezes*, May 1946.
Boylan, W. P. "Affidavit — Loss of the Yorktown." *Sea Breezes*, May 1946, pp. 299–301.
Brown, Alexander C. "Exodus 1947: An Interim Report on the Career of the Steamer President Warfield." *American Neptune*, April 1948, pp. 127–131.
Burgess, Robert H. "Fightin' Steamboats." *Shipyard Bulletin*, Newport News, May 1946.
Hardy, A. C. "More Reminiscences of the Honeymoon Fleet." *Sea Breezes*, December 1946, pp. 402–405.
Hess, Jean B. "Last of Their Kind." *Sea Breezes*, July 1961.
Ritzer, Stanley (as told to Peter Michelmore). "I Ran the Blockade to Palestine: The True Story of the Exodus." *Argosy*, February 1960, Vol. 350, No. 2, pp. 19–21 and 78–80.
Timewell, H. C. "Exodus 1947 Takes on Her Cargo." *American Neptune*, Vol. 9, No. 4, October 1949, pp. 300–301.

Documents, Private Papers and Official Records

Abstract of the log of *President Warfield*, February 25, 1947–February 27, 1947. In the possession of Mr. Samuel Meisel of Baltimore, Maryland.
Collection of clippings and notes of Mr. Samuel Meisel of Baltimore, Maryland.
Court of Claims Reports, Vol. 129. *The Derecktor Case*. Cases De-

cided in the U.S. Court of Claims, July 4, 1954, to March 28, 1954. U.S. Government Printing Office, 1955, pp. 103–136.
Federal Supplement, Vol. 128. *The Derecktor Case*. Cases Argued and Determined in the U.S. District Courts and the U.S. Court of Claims. St. Paul, Minnesota. West Publishing Company, pp. 136–144.
Files of the Zionist Archives and Library, New York.
Great Britain. *Parliamentary Debates*. House of Commons, Fifth Series, Vols. 317–449. London, 1936–1949.
———. *Palestine Royal Commission Report*. London: His Majesty's Stationery Office, 1937.
———. *The Political History of Palestine under British Mandate*. Memorandum by His Britannic Majesty's Government presented in 1947 to the United Nations Special Committee on Palestine. Jerusalem, 1947.
Letters and files in the archives of the British Embassy, Washington.
Maryland Historical Society File No. MS 1023.
Record of the Remarks of Mr. F. Joseph Donohue, National Board Chairman of the American-Israel Society, and Captain Itzak Aronowiecz, at the Annual Luncheon of the Maryland Chapter, Lord Baltimore Hotel, Baltimore, Maryland, Friday, December 4, 1959.
U.S. Martime Commission, Official Records. Ship File on the President Warfield.
U.S. Navy. Official Log Book, U.S.S. *President Warfield* (IX–169).
U.S. Navy. Official Records. File on the *President Warfield*.
U.S. Treasury Department. U.S. Coast Guard. Log of U.S.S. *Cherokee*, February 26–27, 1947.

Newspaper Articles — Unsigned

"A Local Lady Returns from the Wars." Baltimore *Sun*, July 28, 1945.
"Baltimore Ship Reported off Palestine with Refugees." (AP). Baltimore *Sun*, July 18, 1947.
"Ban Hits Refugee Ship." New York *Times*, August 10, 1947.
"British Army Ordered New Security Measures in Poppendorf and Am Stau Camps." New York *Times*, September 13, 1947.
"British Assailed on Refugee Threat." New York *Times*, August 22, 1947.
"British Bid for Aid in the Exodus Case." New York *Times*, August 24, 1947 (AP).
"British Bring Ex-Bay Liner into Haifa After Long Fight." Baltimore *Sun*, July 19, 1947.
"British Fight Terrorists in Jerusalem: Holy Land Disorders Follow Deportation of Warfield's Passengers." Baltimore *Sun*, July 21, 1947.
"Crew Man from the Exodus 1947 Denies the British Met Firearms." New York *Times*, August 9, 1947.
"Exodus and Return." (Editorial). New York *Times*, September 14, 1947.
"Exodus Refugees Begin Forced Trip to German Camps." New York *Times*, August 23, 1947.

"Exodus Refugees Reach Gibraltar." New York *Times*, August 27, 1947.
"Four of Exodus Crew Arrive by Plane." New York *Times*, September 19, 1947.
"France to Renew Invitations to Jews: Will Try Again to Induce 4500 Deported Emigrants to Go Ashore En Masse." New York *Times*, August 1, 1947.
"French Foreign Office Spokesman Said Jews Victims of Fraud." New York *Times*, July 25, 1947.
"From Bay to Battle: A War Diary of the U.S.S. President Warfield." Baltimore *Evening Sun*, March 20, 1945.
"Honduras to Cancel Refugee Ship Rights." New York *Times*, July 25, 1947.
"Jews Sent Back to German Port: 4400 from Exodus Refused to Land in France." Baltimore *Sun*, August 23, 1947.
"Liner Warfield Towed to Port as 60-Mile Gales Lash Atlantic." Baltimore *Sun*, February 28, 1947.
"A Local Lady Returns from the Wars." Baltimore *Sun*, July 28, 1945.
"Miss Louise Lazenby, Social Directress of the President Warfield of the Old Bay Line." Baltimore *Evening Sun*, June 8, 1940.
"Old Bay Line at Century Mark Turns Years Back for Fete: Costumed Participants and Officials Take Part in Celebrating Centenary of Pioneer Ship Service." Baltimore *Sun*, May 24, 1940.
"Old Bay Steamer to Become Floating Museum in Israel." Baltimore *Sun*, March 20, 1951.
"On Board Runnymede Park." New York *Times*, August 31, 1947.
"Rabbi Morris S. Lazaron Asks Toleration, Assails Zionist Extremism, Urges Palestine Homeland." Baltimore *Sun*, September 15, 1947.
"Ship Loses Guard Rails: President Warfield to be Repaired When Bids Arrive." Baltimore *Sun*, March 2, 1947.
"Six Vessels Purchased to Aid Refugees, Say Zionists Here." Baltimore *Sun*, August 3, 1947.
"Trouble Dogs Ship Off for Palestine." New York *Times*, March 31, 1947.
"U.S. Press Barred at DP Camp Survey." New York *Times*, August 10, 1947.
"Utmost Tact to be Used by British in Persuading Jews to Disembark." New York *Times*, September 6, 1947.
"Warfield's Epic Cruise: Passenger Narrates Odyssey of Jewish Refugee Ship." Baltimore *Sunday Sun*, September 7, 1947.
"Warfield, Old Bay Line Queen, Exiled to China as Riverboat." Baltimore *Sun*, January 23, 1947.
"Warfield Ready to Sail for China River Service." Baltimore *News-Post*, February 3, 1946.
"Warfield Repairs Almost Done." Baltimore *Evening Sun*, March 21, 1947.
"Warfield Seen Under Scrutiny: Ex-Bay Liner Said to Carry Jews in Mediterranean." Baltimore *Sun*, July 14, 1947.
"Willie Harris, Bay Boat Waiter to Notables, Dies. A Son of Bay Line Veteran, His Rolling-R Dinner Call Became Famous, Was Hero in Ship Fire." Baltimore *Evening Sun*, September 15, 1942.

"Zionist Abduction of Jews Alleged." New York *Times*, September 6, 1947.
"Zionists Denounce Seizure of Vessel." New York *Times*, July 25, 1947.

NEWSPAPER ARTICLES — BYLINED

Bradley, Holbrook. "Chesapeake Boat Now on Seine River Run." Baltimore *Sun*, June 18, 1945.
Brown, Alexander C. "Former Favorite Bay Steamers Battled Nazi Wolf Pack in World War II." Newport News *Daily Press*, September 25, 1960.
———. "Odyssey of Frustration Began Five Years Ago with Ship Leaving Here." Newport News *Daily Press*, February 24, 1952.
———. "The Three Lives of the Old Bay Line's President Warfield: Bay Boat, Warship, Then the Famous Exodus — But the End Has Come." Baltimore *Sun*, February 9, 1964.
Currivan, Gene. "Refugees Being Returned to France." New York *Times*, July 21, 1947.
———. "Terrorist Tension Reaches New High as Refugees Sent to France." New York *Times*, July 22, 1947.
Clopton, Willard, Jr. "An Old Ship's Big Moment." Washington *Post*, July 17, 1967.
Daniel, Clifton. "Violence Threatens Development of Palestine." New York *Times*, August 3, 1947.
Dulaney, Carroll. Untitled article on S. Davies Warfield. Baltimore *News-Post*, March 1, 1941.
———. "Day by Day" (article on the Chesapeake Bay). Baltimore *News-Post*, May 25, 1940.
Graham, Fred. "Last Convoy Ships Back from Europe: Sailors Swarm Ashore at Norfolk After Seeing Service in Invasion of France." New York *Times*, July 26, 1945.
Horne, George. "Palestine-Bound Mystery Ship." New York *Times*, March 6, 1947.
Hulen, Bertram D. "Futile U.S. Appeal on Exodus Bared." New York *Times*, September 11, 1947.
Kennedy, Paul P. "Exodus Refugees Get an Ultimatum." New York *Times*, August 22, 1947.
MacNees, James. "Model to Honor 'Exodus' Ship." Baltimore *Sun*, July 13, 1967.
Morrow, Edward A. "Exodus Head Calls Battle a Mistake." New York *Times*, September 11, 1947.
———. "Exodus Zionists May Face Charge." New York *Times*, August 30, 1947.
Ramage, Robert C. "Ferry to Palestine — Twenty Century Exodus." Norfolk *Virginian-Pilot*, April 17, 1960.
Rivkin, Ben. "It Began in Baltimore Twenty Years Ago." Baltimore *News-American*, January 15, 1967.
Shaner, J. Jean. "Old Bay Line Gets up Steam." Baltimore *Evening Sun*, February 19, 1940.
Sterne, Mary. "U.S.S. Warfield Back Home from War." Baltimore *Sun*, July 26, 1945.

Twyfoed, Warner. "Lutz, Veteran of the Exodus, Is Home Again." Norfolk *Virginian-Pilot*, November 18, 1947.

Warren, Lansing. "French Bar Using Force on Refugees." New York *Times*, July 31, 1947.

Williams, Harold A. "From Canton to Canton." Baltimore *Sunday Sun*, February 3, 1947.

Index

Picture Credits

The photographs on the following pages are all from a private collection: 68, 142 (*top*), 143 (*both*), 154, 160 (*both*), 180, 181, 237 (*top*), 238 (*second from bottom*), 239, 241 (*top*), 242 (*top*), 247 (*both*), 248, 256. Those on pages 24 (*bottom*), 46, and 52 carry no credit.

Frontispiece: From the collections of the Maryland Historical Society.

Page 8 Courtesy of the Mariners Museum, Newport News, Virginia.

11 (*both*) Courtesy of Raymond L. Jones.

23 Photo by Alexander C. Brown. Courtesy of the Mariners Museum, Newport News, Virginia.

24 (*top*) Photo by Hans Marx. Courtesy of the Baltimore Sunpapers.

33 Courtesy of A. Spencer Marsellis.

50 Courtesy of Raymond L. Jones and the Mariners Museum, Newport News, Virginia.

57 (*both*) Courtesy of Cdr. D. C. DuBrul, USNR.

62 Official U.S. Navy Photo.

121 Photo by the United Jewish Appeal. Courtesy of the Baltimore Sunpapers.

129 Photo by William Klender. Courtesy of the Baltimore Sunpapers.

139 Photo by Hans Marx. Courtesy of the Baltimore Sunpapers.

142 (*bottom*) Photo by Cyril Weinstein.

197 (*top*) Courtesy of Bernard Marks. (*bottom*) Photo by H. C. Timewell. Courtesy of the Mariners Museum, Newport News, Virginia.

198 (*both*) Courtesy of Bernard Marks.

199 Courtesy of Bernard Marks.

237 (*bottom*) Courtesy of Bernard Marks.

238 (*all except second from bottom*) Courtesy of Bernard Marks.

240 Courtesy of Bernard Marks.

241 (*bottom*) Courtesy of Bernard Marks.

242 (*bottom*) Courtesy of Bernard Marks.

250-251 Photo by British Admiralty. Courtesy of the Mariners Museum, Newport News, Virginia.

252 Courtesy of Bernard Marks.

258 Courtesy of the Mariners Museum, Newport News, Virginia.

278-279 Photo by American Express photographer Bob Mathews. Courtesy of Raymond L. Jones.

284-285 Courtesy of the Mariners Museum, Newport News, Virginia.

286 Courtesy of the Mariners Museum, Newport News, Virginia.